THE
INTERESTING
BITS

The History You Might Have Missed

JUSTIN POLLARD

JOHN MURRAY

First published in Great Britain in 2007 by John Murray (Publishers)
An Hachette Livre UK company

6

A CIP catalogue record for this title is
available from the British Library

ISBN 978-0-7195-2420-2

Typeset in Sabon MT by Palimpsest Book Production Limited,
Grangemouth, Stirlingshire
Printed and bound by Clays Ltd, St Ives plc

John Murray policy is to use papers that are natural, renewable
and recyclable products and made from wood grown in sustainable
forests. The logging and manufacturing processes are expected to
conform to the environmental regulations of the country of origin.

John Murray (Publishers)
338 Euston Road
London NW1 3BH

www.johnmurray.co.uk

For Annabel, James, Jack and Matthew

*'How these curiosities would be quite forgott,
did not such idle fellows as I am putt them down'*

John Aubrey, *Brief Lives*

CONTENTS

3 Men of the Cloth

4 Justice

5 Heads

6 What's in a Name?

7 Animal Magic

8 Bedhopping

9 Improbable Lives

10 I Say!

11 Ouch!

12 Magic

13 Where in the World?

14 Unsound Minds

15 All at Sea

16 Bang!

17 Unlucky

18 How Did That Happen?

19 Who?

20 A Bit of Politics

INTRODUCTION

History is *not* more or less bunk, despite what Henry Ford said. In fact he probably only made the comment in the hope that no one would listen to future historians when they said things like, 'Did you know that Adolf Hitler kept a photograph of Henry Ford in his study?'

There is one problem with history, however – there is an awful lot of it. Everyone and everywhere seems to be full of it. This presents a writer with a problem: how do we understand what's going on? How do we make sense of all this . . . stuff? Traditionally there have been two answers:

1. Write a huge number of impenetrable books, each about a tiny bit of history, with titles like *The Custard Cream as Social Metaphor – 1967 to 1971*.
2. Write sweeping narratives in which everything is neatly arranged into lists of places, peoples and dates. A suitable title might be *A Complete History of Civilisation from the Earliest Times, in Thirty-Six Volumes*.

Neither of these approaches is without its problems, and the biggest of these is that there's a real danger that they make the whole thing extremely boring. You end up with too many books that you know you'll never read about subjects you'd like to know a bit about, but frankly not quite *that* much. Or you find yourself with a few huge tomes full of lists of rulers, lists of battles, lists of important pieces of Hebridean highways legislation – and endless lists of dates.

This is why children don't listen in history lessons at school and who can blame them? Where's the fun? Where's the intrigue? Where are the interesting stories of the mad, bad, stupid, wonderful, odd and improbable things that happened to our ancestors? The past is as daft as the present and the people of the past were as daft as us. That's what actually links us.

History is not simply the extension of the present back into the past; it is a very strange and very different country. Nor does history have a grand direction, although many history books imply that it does. History wanders around, often drunk, frequently bumping into things and usually eschewing anything that might look like progress for another sustained period in full reverse.

So rather than try to produce another volume on custard creams or a big *History of Everything*, which won't actually include everything but rather consist of another series of lists that are impossible to remember, *The Interesting Bits* is more of a selection box – a didactic mixture of historical delicacies, stories, events, facts (and a few salacious rumours) that will go no way whatsoever towards helping the reader to pass his or her GCSE History exam. They have no greater meaning, no direction and no overarching theme beyond being, I hope, worthy of note, possibly even memorable and reminding us that the past was no less peculiar than the present. If it must have a purpose, then I suppose it might help in pub quizzes – maybe.

MAY CONTAIN NUTS

All history is a matter of opinion and these are mine. They are gathered from a wide selection of first- and second-hand sources whose accuracy varies from the impeccable to those with frankly far too many fairies in them to be 100 per cent believable. What they have in common is that those who first recorded them had something to say about history – events that they thought worth remembering and people they wished to praise or pull to pieces – and as such are valuable historical documents regardless. I leave it to you to decide whether St Rumwold really did shout 'I am a Christian' when only three days old but if you find anything within these pages that you know to be simply wrong, do please let me know.

Justin Pollard
Westcott, 2007

1

Oops!

'There's been an accident,' they said,
'Your servant's cut in half; he's dead!'
'Indeed!' said Mr Jones, 'and please,
Send me the half that's got my keys.'

Harry Graham, *Ruthless Rhymes for Heartless Homes* (1899)

Which king rode off a cliff?

Alexander III's rule over Scotland was marred by personal tragedy. By 1283 the king had lost his first wife and outlived all of his children. According to the Chronicle of Lanercost, he was not too bothered by loneliness, however, as *'he used never to forbear on account of season nor storm, nor for perils of flood or rocky cliffs, but would visit none too creditably nuns or matrons, virgins or widows as the fancy seized him, sometimes in disguise.'*

This was great fun but it overlooked the fact that he did need an heir. So it was that on 14 October 1285 he married the French heiress, Yolande de Dreux. All looked to be going well and, as he was only forty-four, there still appeared to be time to produce a successor. The following year all that changed. Once again according to the Chronicle of Lanercost, around 19 March 1286, Alexander finished eating a large dinner in Edinburgh and, despite the gathering gloom and the pleas of his nobles, decided to visit his new bride who was a short distance away in Kinghorn. Having crossed the Queensferry,

> he arrived at the burgh of Inverkeithing, in profound darkness, accompanied only by three esquires. The manager of his salt-pans, a married man of that town, recognising him by his voice, called out: 'My lord, what are you doing here in such a storm and such darkness? Often have I tried to persuade you that your nocturnal rambles will bring you no good. Stay with us, and we will provide you with decent fare and all that you want till morning light.' 'No need for that,' said the other with a laugh, 'but provide me with a couple of bondmen, to go afoot as guides to the way.'

This was a mistake. The party continued but just two miles down the road, now in complete darkness, they lost their way and Alexander, in his eagerness to reach the nuptial bed, rode straight off a cliff. The bodies of horse and rider were recovered the next morning. Without a surviving heir, Scotland had no king for the next six years.

Who was killed by a tiger in a pub?

On Tuesday, 23 October 1703, the brightly painted caravans of a travelling fair snaked their way into Malmesbury. For the inhabitants of a small provincial town the fair brought undreamt of excitement. Strongmen, freaks, strange faces from distant lands, and wild and exotic animals from the farthest reaches of the known world, all descended on the mediaeval town. For one day the uneventful circling of the seasons was suspended and the colour and curiosity of the outside world exploded on to this small stage.

For Hannah Twynnoy, aged thirty-three, it had been a wonderful day. She had been born and bred in Malmesbury and her life so far had been sheltered and without event. She had never travelled to London, let alone ventured abroad, and the occasional passing fair or visiting stranger had provided the only glimpses she would ever get into what lay beyond the boundaries of her own familiar county.

That evening, Hannah and her friends sat drinking in the Blue Boar on River Street. The fair was finally closing down. Tomorrow it would be gone but its brief stay would be a talking point in the pubs of Malmesbury well into the winter, more so, in fact, at that moment than they could possibly have imagined. Inside the Blue Boar a fire was burning and Hannah sat close to it, while outside the stalls and stands of the fair were packed into their wagons. Iron cages clanged shut and strange animals let out mournful howls in the gloom whilst her friends eagerly recounted tales of the day's sights.

The noise outside was dying down and the first wagons were moving off when there was a cry from the street. In the Blue Boar the townsfolk thronged around the small windows, peering out as men with burning torches ran back and forth shouting warnings. A local magistrate went to the door and lifted the latch. Hannah looked up. With a splintering crash the door flew open and the crowd scattered as a storm of orange and white fur burst into the pub.

Hannah had only seen a tiger for the first time that day and didn't really expect to see one again quite so soon. A mythical monster, from a land that she could not be sure even existed outside stories, had screamed into her predictable, mundane life and now looked her in the eye. Two worlds stared briefly at each other but before she could move the animal was upon her and, with a single, savage bite, killed her.

Hannah was buried that week in front of the partially ruined abbey that formed the parish church and there she lies still, her gravestone recounting the terrible moment when the exotic East burst in on Hannah's life and wrenched it away.

IN MEMORY OF
HANNAH TWYNNOY
WHO DIED OCTOBER 23RD 1703
AGED 33 YEARS.
IN BLOOM OF LIFE
SHE'S SNATCH'D FROM HENCE,
SHE HAD NOT ROOM
TO MAKE DEFENCE;
FOR TYGER FIERCE
TOOK LIFE AWAY.
AND HERE SHE LIES
IN A BED OF CLAY,
UNTIL THE RESURRECTION DAY.

Who committed suicide twenty-five years after his death?

Field Marshal the Lord Haig is chiefly remembered today for his leadership of British forces in the First World War for which he has been widely criticised as showing a callous disregard for human life. In his own lifetime, however, he remained hugely popular, even amongst the troops in the trenches, and not simply because his father had run the Haig whisky distillery. In particular his tireless fundraising for ex-servicemen after the war had greatly added to his reputation and this happier view of Haig might have continued, were it not for the efforts of his supporters in gathering and publishing his private papers some twenty-five years after his death in 1928. These dealt very frankly with the war, Haig's decisions during it and the inevitable loss of life that he knew his actions would entail.

Military historians still argue over whether Haig followed the only available course for victory or needlessly wasted lives, but in publishing the details of his actions his supporters managed unwittingly to outflank their hero's reputation and turn popular opinion against him. When the press baron Lord Beaverbrook was shown the papers with a view to publishing extracts in his newspapers, he could only sigh that Haig was the only man he knew who had committed suicide twenty-five years after his death.

Who went into exile after breaking wind?

The story of Oxford's embarrassment comes from diarist John Aubrey's *Brief Lives*, a collection of short biographies written towards the end of the seventeenth century. According to Aubrey, Edward de Vere, 17th Earl of Oxford, was bowing particularly low to Queen Elizabeth I one day when he accidentally (and loudly) broke wind. So embarrassed was de Vere that he went into voluntary exile for seven years. Eventually he returned to court and once again found himself in the presence of the Queen. He bowed carefully (and perhaps a little timorously) this time. The intense silence was only broken by Elizabeth commenting, 'My Lord, I had forgot the fart.'

Supporters of the Earl of Oxford, particularly those who believe that he may be the true hand behind the works of Shakespeare, often consider this story a calumny but it was certainly in circulation by the early years of the seventeenth century where it is referenced in the contemporary poem 'The Parliament Fart', which dates from around 1610. Whilst Aubrey's style is gossipy and occasionally a shade saucy, he was usually a meticulous biographer. And anyway, as he put it himself, *'How these curiosities would be quite forgott, did not such idle fellowes as I am putt them down.'*

Why did Thomas Carlyle rewrite the *The French Revolution*?

This had to be one of the most embarrassing incidents in literary history. As Thomas Carlyle and John Stuart Mill were great friends, Carlyle had asked Mill to read and comment on the handwritten manuscript for the first volume of his enormous new book, *The French Revolution*, which ran to over 300,000 words. Mill willingly accepted but, being not the most organised of characters, somehow managed to leave the work amongst waste paper in his kitchen. This was where his maid found it and, believing it to be unwanted, used it to light a fire.

Mill was devastated and quite reasonably so, as it was the sole copy. On the night of 6 March 1835, he turned up at Carlyle's house and, having asked his friend's wife and his own future wife to leave the room for a moment, he owned up. A couple of weeks later Carlyle described in a letter to Mill's sister Harriet how *'to prevent him almost perishing with excess of misery, we had to forbear all questioning on the subject, which indeed was of no importance to either of us [Carlyle and his wife], and to bid him "Be of Courage, never mind, Be certain I can write it again, and will!"'*

Mill did offer £200 towards the cost of rewriting but Carlyle refused to accept more than £100. He was also as good as his word and wrote the entire book from memory, by hand, once again. When he later asked Mill to read his manuscript for the first book of the next volume, Mill refused: *'not that I believe such a thing could possibly happen again, but for the sake of retributive justice I would wear the badge of my untrustworthiness'.*

The manuscript was entrusted to another friend instead.

Which general was accidentally shot by his own troops?

Thomas 'Stonewall' Jackson was one of the most successful and daring Confederate commanders in the US Civil War. He also had a lifelong belief that one of his arms was longer than the other, which it wasn't.

In his last battle, at Chancellorsville in 1863, the Confederate Army of North Virginia won a major victory over the much larger Union Army of the Potomac, following a brilliant outflanking manoeuvre by Jackson. Unfortunately, whilst returning to camp on 2 May Jackson and his staff were waylaid by one of their own regiments (from North Carolina) who mistook them for Union troops. Having given the usual challenge, 'Halt! Who goes there?' the Carolina regiment seem to have opened fire before getting any coherent response. Jackson was shot three times, twice in the left arm and once in the right hand, but did not seem in imminent danger. In the melee, however, he could not get immediate medical attention, nor did being dropped by his stretcher bearers particularly help matters. Eventually Jackson was treated by doctors, having his left arm amputated, but pneumonia had already set in. He died from complications of this on 10 May.

Where is the Great Moghul diamond?

Well, that's a very good question. The fate of the Great Moghul diamond is something of a mystery and one made all the stranger because you might think that people would look after a 787-carat stone a little better. The stone was first seen by Western eyes in 1665 by the famous jewel trader, Jean-Baptiste Tavernier, who reported that it was the largest diamond ever found in India. The stone was supposedly set into the eye of a statue in a temple in Srirangam (some say Mysore) in southern India, from where it was stolen by a deserter from the French army. Tavernier brought the stone to Madras from where it found its way to Delhi. In 1739, however, the king of Persia, Nader Shah, sacked the city and took the stone as part of the spoils of war.

Nader Shah was obsessed by diamonds and also had in his collection two other famous Indian gems, the Koh-i-Noor (Mountain of Light) and the Darya-ye-Noor (Sea of Light) but, as is the tradition with these stones, they brought their owners little luck. Nader Shah became increasingly paranoid with age and, some might say, rightly so, as people did from time to time try to kill him. He was eventually assassinated by his own guards. In the confusion following his death, the Great Moghul was stolen, finding its way into the possession of a shadowy Armenian millionaire called Shaffrass. At that point the stone disappeared, never to be seen again. It's unlikely that Shaffrass could lose a 787-carat diamond so what happened to it? One possibility is that the gem, which was by all accounts stolen from Shaffrass, was recut to make it harder to trace.

In 1774, Count Grigori Orlov purchased a huge diamond for Tsarina Catherine the Great of Russia in an attempt to regain her favour and many said that this was the largest remaining part of the Great Moghul. Perhaps so, for the stone wove the same baleful spell on Orlov that the Great Moghul had on Nader Shah. Orlov died shortly afterwards – out of favour, obsessed with money and insane. The Orlov diamond remained in the Romanov collection until the death of Nicholas II and his family during the Russian revolution when it was transferred to the Russian Diamond Fund. It remains there to this day.

Where does the Bible recommend adultery?

The book making this rather surprising suggestion is the 1631 edition of the Holy Bible published by the printers Lucas and Barker. Their version, now a rare collector's item, omits the word 'not' from Exodus 20: 14, leaving us with the commandment: '*Thou Shalt Commit Adultery.*' Thanks to this omission their version is now known as the 'Wicked' Bible, and Lucas and Barker received a hefty fine from King Charles I.

And Lucas and Barker were not the only ones that Charles had his eye on. The 'Fool's Bible' brought its printer a £3,000 fine for reading: '*The fool hath said in his heart, there is a God*' in Psalm 14: 1 instead of '*The fool hath said in his heart, there is not a God.*' The 'Unrighteous Bible' of 1653 used the words, '*Know ye not that the unrighteous shall inherit the kingdom of God*' in I Corinthians 6: 9, again omitting the all-important word 'not'.

In the 'Ears to Ears' Bible of 1807, the line in Matthew 13: 43, '*Who hath ears to hear*', reads '*Who hath ears to ears,*' whilst the 'Standing Fishes' Bible of the previous year replaces Ezekiel 47: 10, '*that the fishers shall stand*', with '*that the fishes shall stand*', conjuring an interesting image.

More modern misprints have some of the cynicism of the age. In a 1966 first edition of the Jerusalem Bible, Psalm 122: 6 reads, '*Pay for peace*' instead of 'Pray', whilst a 1970 first edition of the King James II New Testament has John 1: 5 reading, '*And the light shines in the darkness, and the darkness overcomes it*', instead of '*And the light shines in the darkness, and the darkness does not overcome it.*'

What was Mummolus's great mistake?

Mummolus was a prefect under the rule of King Chilperic I of Soissons in the early eighth century. According to Gregory of Tours in his *History of the Franks*, Chilperic's Queen Fredegund believed that Mummolus had had a hand in the death of her infant son Theodoric and she went about investigating in the way that only an eighth-century Frankish queen could: '*she apprehended some women of Paris and plied them with tortures and strove to force them by blows to confess what they knew. And they admitted that they practised magic and testified that they had caused many to die, adding . . . "We gave your son, O Queen, in exchange for Mummolus the prefect's life."'*

She then had the women either broken on the wheel, burnt alive or drowned before telling all to her husband. Mummolus was eventually captured and arrested and, as you might expect from the treatment of the ladies of Paris, tortured. *'He was suspended from a beam with his hands tied behind his back and asked what he knew of "the evil arts", but he confessed nothing concerning the death of the infant prince.'*

It was now that Mummolus made his big mistake. Having carefully refused to admit to being a sorcerer whilst dangling from the ceiling, he couldn't help but have a bit of a dig at Chilperic when he was let down again, so he called a messenger and told him to send a message to the king, saying: *'Tell my master the king that I feel no ill effect of the tortures inflicted on me.'* To say that this was a vain boast would be an understatement. Hearing it, the king not unreasonably replied: *'Is it not true that he practises evil arts if he has not been harmed by these tortures?'* So Mummolus was hauled back into the torture chamber to see whether they couldn't revise his opinion of their work: *'Then he was stretched on the wheel and beaten with triple thongs until his torturers were wearied out. Then they put splinters under his finger and toe nails.'*

After this he was finally released, probably wishing he'd kept his mouth shut in the first place. Clearly the strain of it all was beginning to show, however bold his statements to the contrary, and on the journey home to Bordeaux he died of apoplexy.

Why couldn't you read Marie Curie's lab notes until the 1990s?

Marie Curie is the only woman ever to win two Nobel prizes, the first person ever to win two, and one of only two people to have won Nobels in different fields (the other being Linus Pauling for Chemistry and Peace).

Her two citations for the prizes give a good clue as to why her lab notes have remained inaccessible. Her 1903 Physics prize, awarded with her husband Pierre Curie and Henri Becquerel, was 'in recognition of the extraordinary services they have rendered by their joint researches on the radiation phenomena discovered by Professor Henri Becquerel', whilst her 1911 Chemistry prize was 'in recognition of her services to the advancement of chemistry by the discovery of the elements radium and polonium, by the isolation of radium and the study of the nature and compounds of this remarkable element'.

When one of Marie's daughters and her granddaughter donated Marie's diaries, journals and workbooks to the Bibliothèque Nationale in Paris in the mid-1990s, it was, perhaps not surprisingly, discovered that they were all still highly radioactive. It took two years to decontaminate the paper before the bequest could be accessioned.

At the outbreak of the First World War, Marie cashed in her Nobel gold medals to help the war effort. She died of leukaemia in 1934, almost certainly caused by her massive exposure to radiation.

2

Surprise, Surprise!

Old age is the most unexpected of all things that happen to a man.

Leon Trotsky, *Diary in Exile* (1959), 8 May 1935

Who was Miss Canary Islands 1936?

In the run-up to the Spanish Civil War, General Franco had been sent to a military command on the Canary Islands, mainly to get him out of the way as the government was suspicious that a Nationalist uprising might be on the cards. At this time Franco did indeed come into contact with the conspirators who were planning the revolution that would eventually sweep him to power, but he remained ambiguous about his support for it. Whilst tacitly going along with the plans being made in the spring and early summer of 1936, he was also writing to the government offering to help suppress Nationalistic unrest in the army. By June the Nationalist leaders, José Sanjurjo and Emilio Mola, had set a date for the rising, 18 July, which, they informed Franco, would happen with or without him. It was at this time, as he continued to vacillate, that the Nationalist high command gave him the nickname 'Miss Canary Islands 1936'. Nevertheless, it would not be a title he would hold for long. When the rebellion broke out a day early, Franco seized control of the Canary Islands before flying to Spanish Morocco to take command of the Army of Africa. The quick coup that they had hoped for was botched, however, and a civil war ensued. At the end of it one man would have supreme power – Miss Canary Islands 1936: Francisco Franco.

What did Jethro Tull do with his organ?

Jethro Tull was a gentleman farmer who had always fancied a life in politics. After studying at Oxford and Gray's Inn, however, he found that his father's debts and lawsuits prevented him from taking public office so he set about farming his father's land at Howberry in Oxfordshire.

Tull was quite a meticulous man with his own ideas about how to improve crop yields. He had decided around 1700 to plant a forage crop called sainfoin on a part of his land and insisted that his labourers must plant it at a certain depth, in evenly spaced rows. They disagreed and went on strike, so Tull decided to *'contrive an engine to plant St Foin more faithfully than such hands would do'*. Using some bits from an old musical organ and parts of two other unidentified machines 'as foreign to the field as the organ is', he managed to come up with the seed drill. Despite some rather sniffy comments from other farmers and not a bit of dissension amongst farm labourers who thought that this might put them out of a job, the drill was a great success. In 1731, Tull rather reluctantly published his ideas for the drill, as well as information on improved farming methods that he had gleaned from a tour of the continent, in *Horse-Hoeing Husbandry*. By now his techniques were proving their worth and he had moved to the aptly named Prosperous Farm although his profligate son did his best to dent Tull's prosperity. He died in 1741, claiming, *'I owe my principles and my practice originally to my travels, as I owe my drill to the organ.'* He was buried in Basildon and left his son just one shilling in his will.

What did Queen Victoria think 'lacked fire'?

Some might consider it a little ungrateful but when Queen Victoria was presented with the Koh-i-Noor diamond, she wasn't very impressed. No gem has a longer or more controversial history than the Koh-i-Noor or 'Mountain of Light'. The stone's early history was as a source of strife between the powerful rulers of India's many warring states. Early sources say that the stone belonged to the raja of Malawa for many generations before the Sultan Ala'-ud'Din Khalji took it from him in 1304. Others claim it was given to Babur, the son of the founder of the great Moghul Empire, by the raja of Gwalior in return for his life.

Like many great stones, the Koh-i-Noor formed part of the loot taken by Nader Shah, the king of Persia, when he sacked Delhi in 1739 (see pages 8–9) and, after his assassination, it passed to his general, Ahmad Shah, founder of the greatest Afghan dynasty. But like its former master, the Koh-i-Noor brought the Ahmad dynasty little good fortune. When his great-grandson escaped to India he was forced to hand it over to the Sikh ruler, Ranjit Singh, to persuade the 'Lion of Punjab' not to return him to the warlike Afghan tribes who had deposed him. In 1849 the British annexed Punjab and amongst the many spoils that came to England was the Koh-i-Noor. Queen Victoria, however, proved the diamond's most apathetic owner and said she thought the stone lacked 'fire' so she ordered the royal jeweller Garrard to recut it from 191 carats down to 109. The results were indifferent and Victoria took little further interest in the gem. Only in 1937 did the Koh-i-Noor achieve the fame it deserved, being placed in the queen's state crown for the coronation of the present queen's late mother.

What was the star attraction at the Bronx Zoo in 1906?

The story of Ota Benga is one of the darkest episodes in the history of black America. Born in the Congo in 1883 during the savage personal rule of King Leopold II of Belgium (see pages 127–8 for this King's lighter side), he was 'discovered' by the American missionary, Samuel Verner, who found him hiding amongst the Batwa people after Belgian agents had murdered his family. Verner had been sent to the country to look for pygmy specimens to display at the World's Fair in St Louis as part of the craze for 'ethnological expositions' in which 'primitive' peoples were displayed in mock-ups of their own villages. In Ota Benga he found just what he was looking for. Brought back to America, Benga was displayed in the 'University of Man' exhibit at the 1904 fair along with Inuit, Filipinos, Japanese tribal peoples, Zulus and, the star of the show, the native American, Geronimo, who was labelled 'The Human Tiger'.

After the fair Verner returned all his human exhibits to Africa but Ota Benga found difficulty in returning to his former life, particularly as many of the Batwa he had previously known had been massacred in his absence. After a few months he asked Verner whether he could return to the USA with him and Verner agreed.

Back in the USA, Verner seemed unsure what to do with Ota Benga until it was suggested that he could become a living mascot for the American Museum of Natural History. The museum provided him with a white suit and engaged him to make small talk with visitors. For a brief moment he became a high-society celebrity until an incident when he threw a chair at Florence Guggenheim brought the headline in the *New York Times*, 'Benga Tries to Kill!' and his immediate dismissal.

It was now that Verner took Benga to the Bronx Zoo where initially he was allowed to roam the exhibits and help to feed the animals. It was not long, however, before it became clear that the zoo didn't see Benga as an employee but as an exhibit. He was first asked to hang his hammock in the monkey house and then, on 8 September 1906, a sign went up describing the zoo's newest acquisition, an African pygmy called Ota Benga. Some 40,000 people are estimated to have come to see the man now variously described as an elf, a cannibal, a dwarf and a savage, before a group of African-American ministers mounted a successful press campaign to end the spectacle.

Ota Benga was then moved to the Howard Colored Orphan Asylum where he was taught English and Scripture. Once it was considered that he had learnt all he could, his ritually filed teeth were capped and he was sent to Lynchburg, Virginia, under a new name, Otto Bingo, where he worked in a tobacco factory. Although this was better treatment than he had received in New York, Benga found it hard to settle into his new life and became depressed when he realised that he could never save enough money to return to Africa. On 20 March 1916 he took a friend's pistol and shot himself through the heart. He is buried in an unmarked grave.

Which monument was bought as a birthday present?

There are many types of stone that a man might buy his wife for her birthday but Sir Cecil Chubb, the self-made son of a saddler, wanted something a bit special. The stone, or rather stones, that he intended to purchase had an ancient history although no one was quite sure who had originally owned them. They had certainly belonged to the nuns of Amesbury Abbey before the Dissolution of the Monasteries and after that they came into a number of noble hands, including those of the Duke of Somerset and the Marquess of Queensberry, before finding their way into the Antrobus family. The Antrobuses held on to these treasures right up until the First World War. Then, tragically, in the opening months of the war, Edmund Antrobus, the heir to the family fortune, was killed and his father decided to sell up. Messrs Knight Frank and Rutley were called in to catalogue and sell the whole estate. It was into this auction, in the Palace Theatre in Salisbury, that Cecil Chubb walked on 21 September 1915. Shortly after, he emerged some £6,600 pounds poorer but the proud possessor of a unique birthday present for his wife – Lot 15: Stonehenge with about thirty acres, two rods and thirty-seven perches of adjoining downland.

Chubb later admitted that he had had no intention of buying the monument when he went into the sale but thought that, as a local boy made good (he was the owner of a successful asylum and several racehorses), perhaps he ought to buy it. Three years later he, or rather his wife, formally gave the monument to the nation on the condition that the gate money should go to the Red Cross for the duration of the war and that the people of local parishes should be able to visit for free, which they still can. The following year Chubb was created a baronet and took as his arms one of the distinctive trilithons of Stonehenge.

Which German dedicated a symphony to a French dictator?

Beethoven composed the 'Eroica' or Heroic Symphony between 1803 and 1804, and on the original title page dedicated the work to Napoleon Bonaparte. At the time Napoleon was First Consul of the French Republic, a nation that Beethoven rather admired, and whose consul he thought of as a champion of ordinary people and democracy.

However, on 18 May 1804, Napoleon rather disappointingly chose to declare himself emperor. Beethoven was furious. According to his friend and biographer Ferdinand Ries, who told him the news (either that May, or possibly in December after Napoleon's coronation), he shouted: *'So he is no more than a common mortal! Now, too, he will tread under foot all the rights of man, indulge only his ambition; now he will think himself superior to all men, become a tyrant!'* Which wasn't all that far from the truth. Beethoven then marched to the table where the completed manuscript lay and scratched out Bonaparte's name on the front sheet, with such venom that he made a hole in the paper. When the symphony was published it had a new dedication: *'Sinfonia eroica composta per festeggiare il sovvenire d'un gran uomo [Heroic Symphony composed to celebrate the memory of a great man].'*

And ever since the work has been known as the 'Eroica' Symphony.

What was Oliver Cromwell's name?

Oliver Cromwell could have called himself many things, perhaps the least likely of which was Oliver Cromwell. He was a descendant of a Welshman, Morgan ap Williams, so if he had used the Welsh form of his surname he should have been 'Oliver son of Robert (his father)' or Oliver ap Robert. Instead he kept the family name of his great-great-grandmother, Catherine Cromwell, who had married the Welshman. But if we allow that this marriage formed a new Anglo-Welsh family, Oliver's real surname should have been Williams. So how did all this confusion come about?

Catherine Cromwell was born around 1483 and was the older sister of Tudor statesman Thomas Cromwell. Despite marrying into the Tudor line, she and her descendants chose to keep the Cromwell name and there are two theories as to why this might be. One states simply that the family wished to maintain their connection with their illustrious Tudor ancestor Thomas, even though that passed down only on the female side. However, it might also have been to disguise the male side of the family's heritage. This, rather embarrassingly for a republican like Oliver, connected them to the houses of Tudor, de Valois and Wittelsbach: the three royal dynasties of England, France and the Holy Roman Empire respectively. This may seem unlikely but it is easily explained.

Cromwell's alleged paternal ancestor, Jasper Tudor, was the uncle of Henry VII of England. Both Jasper Tudor and his brother Edmund were sons of Owen Tudor and Catherine of Valois, daughter of the slightly inflammable Charles VI of France (see page 225) and the unfortunate Isabeau of Bavaria (see pages 100–1). Catherine was also the widow of Henry V of England. Her mother, Isabeau, was the daughter of Stephen III, Duke of Bavaria-Ingolstadt and Thaddea Visconti.

Interestingly after the Restoration, when it was not a good idea to be seen to have close links with Oliver Cromwell, some members of the family reverted for a time to calling themselves Williams.

Who gave all three of his sons the same name?

Karl I Alexander, Duke of Württemberg, fought under Prince Eugène of Savoy in the War of the Spanish Succession (1701–14), a spat that started over who should succeed to the Spanish throne after the death of the last Habsburg king. However, it rapidly mushroomed into an attempt by the Holy Roman Empire, England and the Dutch to prevent the crowns of Spain and France from uniting. It was in this war that the Duke of Marlborough made his name in England and Prince Eugène of Savoy made his in Austria. Karl Alexander was therefore delighted to serve with the illustrious prince. So impressed, indeed, was Karl with his military commander that he named all three of his sons Eugène (or rather Eugen in German). Whilst giving more than one child the same name was not unusual if one had died in childhood, all Karl's boys survived. Fortunately he had also given them other names – Karl, Friedrich and Ludwig – so everyone knew where they stood.

Who built Cleopatra's Needle?

Strangely enough, Cleopatra's Needle has absolutely nothing to do with Cleopatra although it does have an interesting history. The needle, which is one of three obelisks, was commissioned by the Pharaoh Tuthmoses III some 1,400 years before Cleopatra was even born. Cut from red granite mined near what is now Aswan, they were erected outside a temple in Heliopolis, an ancient capital that stood at the apex of the Nile delta. A couple of hundred years later the Pharaoh Rameses II decided to have inscriptions carved on them, something he liked to do to any spare piece of stonework lying around in his kingdom that didn't already make mention of his great deeds.

It was only under Roman rule, in 12 BC, that the obelisks were taken from Heliopolis to the city that until recently had been Cleopatra's capital, Alexandria. Here they were erected again outside a building that Cleopatra had begun in honour of Mark Antony but which Augustus, after their deaths and his promotion to the title of emperor, finished in his own honour and renamed after himself.

Their setting is described by a Jewish scholar living in the city in the first century AD as *'huge and conspicuous, fitted on a scale not found elsewhere with dedicated offerings, around it a girdle of pictures and statues in silver and gold, forming a precinct of vast breadth, embellished with porticoes, libraries, chambers, groves, gateways and wide open courts and everything which lavish expenditure could produce to beautify it'* (Philo of Alexandria, *The Embassy to Gaius*, 15).

It was here that the obelisks stayed, although toppled by a series of earthquakes, until the nineteenth century. In 1801 the Ottoman viceroy of Egypt gave Britain what had by then come to be called a needle in thanks for British victories over the French at the Battle of the Nile and the Battle of Alexandria. The British government, however, was not prepared to pay for the huge monument to be brought to London. It was only in 1877 that a wealthy English dermatologist paid for the needle to be shipped over at the staggering cost of £10,000. The obelisk was encased in its own barge, an iron tube called *Cleopatra*, to be towed to England but it capsized in the Bay of Biscay during a storm, killing six men. It was eventually picked up, floating free in the open sea, and finally erected on the Embankment in London in August 1879.

The needle in Paris was originally from the Luxor temple in what was ancient Thebes and, not surprisingly, is also covered in hieroglyphics praising Rameses II. It was given to France by another Ottoman viceroy of Egypt (in 1829). He presumably took a different view from his predecessor who had donated the other one to Britain for having expelled the French. It now stands in the centre of the Place de la Concorde.

New York's needle was also a gift of the ruling Ottoman dynasty in Egypt, this time from the Khedive Tewfik Pasha in 1879. He didn't care whether the French were coming or going but just wanted to improve trade relations. Its move to New York took over a decade to achieve and was funded by the railroad magnate, William Vanderbilt. It, too, is covered in self-congratulatory inscriptions to a certain Rameses II.

3

Men of the Cloth

It's great being a priest, isn't it, Ted?

Graham Linehan and Arthur Mathews, *Good Luck, Father Ted* (1994), episode from the series *Father Ted*

Whom did Edward Gibbon accuse of piracy, murder, rape, sodomy and incest?

These were Edward Gibbon's comments in his *Decline and Fall of the Roman Empire* on the man who called himself Pope John XXIII and who is today known by the Catholic Church as Antipope John XXIII.

The distinction here between antipope and pope is important as there is also a Pope John XXIII who held the Holy See from 1958 to 1963. When he became pope there was some question as to whether he might take the title John XXIV to avoid any association with Gibbon's murderous pirate but he announced that he would be Pope John XXIII in order to make it clear that the murderous pirate was not a proper pope and so the number twenty-three was still available. Interestingly enough, he could also have chosen to be Pope John XX as, due to a clerical error, no Pope John ever had that number.

So what did Antipope John XXIII do to get such a bad press? Well, partly it was a matter of politics. John was one of three people claiming to be pope in the early fifteenth century during the split known as 'The Great Schism', each of whom had the support of a few cardinals and, most importantly of all, that of one or more of the European rulers who really held the power. John was certainly a little worldly, having managed a stint as a pirate and run a protection racket at the University of Bologna before deciding to become religious. In fact at the time of his 'election' as pope, he wasn't even a priest and had to be ordained quickly before he could be enthroned. But in many ways he was no worse than the others – just wholly unsuitable as pope.

Eventually everyone in Europe got rather tired of all these popes who kept popping up and a council was called at Constance between 1414 and 1417, which decided to get rid of all the current popes and antipopes. Gregory XII saw which way the wind was blowing and retired gracefully; Benedict XIII retreated to Spain, still claiming it was really unfair; but John XXIII ran away, only to get caught and dragged back before the Council. Still, at least he was alive (see pages 196–7). The charges brought before him at the Council, as described by Gibbon, were certainly exaggerated but they had enough of a ring of truth about them to ensure his deposition and imprisonment. Once the Council had agreed on a new pope, Martin V, everyone felt a little more forgiving, however, and John, now just plain old Baldassarre Cossa, was released. This was a good result for the antipope really, since he had been charged with nearly every major crime in existence and was sentenced to a mere three years in prison. Jan Hus, who was also condemned at Constance, had agreed to recant all the theological statements he had made if they could be proved wrong and they burnt him at the stake anyway. After his release the former antipope was made Cardinal Bishop of Tusculum by Martin V and moved to Florence, where he died in 1419. Cosimo de Medici, a big patron of the arts, commissioned Donatello and Michelozzi to prepare a magnificent tomb for him, which survives to this day.

Which famous monk married a nun?

In the mediaeval period the marriage of monks or nuns, let alone one to the other, was generally frowned upon. Even popes hadn't taken wives since the time of Adrian II in the ninth century (although a few of the less reliable popes had taken a mistress or two and some were possibly even secretly married). All marital prospects therefore suddenly declined for one young man returning from the University of Erfurt who was struck by lightning. According to his own testimony he immediately shouted, 'Help, St Anna, I will become a monk,' and was immediately as good as his word.

Martin Luther wasn't going to be a normal monk, however. His own personal devotion didn't tally with the apparent venality of the Church, evidence of which he now saw all around him, leading him to write to the archbishop of Mainz and Magdeburg, complaining about the sale of indulgences and attaching his ninety-five theses (which, legend has it, he also handily nailed to the door of the castle church in Wittenberg the same day). The archbishop was at the time using part of the money from indulgence sales to pay off his bribery debts so he wasn't best pleased about Luther's complaints. He had the theses checked for heresy and sent the lot off to the pope without bothering to reply. One thing led to another and, before you knew it, Luther had been excommunicated and outlawed, and the Reformation had kicked off.

By now Luther was getting regular requests from nuns who wanted to escape from their nunneries. On 7 April 1523 a group of nine of these escapees arrived at Luther's home, having been smuggled out of the Cistercian monastery of Nimbschen in herring barrels. Amongst them was Katharina von Bora. The other eight ex-nuns were soon married to locals in Wittenberg but Katharina let it be known that she wanted to marry Luther himself. He was initially reluctant, taking the view that, as an excommunicant and outlaw, he wouldn't make an ideal husband. She prevailed, however, and he married the woman he would later fondly call 'My Lord Katie' on 13 June 1525. They had six children – three girls and three boys – and lived in 'the Black Cloister', a former Augustinian monastery in Wittenberg, which the Elector gave them as a wedding present.

What is unusual about Pope Sylvester's tomb?

Sylvester was the first French pope and the man with the tricky job of guiding Christian Europe through the start of the first millennium when many people believed the world would end, which it didn't. Sylvester was a great scholar and one of the few Christians to have studied the academic heritage of the Muslim world, which had preserved a great deal of the scientific knowledge of classical civilisations, much of which was long lost in the West. This knowledge made people suspicious, however, and rumours began to circulate that he was in league with the devil, acquiring his wisdom from forbidden Moorish books that he had stolen whilst in Spain and receiving answers to difficult questions from a magical bronze head that could give 'yes' or 'no' answers. All these rumours grew out of Christian mistrust of Arab scholars, the turbulent politics of the era (in which Sylvester was heavily involved) and a general feeling of unease that Armageddon was nigh.

In truth Sylvester was a brilliant man who saw Europe through the millennium without the expected apocalypse and whose last years were marred only by his expulsion from Rome following a political revolt. What is unusual about his tomb is not that it contains the remains of a necromancer but that the bones inside are said to rattle whenever a pope is about to die. This story might appear to be some half-memory of Sylvester's supposed astrological powers but is in fact simply a mistranslation of what's written on the lid. The Latin inscription states that the tomb will yield up its contents to the sound (of the last trumpet) of the advent of the Lord. The Latin here being a little obscure, this was misread as saying that the tomb itself will make a sound at the advent of the Lord, which was taken to mean that when a pope nears death, its contents will rattle, which they don't.

Which war was caused by an argument over a key?

Nearly 280,000 people were killed, wounded or died of disease during the two years of the Crimean War, yet the entire conflagration was sparked by nothing more than a tussle over the ownership of a key.

In all fairness it was a golden key and it did open something rather special – the doors to the church of the Nativity in Bethlehem – and behind this apparently inoffensive item lay all the political muscle flexing and posturing that so often precedes a war. The question of the moment in the early 1850s was, who is the protector of Christians in the Ottoman Empire (which then included the Holy Land)? According to Napoleon III and the French it was them and the Roman Catholic Church. Initially, at least, the sultan in Istanbul went along with this and the golden key to the church of the Nativity, which represented this hegemony, was handed over to the Roman Catholic monks in Bethlehem. The Russian tsar, however, was not at all happy about this and pointed out to the Ottomans that two eighteenth-century treaties stipulated that Russia (and the Greek Orthodox Church) should be the guardians of Christians in the Ottoman Empire. The sultan took his point and so the ownership of the golden key reverted to the Orthodox monks of Bethlehem. France, now furious, sent a warship to the Black Sea in direct contravention of the London Straits Treaty, which prevented military shipping using the Bosphorus.

This sabre-rattling worked, with the result that the sultan changed his mind yet again. France and the Roman Catholic Church were once more back in charge and the Orthodox monks in Bethlehem were keyless. But this forceful diplomacy had left Tsar Nicholas I with few options if he wanted to regain influence with the Ottomans. At this point he decided that the only course left was to force the authorities in Istanbul to change their minds by mobilising against them. Attempts at brokering a peace in Europe failed and the European powers, namely France and Great Britain, aligned themselves with the Ottomans against the Russians. And so it was cardigans at dawn (see pages 263–5) as a golden key started the Crimean War. The French statesman, Adolphe Thiers, later said that it was '*a war to give a few wretched monks the key of a grotto*'.

Was there really a female pope?

A number of women have played an important role in the development of the papacy. Up until the reign of Adrian II (867–72), popes could and sometimes did marry although Adrian was the last to do so and he put his wife aside when he got the top job. During the Renaissance a number of popes were heavily influenced by their aristocratic mothers and mistresses – not least the

Borgia pope Alexander VI – but, sadly, the most famous of all, Pope Joan, is entirely fictional.

According to legend, after the death of Leo IV in 855 (some sources say after Victor III) a pope was quickly elected who took the title John Anglicus – John the Englishman. His reign was to be short, however. During an Easter procession between St Peter's and the Lateran Palace, an excitable crowd accidentally pushed him from his horse. The shock of the fall brought on premature labour and 'John' promptly gave birth to a baby. John was in fact Joan – a woman – and an Englishwoman at that, who had usurped the papacy by dressing as a man. Her undoing had been her failure to remain chaste and with her secret revealed the crowd took its revenge. They dragged her through the streets of Rome tied to a horse, then stoned her to death, thus making their opinion of female popes abundantly clear.

Why this story grew up is still something of a mystery. It first appears in the Universal Chronicle of Metz written around 1250, some 400 years after Pope Leo IV's death, and it remained popular until the seventeenth century when it was finally disproved. It may have originated as a satire on the papacy put around by the court of the Holy Roman Emperor, Frederick II, who had annoyed a lot of thirteenth-century popes by sidestepping their attempts to make him go on a crusade. They, in turn, had excommunicated him, so he responded by telling stories about how worldly and unholy the papacy was, which wasn't that far from the truth. And what better story than that the pope had once – horrors of horrors – been a woman, and an unchaste woman at that?

But why is Joan said to have been English and why place her way back in the ninth century? After the death of Leo there had been clashes between the Holy Roman Emperor and the papacy that had involved the usual excommunications and election of antipopes, so perhaps for the compiler of the Universal Chronicle it seemed to be an era with startling similarities to his own. Strangely enough it was also a time when an important English delegation was in Rome, led by Æthelwulf, king of Wessex, and his son Alfred (later to become Alfred the Great), so perhaps the insistence that Pope Joan was English is a confused memory of the rare presence in the city that year of an important party of English pilgrims.

Who cremated Jesus Christ?

Dr William Price was an unusual man by the standards of late nineteenth-century Wales. In an age of fervent Christian belief, Price claimed to be the reincarnation of a Celtic priest who had died some 10,000 years before. In other words, a druid.

This was in itself enough to enrage many a decent chapel-goer but it was not this that would get Price into trouble. Nor was it his assertion that the ancient Welsh (and the modern ones too if he could persuade them) enjoyed open marriages, naked sunbathing and vegetarianism. It was not even his habit of carrying a stick marked with arcane Greek insignia and topped with a crescent moon, or the fox skin that he always wore on his head – with the animal's head still attached. What enraged the public of 1883 has today become part of everyday life.

William Price had a son who, not surprisingly for someone as eccentric as himself, he had christened Jesus Christ. There was nothing to actually stop him using that name although it probably made the poor boy's life a bit difficult.

The real problems for William Price and Jesus Christ only came after Jesus' death. When Jesus died William refused to register the death. Instead he took his son's body to a nearby field where he built a huge bonfire. This attracted quite a lot of local attention and a fair few people came to see what he was up to. When they saw him put his son's body on the bonfire and set light to it, there was a riot.

In late nineteenth-century Britain the dead were always buried. The thought of burning them horrified the gathered crowd. They surged past Price towards the flames and pulled the charred body from the pyre. The police were called. William was arrested and charged with burning a body in an attempt to prevent an inquest.

But it was a flawed prosecution. Nobody had claimed that William was burning the body to hide evidence of wrong-doing. His son had died under perfectly normal circumstances. In court his barrister argued that there was no law to say that a body had to be buried, not cremated, and he was quite right. At the time people thought that burial alone was decent but no law existed to prevent any other means of disposing of the dead. So William Price walked free, fox-skin hat and all. When he died nine years later at the ripe old age of ninety-one he was, of course, cremated. Nearly 20,000 people came to watch. He'd started a fashion.

Four years after his death Britain's first crematorium was opened. Today seven out of ten bodies are cremated instead of buried – though not usually in open fields. William Price's most eccentric idea has become the normal way of doing things.

Who made 200 monks jump?

Jean-Antoine Nollet was trained for the religious life, which is why he generally liked to be known as Abbé Nollet, and as such could probably have made any number of monks jump whenever he chose, but what he really wanted to do was demonstrate an important scientific point. Although nominally a man of the cloth, Nollet was also a great scientist with a particular interest in the strange phenomenon of electricity that, at the beginning of the eighteenth century, still hadn't been properly explained. In 1745 he developed the theory of electrical attraction and repulsion, which he thought came from there being two types of electricity – positive and negative. This brought him into direct conflict with Benjamin Franklin, founding father of the USA and extreme kite flyer, whose ideas would eventually supplant his own.

What Nollet and Franklin had in common, however, was the ability to turn an experiment into a great show. Whilst Franklin flew kites in electrical storms to prove that lightning was electrical (and still found time to invent a flexible urinary catheter), Nollet had developed an amusing way of showing how electrical conductivity worked. Having been appointed Preceptor in Natural Philosophy to the royal family, he was required to demonstrate physics experiments for the education and amusement of King Louis XV and his entourage. At Versailles in 1746 he persuaded 180 royal guards to line up whilst he connected them together with a thin wire. He then attached each end of the line to a Leyden jar. This was an early form of capacitor, which stored an electrical charge. When the unfortunate soldiers at the end of the line were attached to it, the electricity discharged through them via the whole line, making all the soldiers jump in the air. This demonstration of the action of electricity on human bodies greatly amused the royal party but also made an important point.

Nollet had greater ambitions and back in Paris he used his ecclesiastical authority to arrange a yet more spectacular public demonstration in the hope of discovering the speed of electrical transmission. For this he summoned 200 (some sources say over 1,000) monks from the Carthusian Grand Convent in Paris whom he placed in a line over a mile long, all connected together by iron wires twenty-five feet long. Nollet then attached a series of large Leyden jars to one end of the line and discharged them, sending a few hundred volts through the unsuspecting monastic daisy chain. Apparently instantaneously, all the monks jumped in the air, shouting and cursing with the same force, suggesting to Nollet that electricity passes instantaneously and can travel over long distances. This experiment has since been claimed as the origin of the telegraph.

How old was the youngest pope?

It's not easy to find out how old some of the earlier popes were at the time of their election as there was little in the way of good birth records. A claim is often made that Benedict IX became pope at the tender age of eleven but that calculation is based on the fact that we have absolutely no idea when he was born. The more sober *Catholic Encyclopaedia* estimates that he was around twenty, which seems more likely. If so, he is beaten to the title of youngest pontiff by John XII who was certainly only eighteen when he got the top job. What both popes have in common is that they got the post through nepotism and they were both wholly unsuited to the role. In his splendidly vitriolic *Book of Gomorrah*, St Peter Damian accused Benedict of being a homosexual devil who practised bestiality. Whilst this might be going a bit too far, Benedict certainly managed to be pope three times (having been kicked out twice), was probably married and once sold the papacy to his godfather.

John XII wasn't much better. He was accused of invoking demons whilst playing dice, toasting the devil with wine, and sleeping with scores of women, including his father's concubine and his own niece. He was also accused of murders, blindings and of ordaining a ten-year-old as a bishop. He died aged twenty-seven, possibly killed by the irate husband of one of his lovers – a fate he shared with Pope Benedict VII.

What was Jesus' younger brother doing in China?

He was starting the second-bloodiest conflict in world history. The mid-nineteenth century Taiping rebellion isn't very well known outside China and yet a conservative estimate of the death toll amongst soldiers and civilians is 20 million people. The rebellion had its origins in dissatisfaction with the ruling Qing dynasty who had suffered a series of natural disasters and defeats by foreign powers, notably the British in the First Opium War.

Leading the backlash against the Qing, two men emerged – Hong Xiuquan and Yang Xiuqing – who led their followers to found the 'Heavenly Kingdom of Great Peace', carved out of huge tracts in the south of the country. The main problem with the Heavenly Kingdom of Great Peace, however, was the complete lack of any sort of peace as the imperial armies continued to attack it. Even within the kingdom, rule was absolute and militaristic. The leaders were Christian converts who took a literal interpretation of the Bible in which they cast themselves as supreme intermediaries between God and man. Yang Xiuqing, a former firewood salesman, was the mouthpiece through whom God spoke directly to the Taiping rebels, whilst Hong Xiuquan declared himself to be the younger brother of Jesus and hence the new Messiah.

Despite these rather unusual ideas the rebellion garnered a massive following, which probably goes to show how unpopular the imperial court really was. At its height there were over 1 million soldiers in the Taiping 'Army of Love', which, contrary to what the name might suggest, was renowned for its fanaticism and bloody determination. At the third Battle of Nanking, 100,000 people lost their lives in just three days of fighting.

Within their kingdom, of which Hong Xiuquan was the supreme and absolute ruler, there were a number of innovations (by nineteenth-century standards) including political and gender equality; the abolition of foot binding; the banning of gambling, prostitution, slavery, opium, tobacco and other such vices; the adoption of a solar calendar; and an insistence on monogamy. The application of the rules was arbitrary, however, and the situation was not helped by Hong Xiuquan's increasingly delicate mental condition. In 1853, like so many autocratic Messiahs, he decided to withdraw from the deteriorating situation in his Heavenly Kingdom and spend more time with his harem.

With the middle classes increasingly disturbed by the rebellion's fundamentalism and administrative corruption, support for its leaders began to wane and imperial forces seized the opportunity to advance, aided by Charles Gordon (later of posthumous Khartoum fame – see page 253). By 1864 most of the country was back under imperial control and the Taiping capital at Nanking was besieged. Hong died from food poisoning, caused by eating wild food that had been gathered when supplies in the city ran out, and he was buried in the old Ming imperial palace. When the city fell, his body was exhumed and cremated before being fired from a cannon to prevent any one place becoming a shrine to his memory.

When did the pope become infallible?

The idea of infallibility seems rather mediaeval today and so you might expect to find that popes decided that they were infallible many centuries ago. In fact the doctrine of infallibility was only actually codified at the First Vatican Council in 1870 and it certainly doesn't imply that whatever the pope says is beyond argument. For the pope to make an infallible statement, he has to be speaking *ex cathedra,* i.e. in his official capacity as pastor of all Christians, not as a private individual (so he can't use his infallibility to win arguments). He must also make it clear that he is promulgating a doctrine of faith or morals and that this is the last word on the matter. Finally he must make it clear that he intends to bind the whole Church by the statement and that everyone must agree on pain of what the Catholic Church calls 'spiritual shipwreck'.

Interestingly, infallibility is a personal thing for popes, being something handed down to them from St Peter. Whilst they can issue infallible statements themselves, statements that have come from councils of cardinals or elsewhere – even if the pope has approved them – can never be considered infallible. Nor is the whole of a statement made *ex cathedra* necessarily infallible. In Pope Pius IX's statement of dogma on the Immaculate Conception, only one or two sentences are considered infallible. The last time that a pope made an infallible statement was in 1950 when Pius XII issued a dogmatic statement *ex cathedra* on the Assumption of Mary.

4

Justice

This ain't the shop for justice.

Charles Dickens (said by the Artful Dodger), *Oliver Twist* (1838), chapter 43

Who was buried with a stake through the heart?

Not Draculas (see pages 93–4) nor, indeed, any other vampire but, in Great Britain at least, suicides. The Christian view of suicide as a crime against the self dates back at least to St Augustine of Hippo but the rather harsh treatment of suicides in Britain goes right back to the Anglo-Saxon period. Suicides were separated into two types. First there were those who killed themselves when of unsound mind. They were treated with some compassion as the 'crime' wasn't really their fault. Those who had coolly and sanely killed themselves, however, were guilty of a felo de se – a crime against the self, or self-murder – and this deserved punishment. Obviously it's quite difficult to punish someone who's dead but you could penalise their family, desecrate their memory and, assuming they were Christian, destroy their hopes of salvation.

Those found guilty of a felo de se were to have an ignominious burial. Their bodies were often dragged through the town and then buried without Christian rites in an unconsecrated place, usually a rural crossroads. For good measure a stake was then driven through their hearts. Executed criminals, too, were often buried at crossroads, a location that may have been chosen partly because it lay on the fringes of a community (like the behaviour of criminals and suicides) and partly to prevent their malign spirits from haunting the living. Crossroads were thought to confuse the avenging spirit who, with any luck, might wander off in the wrong direction. *The Gentleman's Magazine* of 1784 records that a coroner recommended that a female poisoner who had also poisoned herself should be buried at a crossroads with a stake through her heart to prevent her haunting the locals, although the locals actually buried her on the seashore instead. From a Christian perspective, burial outside a consecrated churchyard additionally implied that such folk would not be amongst the saved come Judgment Day.

Things were pretty bad for the family of a suicide as well. They were still around, and could therefore be punished. So they were.

Someone guilty of a felo de se could have their entire estate confiscated and handed to the Crown, effectively disinheriting any heir.

Surely all this mediaeval barbarism was abolished a long time ago though? Not really. In seventeenth-century England the law was changed to confiscate only the suicide's personal property, leaving their land to their heirs, but crossroads burials were abolished by Act of Parliament only in 1823. This came about partly due to unrest caused by the difference in the treatment of two suicides: Viscount Castlereagh, who was declared 'of unsound mind' after an unfortunate incident with a letter-opener (see pages 133–4), yet was buried with full rites in Westminster Abbey, and one Abel Griffiths, who was interred without rites in 'drawers, socks and a winding sheet' at the crossroads formed by Eaton Street, Grosvenor Place and King's Road in London less than a year later. The *Annual Register* for that year did at least conclude that *'the disgusting part of the ceremony of throwing lime over the body and driving a stake through it was dispensed with.'* The forfeiture of personal property remained on the statute book until 1870, however. Suicide technically continued to be a crime in the UK up to 1961 and doctors dealing with suicides were meant to inform the police. Ireland repealed its suicide laws only in 1993.

Which uncle of Queen Victoria was suspected of murder?

Field Marshal His Royal Highness the Prince Ernest Augustus, KG, KP, GCB, GCH, Duke of Cumberland and Teviotdale and Earl of Armagh, later His Majesty Ernest Augustus I, King of Hanover and Duke of Brunswick-Lüneburg, was not a popular man, even considering his enormously long title. He was the eighth child of George III and despite the very poor reputations of his brothers, particularly the Prince Regent (for more on which see pages 101–2), he still managed to be the least liked of the whole brood. He was an extreme Tory, opposing just about every bit of reforming legislation put forward, including the Catholic

Emancipation Bill (see pages 271–2) proposed by the Duke of Wellington, who was then Prime Minister, and the 1832 Reform Act (see pages 273–4).

But it was in his private life that he really gained notoriety. Despite a string of chivalrous titles (he was a Knight of the Garter, Knight Grand Cross of the Order of the Bath, Knight of St Patrick and eventually Sovereign and Grand Master of the Royal Guelphic Order), his attitude towards women was usually less than chivalrous. In the scrupulous contemporary memoirs of Charles Cavendish Fulke Greville, which Lord Winchelsea unkindly likened to a life of the apostles written by Judas Iscariot, he records the exploits of Cumberland, whom he describes as 'the most audacious villain in the world and totally without fear or shame'. The duke was known to have had an affair with Lady Graves, shortly after which Lord Graves cut his own throat (although the coroner refused to connect the events and recorded a verdict of insanity).

The Sellis incident was stranger still, however. Around 2.30 a.m. on 31 May 1810, in his rooms at St James's Palace, the duke claimed that he awoke to find a man attacking him with his own regimental sabre. He attempted to defend himself and in the process was severely cut on the hands and wrists. Nevertheless, he managed to call out for help and his valet Cornelius Neale arrived. At this point his assailant vanished. A doctor was called and, as his wounds were being dressed, the duke asked for his other valet, a Sardinian by the name of Joseph Sellis. Two servants were dispatched to fetch him but on entering his rooms they found him lying dead on the bed, his throat cut from front to back as far as the spine. An inquest was held and it was rapidly (many say too rapidly) concluded that Sellis had attacked his master, for reasons unknown, and, being disturbed, had then retired to his room where he had almost completely cut off his own head with a razor.

Perhaps not surprisingly, the public – and, indeed, Cumberland's political enemies of whom he had an impressive number – did not really believe the story. A basin containing bloodied water was found in Sellis's room, suggesting he'd washed his hands after nearly severing his own head. It was also questioned whether one could really inflict an injury that severe on oneself without help. There was also no sign on the valet's body of the frenzied attack that he had allegedly inflicted on Cumberland.

Court rumour suggested a more likely scenario – that Cumberland had killed his valet, either whilst he slept or when Sellis confronted him. But what was Sellis to confront his master with? Rumour had it that Cumberland had been having an affair with Sellis's wife and the two had been caught in flagrante delicto. The furious Sellis had attacked his master but Cumberland, an excellent swordsman, had dispatched him. Some London pamphlets reported that it was Sellis's daughter rather than his wife who had been raped by Cumberland and the duke, threatened with exposure, had cut his valet's throat as he slept. Perhaps the most extraordinary claim, and one that, considering the duke's known predilections, probably has more to do with spite than fact, claimed that Sellis caught Cumberland involved in a 'grotesque act' with the other valet Neale and had to be silenced.

Which highwayman stole from the rich and gave to the poor?

James Hind was the only highwayman to *give* money to his victims. He seems to be the origin of our rather unusual attitude towards highwaymen. Whilst anyone doing today what highwaymen did a few hundred years ago would probably be dismissed as a mugger, we take a kinder and more romantic view of them.

Hind, according to his own words, was a highwayman with a conscience who really did steal from the rich to give to the poor. He was active during the English Civil War and was a fervent Royalist. As such, he would interview his chosen victims before robbing them to see whether they were suitable targets. In his 'Declaration' published in 1651, he wrote: '*Neither did I ever take the worth of a penny from a poor man; but at what time soever I met with any such a person, it was my constant custom, to ask, Who he was for? if he reply'd, For the King, I gave him 20 shillings: but if he answer'd, For the Parliament, I left him, as I found him.'*

Of course not everyone got away so lightly. In his speech in Newgate gaol he admitted: *'Neither did I ever wrong any poor man of the worth of a penny: but I must confess, I have (when I have been necessitated thereto) made bold with a rich Bompkin, or a lying Lawyer, whose full-fed fees from the rich Farmer, doth too too much impoverish the poor cottage-keeper.'* But according to his none-too-reliable biographer George Fidge, who published *The English Gusman* in 1652, Hind always returned some of the money he stole, even from 'rich bompkins', to cover his victims' travelling expenses.

Sadly such generosity did not save him. Whilst he might have been the first 'gentleman thief', he was also a Royalist robbing the streets of Cromwell's England. He was betrayed, tried and hanged at Worcester in 1652.

What could you buy with a 'Tyburn Ticket'?

Although not as much fun as one of Willy Wonka's Golden Tickets, a Tyburn Ticket was still worth having. The Ticket was introduced under William III as a way of encouraging have-a-go heroes. It was granted to individuals who caught and successfully prosecuted a felon, leading to their execution. The Ticket granted certain benefits to its holder, including exemptions from duties in the parish where the crime had taken place. It was also transferable and hence could be bought and sold. Indeed, 'thief-catchers' like Manchester's notorious Joseph Nadin traded in them. It was clearly a valuable business, as on 27 March 1818 the *Stamford* announced the sale of one of these Tickets for £280. Although the issuing of Tyburn Tickets was repealed in 1818, as late as 1824 a judge in Hertfordshire granted William Hale a Ticket for apprehending and prosecuting a burglar who broke into his father's house. Even later, trading in them continued and, according to the magazine *Notes and Queries*, someone was claiming an exemption from jury service as late as 1856 on the grounds that they held a Ticket.

What made the king of Hungary's wedding a disaster?

The fourteenth-century Hungarian court could be a dangerous place as the tale of Felician Zach demonstrates. On 6 July 1320, King Charles Robert I of Hungary married his third wife, Elizabeth, daughter of King Casimir III of Poland. As you might expect, the father of the bride came along to the festivities but then, as is so often the case with families, things started to go wrong.

During the celebrations Casimir 'insulted' (which we can probably read as raped) a maid of honour at Charles's court, the daughter of a powerful magnate called Felician Zach. Zach was rightly furious and decided that the only acceptable response was to assassinate Casimir. Whether through bad luck or poor navigation, however, Zach and his friends could not find Casimir in the palace but they did run across the hapless new queen, Elizabeth, cutting off four of her fingers before trying to assassinate Charles himself and murder his sons for good measure.

Needless to say, Charles was less than pleased. At this point the two versions of the story diverge. In one, Zach was killed on the spot by a brave royal tutor who didn't want to see all that tutoring of the princes go to waste. The other, as recounted by Dr Doran in his rather excitable 1857 tome *Monarchs Retired from Business*, states that Zach was captured and executed by being cut into small pieces. Always keen to do a thorough job, Charles then ordered Zach's son to be tied to the tail of a horse and dragged to death, his second daughter to be beheaded and her husband (who didn't really have much to do with this) starved to death. The rest of the family were then disinherited and banished. Zach's raped daughter, who might by kinder souls be considered the real victim in all this, was paraded through the streets after having her nose, fingers and lips cut off.

What was Michael Barrett the last man to do?

Poor old Michael Barrett was the last man to be publicly hanged in Britain and, to rub salt into the wound, he was almost certainly innocent. Barrett was an Irish Nationalist in the mid-nineteenth century at a time when there was a groundswell of popular opinion in England that the 'Irish question' had to be resolved, probably through home rule.

With public opinion very much behind them, the last thing the Nationalists (or Fenians as they were known) needed was a PR disaster but that's exactly what they managed to engineer for themselves. On 13 December 1867 an attempt was made to break out Fenian prisoners from Clerkenwell prison. An explosive charge was placed in a wheelbarrow next to the perimeter wall in the hope of blowing a hole in it but the quantity of explosives had been badly miscalculated. Instead the explosion not only knocked down the wall but demolished a row of houses opposite it, killing twelve people and injuring over fifty.

Not surprisingly there was a huge anti-Irish backlash in England. The government enrolled an extra 50,000 special constables, Queen Victoria was all in favour of stringing up any Fenian that could be found and, as Karl Marx put it: *'The London masses, who have shown great sympathy towards Ireland, will be made wild and driven into the arms of a reactionary government. One cannot expect the London proletarians to allow themselves to be blown up in honour of Fenian emissaries.'*

The government needed a result quickly and Michael Barrett – a known Fenian sympathiser, who had been arrested previously in Glasgow for firing a gun – was hauled in for questioning. Shortly after, the specimen charge of the wilful murder of Sarah Jane Hodgkinson (a victim of the Clerkenwell bombing) was brought against him. Despite the lack of evidence against him and a very strong alibi that he was in Scotland at the time, something his friends could prove, Barrett was found guilty. The *Daily Telegraph* reported his speech from the dock prior to his sentencing, saying that he '*delivered a most remarkable speech, criticising with great acuteness the evidence against him, protesting that he had been condemned on insufficient grounds, and eloquently asserting his innocence*'. Despite this, and many appeals for clemency, Barrett was hanged outside Newgate prison on 26 May 1868. The following day *The Times* reported:

> Yesterday morning, in the presence of a vast concourse of spectators, Michael Barrett, the author of the Clerkenwell Explosion, was hanged in front of Newgate. In its circumstances there was very little to distinguish this from ordinary executions. The crowd was greater, perhaps, and better behaved; still, from the peculiar atrocity of the crime for which Barrett suffered, and from the fact of its being probably the last public execution in England, it deserves more than usual notice . . .

How could Margaret of Hell help your court appearance?

In 1529, Henry VIII finally became fed up with the miserable conditions in the palace of Westminster (which also had an annoying habit of catching fire) and so decided to move his main London residence to Whitehall. Until then Whitehall had been the site of York Place, one of Cardinal Wolsey's many lavish homes, but thanks to the cardinal's fall from grace and his subsequent death it now became Henry's.

What Henry was getting away from was the filth and din of mediaeval Westminster and places like Margaret of Hell. The area was a mass of taverns, drinking dens and cockfighting pits, and its streets were full of horses, poultry and pigs, the latter of which were known to occasionally kill small children. On King Street there were carpenters, tailors, cutlers, cordwainers, brewers, masons, yeomen of the king's chamber, weavers, barbers, flax wives, embroiderers, glaziers, skinners, tillers, spurriers, watermen, butchers, smiths, pewterers, sawyers, saddlers, coopers, goldsmiths, haberdashers, parchment makers, bookbinders, illuminators, chandlers, grocers, cooks, poulterers, fishmongers, hardwaremen, ushers of the king's exchequer and drapers.

There were other less 'virtuous' trades as well. When Henry VIII turned the women out of St James's Hospital it was found that, despite the requirements of that institution's charter, they were neither poor nor leprous and they most certainly were not maidens. On the approach to the gates of the palace there were other dubious institutions, including rows of 'tipplers' (off-licences) and a warren of illegal pavement cafés selling spare ribs. Finally, just by the gates themselves were unlicensed drink stalls, where visitors to the law courts in the once great palace of Westminster could have a final stiffener before entering. They were wryly named after the three options available after plunging through life's last portal – Jane Paradise, the Wife of Purgatory and Margaret of Hell.

Why was the patron saint of businesswomen crushed to death?

Margaret Clitherow was deliberately compressed to death in one of the more unpleasant incidents in the growing Tudor struggle between Catholics and Protestants. Margaret was a respectable businesswoman in York who in 1571, aged eighteen, had married a wealthy butcher (and chamberlain of the city). Her husband John was a good Protestant but his brother was a Catholic priest and, just three years after her marriage, Margaret too converted to Catholicism.

The 1570s were not a good time to become a Catholic. On 25 February 1570 the pope had issued the Bull Regnans in Excelsis, which declared Elizabeth I a heretic and absolved her subjects from any allegiance to her. This effectively meant that any Catholic in England was automatically suspected of treason and the government acted quickly to suppress all Catholics. Margaret, meanwhile, was holding secret masses in her house in the now famous butchers' street in York, known as the Shambles, for which she was frequently imprisoned. Her husband, who remained a Protestant, was also often fined for her non-attendance at church. Indeed, he said his wife's only two failings were her excessive fasting and refusal to go to church with him. In 1585 the situation worsened when harbouring Catholic clergy became a capital offence. This didn't seem to bother Margaret and she continued to hold secret masses.

Her Catholic sympathies were well known, however, as she made little attempt to hide them, and on 10 March 1586 her house was searched. In the process a young boy was frightened into revealing the whereabouts of a priesthole that also contained vestments for the mass. Margaret was arrested.

Four days later she appeared before the York Assizes where she took an extraordinary step. Instead of pleading innocent or guilty, and either way perhaps getting off with a fine, she refused to plead at all, claiming that she had done nothing wrong and hence had no case to answer. In truth she was probably trying to protect her children, servants and any fellow Catholics whose names might come out in court. English law took a dim view of refusing to plead as it made the legal process very tricky. In fact, to discourage defendants from taking this course the law dictated that those who refused to plea could suffer *peine forte et dure*. Helpfully, Margaret's judge, a man called Clinch, described to her what this actually meant:

> If you will not put yourself to the country this must be your
> judgment. You must return from whence you came, and there,
> in the lowest part of the prison, be stripped naked, laid down,
> your back upon the ground, and as much weight laid upon you
> as you are able to bear, and so to continue three days without

meat or drink, except a little barley bread and puddle water, and the third day to be pressed to death, your hands and feet tied to posts, and a sharp stone under your back.

And they were true to their word. On Good Friday 1586, Margaret was taken barefoot to the tollbooth at Ousebridge. Here she was laid on her back with a sharp rock under her spine, a door was placed on top of her and this was loaded with stones. She died within fifteen minutes, her last words being recorded as, 'Jesu, Jesu, Jesu, have mercy upon me!' She was around thirty-three years old.

To Catholics, Margaret soon became a martyr. Indeed, her biographer, Father Mush, was one of those who recovered her body from a dung heap (where it had been buried after her execution) to report that even after six weeks it was uncorrupted. She was beatified in 1929 and finally became a saint on 25 October 1970. Her right hand is still preserved as a relic in St Mary's Convent in York and she is now the patron saint of business-women.

But Margaret Clitherow's death may have had a yet greater effect on British history. Her terrible end certainly caused a sensation at the time. Whilst Catholics fêted her, many in the city could not believe how willingly she had gone to her death. Her step-father, Henry May, Lord Mayor of York, actually accused her of effectively committing suicide and abandoning her family. But there was one young and impressionable man in York who was very impressed with Margaret's faith. A new convert to Catholicism, he was probably present at the execution. His name was Guy Fawkes.

What was the least successful revolution in British history?

Perhaps the least successful uprising in British history revolves around the sorry tale of Bartholomew Steere. One night in the autumn of 1596, Bartholomew climbed Enslow Hill, near Bletchingdon in north Oxfordshire, to start a revolution. For several weeks he had been talking to a lot of the local people, particularly those like him: young men whose families for centuries before had been peasant farmers in the area or servants in the big houses. They all felt the same: the life that they'd been sold was a lie and now Bartholomew intended to do something about it.

What he wanted was a life like his father's, which, if not particularly exciting, had its moments. The Steeres were farmers who rented land from the local landowner and worked it to grow the food they needed for their families. In good years, there might even be something extra to sell to pay for little luxuries – like shoes. It was a life regulated by the Church, which laid down the feast days and holidays (quite a few of them) that marked out the staging posts of the year and provided a safety net in the form of charities for those who were too ill or old to work. But this wasn't going to happen for Bartholomew. A new entrepreneurial age was dawning and landlords were realising that there was more money to be made turning over their lands to sheep pasture than collecting meagre rents from a bunch of peasants. So they began enclosing their fields and kicking their farmers out. Henry VIII's chancellor, Sir Thomas More, thought it a bad idea too: '*Your sheep that were wont to be so meek and tame, and so small eaters, now, as I hear say, be become so great devourers and so wild, that they eat up, and swallow down the very men themselves.*'

Thus it was that Bartholomew asked his supporters to go round the villages finding like-minded souls prepared to join him at a rendezvous that night on Enslow Hill. That was where the people of north Oxfordshire would usually gather and, the next day, that was where the revolution would begin.

And so as the sun went down the first of the rebels began to arrive – ten men and boys, variously armed with a selection of antique pikes, one rather fetching rusty sword and a dog. On top of the hill they gathered round a fire to wait for people to swarm out of their homes under cover of darkness to join them.

The next morning brought a scene that none of them had been expecting. There, arrayed on Enslow Hill, were – ten men, a handful of pikes, one rusty sword and a dog. No one else had come. So they put out the fire and went home. The North Oxfordshire Uprising was over.

The North Oxfordshire Uprising might have been a bit of a damp squib but the official response to it was not. Bartholomew and his friends might well have got away with what was, after all, in reality nothing more dangerous than a slightly unpopular picnic, had it not been for a local vicar with a broken bookshelf. He had called in the local carpenter, Roger Symonds from Hampton Gay, to mend it and, as he sawed and hammered, he chatted in the way that workmen are wont to do, making mention of the 'rebellion'.

The result of this little tête-à-tête was absolute mayhem. Panic swept through the enclosing landowners and many took to their beds for weeks, feigning illness in the belief that the roads seethed with cut-throat peasants baying for their blood. News of it reached London where the government was growing nervous about the numbers of rural poor who, because of the enclosures, had nowhere to go and nothing to do.

Warrants were immediately sent out for the arrest of the 'ring-leaders' and four men, including Bartholomew Steere, were captured. So fearful was the government that the nation was on the brink of some brilliantly engineered peasants' revolt that specific instructions were sent out, ordering the men to be lashed to horses for the journey to London to prevent them talking to each other or getting word to their fellow conspirators and effecting a rescue. They needn't have bothered. Bartholomew and his friends arrived in London for their trial without incident.

Before being tried, they were 'softened up', torture being officially sanctioned here for one of the last times in British history. This saved the hangman a job, at least in Bartholomew's case. He and one of his friends both died under interrogation. The other two were sent before the judges and duly sentenced. Both were then taken back to Enslow Hill where they were hanged, drawn and quartered. And that was that.

How did a comma save a life?

There are many advantages to being a supreme ruler and one of them is to hold the power of life and death over your subjects. Russian tsars had long enjoyed that privilege when Alexander III came to the throne in 1881. Even by the none too jolly standards of the Romanovs, he was a famously dour and sombre individual whose chief hobby was preparing planks for cabinetmakers. When catching his eye, a Russian theatre critic described his look as being '*as cold as steel, in which there was something threatening, even frightening, and it struck me like a blow*'. His wife, Maria Feodorovna, could not have been more different, however. Born a princess of Denmark, she had originally been engaged to the Russian heir-apparent, Nicholas, and on his sudden death was rapidly betrothed and married to his younger brother, Alexander.

These were troubled times in Russia. Alexander's father was assassinated by nihilists, and there was growing discontent with the absolute power of the tsars and the accompanying corruption of the government. Several assassination attempts were uncovered, including one by students who planned to fill books with dynamite and throw them at the royal couple. Five students, including one Alexander Ulyanov, were caught and hanged before the plan could be realised. This event might go some way to explaining the attitude towards the royal family of Alexander Ulyanov's little brother, Vladimir. He would later take the alias Lenin and be revenged on them (see pages 269–70).

Tsar Alexander's response to these rebels was to crack down further, preventing any of the democratic reforms that his father had toyed with, and increasing the number of executions and deportations to the savage Siberian work camps. Whilst Maria

Feodorovna rarely interfered in politics it was on one of these occasions that she famously saved a prisoner from a fate worse than death. Alexander, wearily going through another list of suspected traitors and criminals, had written against one name, 'Pardon impossible, to send to Siberia'. Maria changed this to 'Pardon, impossible to send to Siberia' and so saved a life with a solitary comma.

5

Heads

So the heart be right, it is no matter which way the head lies.

Sir Walter Raleigh (at his execution, on being asked which way he preferred to lay his head)

What did Walter Raleigh's wife keep in her handbag?

The story of Sir Walter Raleigh is one of fortunes both won and lost. He was for a time the epitome of the Elizabethan court – daring and dazzling, a rich adventurer with the ear of the queen and the hand of one of her ladies. But on Elizabeth's death his fortunes and those of his wife, Bess, began to change. In the new Stuart era he was considered something of a throwback, a flamboyant and annoying reminder of the old century. Getting rid of him proved all too easy for King James and his followers who hated the old explorer. Raleigh was arrested and tried as a conspirator in a planned Catholic uprising known as the Main Plot. He was found guilty (although on pathetic evidence, even by those days' standards), sentenced to death and sent to the Tower where he stayed until 1616. In that year he was released on condition that he search for the second time for El Dorado – the fabled City of Gold. Raleigh set off for Guiana. Here the endgame began to play out. Off the South American coast Raleigh's men, against his orders, attacked the Spanish outpost of San Thome during which his son Wat was shot dead. On his return there was worse to come. Not only had he not found El Dorado but the Spanish ambassador was furious about the attack, as England and Spain had now signed a peace treaty. The ambassador insisted the original death sentence on Raleigh from 1603 be reinstated and King James agreed.

Raleigh was beheaded on 29 October 1618 and his body was buried in St Margaret's church (next to Westminster Abbey). His head, however, was not. As was the custom, this was embalmed and given to his wife as a sort of grisly memento. Bess seemed rather fond of it, however, and from then on carried it around everywhere with her in a red bag. It was reported that when people came to the family home she would even ask them whether they would like to see Walter, at which point she would produce the bag with the head in it. For all this eccentricity, Bess spent the

best part of the next thirty years vigorously pressing for the reha-
bilitation of her husband's reputation and, in the process, helped
to undermine the Stuart monarchy in the run-up to the Civil War.
By the time of her own death around 1647 her lobbying (and his
head) had helped to make Raleigh a hero again. The head was
then passed to Raleigh's son and was finally buried in his grave
with him in London in 1668.

How did an Emperor lose a nose?

The Emperor Justinian II (669–711) was a harsh and generally
disliked ruler in Constantinople. In particular his choice of admin-
istrators was greatly despised. His treasurer Stephen, who is said
to have flogged the emperor's mother in his absence, and
Theodotus, the public logothete (or chancellor), who extorted
money by suspending individuals over fires, undermined the
emperor's position. The brutality of these men eventually led to
an uprising. The commander of the army, Leontius, a soldier who
had previously been imprisoned for three years, led his men, plus
a sizeable mob from the city, to the cathedral where they received
the (forced) sanction of the Patriarch.

At daybreak the throng rushed to the circus where the emperor,
deserted by all his followers, was dragged. The crowd bayed for
his blood but Leontius satisfied himself by cutting off the emperor's
nose and removing his tongue. Now noseless, Justinian II received
the nickname 'Rhinometus', that is 'the noseless', and was banished.

Despite numerous attempts on his life, Justinian survived and
eventually gained enough support to retake Constantinople. His
revenge was brutal. Leontius (who by then had also been over-
thrown and de-nosed) and the new Emperor Tiberius were dragged
to the circus where Justinian sat, one foot on each of the traitors'
necks. They were then decapitated. Justinian's other enemies were
rounded up and hanged, or beheaded, or thrown into the sea in
sacks. Others were blinded and banished.

Justinian the Noseless was not safe on the throne, however. His enemies retook Constantinople and although the emperor and his army had slipped away, his wife and child were not so lucky. She took her son to the church of the Virgin at Blachernae and, wearing protective amulets, made him hold the pillar of the altar with one hand and a piece of the true cross with the other, in the hope that this would save him. It was in vain. The little boy was carried out of the church to a postern gate where his throat was cut.

Meanwhile the new (self-proclaimed) emperor had caught up with Justinian's army. On the promise of immunity, Justinian's men deserted. The noseless emperor was captured and beheaded.

Who hung the world's most famous painting in his bathroom?

Francis I of France wanted nothing more than to be the perfect Renaissance monarch and in many ways he was. As a great patron of the arts it was Francis who invited the aged Leonardo da Vinci to leave Italy and come to join him at his chateau at Amboise in 1516. It was a good deal for da Vinci – the offer of a manor house close to the chateau and very generous terms for himself and his staff – and so he accepted.

Amongst the possessions that he carried over the Alps to France with him was a particular painting, a mysterious piece for which there is no record of the commission, no name for the sitter and not even a signature – the *Mona Lisa*. It remains unclear why da Vinci had kept it instead of giving it to whoever had commissioned it (assuming that it was, like most portraits, a commission) but once in France he did agree to sell it to Francis I. The French king first hung the portrait in the chateau at Amboise before moving it, with his court, first to Fontainebleau and then to Paris. In Paris, this small and at the time not well-known work had to vie with many other paintings in what would become the Louvre art collection. Because the king's palace walls were overcrowded it was hung in a bathroom.

There the *Mona Lisa* remained until Louis XIV moved it,

together with his whole court, to the newly built palace of Versailles. His son, Louis XV, disliked the painting and had it sent back to Paris, where it stayed until Napoleon Bonaparte declared himself emperor. He rather liked the painting and had it hung in his bedroom, where it took pride of place until he was removed from office, when it went back to the Louvre.

The painting's last journey took place in 1911 when an Italian house painter called Vincenzo Peruggia managed to steal it, believing it to have been illegally taken from Italy by the Duke of Wellington's least-favourite relative (see pages 278–9), Napoleon, which it hadn't. He returned the painting to the place it had originated from, Florence, where he tried to sell it to an art dealer and, as might be expected, was instantly arrested. The painting did not immediately return to France, however, but toured Italy first. This was no great loss to the Louvre, which, surprisingly, had seen ticket sales increase in the two years that the painting was missing. This was because more people paid to come and see the spot where the *Mona Lisa* was stolen from than had come to see the masterpiece itself.

Why did Grace Darling nearly go bald?

Grace Darling was a victim of her own admirers. Grace and her father were living in the Longstone lighthouse on the Farne Islands off the Northumbrian coast when, on the night of 6 September 1838, a furious storm blew up. During this a ship, the SS *Forfarshire*, carrying around sixty crew and passengers, foundered on the Big Harcar rock about three-quarters of a mile off the lighthouse. Nine of the survivors managed to make it to a lifeboat but another nine hung precariously to the rocks themselves, in danger of being swept out to sea at any moment.

At dawn, realising that the weather was still too rough for the lifeboat to launch, William Darling decided that he must brave the huge seas in his rowing boat to try to rescue the survivors. Unfortunately his sons, who would usually provide the rowing power for such a trip, were not at home and so it fell to the twenty-two-year-old Grace to land her father on Big Harcar to assess the situation whilst she tried to keep their little wooden boat from being smashed to matchwood in the huge surf around its base.

The rest, as they say, is history. Thanks to the magnificent seamanship of Grace Darling, the nine survivors were rescued and an adoring public turned her into a newspaper celebrity. But for Grace, like so many celebrities, fame was a two-edged sword. Whilst money and medals were forthcoming (Queen Victoria was so impressed that she sent £50), so too came requests for that most treasured of Victorian keepsakes – a lock of her hair. And Grace, being a generous soul, obliged to such an extent that by the following spring one of her sisters wrote that she feared Grace would have to buy a wig as she was giving her hair away faster than it could grow.

Grace Darling did not have to suffer the pitfalls of celebrity long, however, despite the newspaper articles, the marriage proposals and even a poem by Wordsworth. She died in her father's arms just four years later, having contracted tuberculosis. Today her memory is perhaps best served not by the huge quantity of her hair in circulation but by the RNLI's custom of always having in service a lifeboat named after her.

Who thought there was a woman in the moon?

The first moon race was not to see who could land a human there but to see who could map its surface. The winner was the Italian astronomer, Giovanni Domenico Cassini. Having been Professor of Astronomy at Bologna University, he took the post of Director of the Paris Observatory in 1671. Here he combined the roles of Royal Astronomer and Royal Astrologer to the Sun King, Louis XIV, although his interest in astrology waned as his discoveries in astronomy gathered pace. Along with Robert Hooke he is credited with first observing the Great Red Spot on Jupiter, and he alone discovered the division in Saturn's rings that now bears his name.

Cassini was also something of a cartographer, having made the first informed estimate of the actual size of France, a country that turned out to be somewhat smaller than Louis XIV had been led to believe, and which led the king to quip that Cassini had robbed him of more land than he had won in all his wars. Cassini also began a topographical map of France – the first topographical map of an entire country in history – which his descendants would finally deliver in 1789.

But in 1679 the race had been to accurately map the moon, something that had become possible thanks to rapid improvements in telescope technology. Indeed, when Cassini published his detailed map that year it would be fair to say that Europeans had a better knowledge of the surface of the moon than they did of their own planet. But Cassini's map is not perfect or, at least, it contains one strange feature. On one edge of the Mare Imbrium (the Sea of Rains) lies the Sinus Iridium, or Bay of Rainbows, and at one end of this lies Cape Heraclides, which juts out into the smooth dark basin of the bay. But on Cassini's map either he or his engraver, Claude Mellan, have drawn not a rocky cape but the face of a young girl, her hair streaming out as she gazes towards the sun across the bay. Why she is there and whether she is a joke by Cassini, or a feature that he actually believed he had seen, remains a mystery but this unique map feature is known to this day as the Moon Maiden.

Where can you meet Archbishop Sudbury?

Archbishop Sudbury had the misfortune to be one of the main scapegoats of the peasants at the time of the Peasants' Revolt in 1381. Having had a splendid evening setting fire to John of Gaunt's lavish London palace, the Savoy (now the site of the Savoy Hotel), the main body of the rebels, led by Wat Tyler and John Ball, were having a quiet chat with Richard II at Mile End. Meanwhile another group of rebels were on the lookout for the men they really blamed for their troubles, the great officers of state, Treasurer

Sir Robert Hales and Archbishop Simon Sudbury. The archbishop also happened to be the chancellor and was hence technically responsible for the poll tax that began the revolt.

Sudbury and Hales were not at their king's side that day but had holed up in the Tower of London in the hope that things would cool down if they kept out of sight. However, they were out of luck. Just what sort of a fight the Tower guards put up is not recorded but a group of rebels easily broke in and headed for the royal apartments. They seem to have been in a rather good mood and the shocked chronicler, Thomas Walsingham, noted: *'Who would ever have believed that such rustics and most inferior ones at that would dare to enter the chamber of the King and of his mother with their filthy sticks. They arrogantly lay and sat on the King's bed while joking and several asked the King's mother to kiss them.'*

Walsingham does not record whether the king's mother was amenable, but the mob were not simply there to joke, as Sudbury knew only too well. The king had told the rebels that he would execute any traitors he found around him. The rebels had already decided that that meant Hales and Sudbury and they had come to carry out the sentence. In a last desperate bid to escape, Sudbury made a dash for the Watergate that led on to the Thames but was seen by a woman and stopped. He and five other 'traitors', including Hales, were then unceremoniously dragged away to Tower Hill and beheaded.

Sudbury's body was left unburied for two days. His severed head, with his episcopal cap nailed to it, was placed, like those of all traitors, on London Bridge. Yet Sudbury was not a universally hated man. Indeed, he'd been quite a conscientious archbishop, if a rather pliant chancellor, and his friends soon removed his head from the bridge. This was preserved and smuggled back to Sudbury in Suffolk. With his body buried in Canterbury Cathedral, the local priest at Sudbury clearly didn't know quite what to do with this unusual relic and so put off making a decision. Over 600 years later, Simon Sudbury's head is still awaiting burial, and currently resides in the town with which he shares his name, in a niche in the vestry wall of the church of St Gregory with St Peter.

How did one man's ear start a war?

The 1729 Treaty of Seville allowed for Spanish coastguards to board British ships in the Caribbean to check whether they were breaking the terms of the treaty, which forbade trading with Spanish colonies. So it was that on 9 April 1731 a Spanish boarding party came alongside the brig *Rebecca* just off Havana, as she made for Jamaica. The Spanish coastguard clearly believed that the *Rebecca* was carrying contraband but her captain, Robert Jenkins, denied this. According to Jenkins, the Spanish began physically abusing him to try to get him to tell them where the loot was. He was half strangled and beaten up. Then the Spanish commander cut off a part of his ear, 'bidding him to carry it to his Master King George'. The ship was plundered and sabotaged with the intent, so the Royal Navy claimed, of ensuring that she would never make it back to port. Miraculously the *Rebecca* did survive, however, bringing back home to England the beaten, bruised and partially earless Jenkins in June of that year.

Whilst there was some sympathy for Jenkins at the time, and representations were made to the Spanish authorities about this and other alleged cases of Spanish intimidation, no real action was taken until 1738. By then Britain's relations with Spain had soured further and Jenkins' mutilation provided the perfect rallying point for anti-Spanish sentiment. Jenkins was called to attend a House of Commons Committee examining Spanish predations. According to one version of the story, he turned up brandishing his now famous ear, which he had pickled and put in a jar. Sadly there's no independent evidence that he even attended the committee, let alone that he brought his ear with him. The following year, the political opposition to Robert Walpole's government, which had used Jenkins' ear as a symbol of Spanish aggression and cruelty, finally got their way and war was declared on Spain.

The fighting in what became known as the War of Jenkins' Ear took place in the Caribbean, culminating in the successful British capture of Puerto Bello in Panama, in recognition of which Portobello Road in London was named. The British admiral in charge of the expedition, Admiral Vernon, was also a great navy moderniser. His insistence on watering down the rum ration so that his sailors were sober enough to sail, and his habit of always wearing an old grogram coat, gave the world the term grog for watered-down rum. By 1742 the war, although still being fought, had become no more than a sideshow in the War of the Austrian Succession, which was by then raging in Europe, engulfing Spain, Britain, France, Russia and the Holy Roman Empire.

Which general gave his name to facial hair?

General Ambrose Everett Burnside was not, by his own admission, one of the best Union Army generals. If he had a failing it was that he was remarkably amiable and easily befriended those around him, which made him very popular. This, and his impressive physical appearance, led to his rapid rise through the ranks of the Union Army during the American Civil War, leaving him in a position of command that he didn't want and wasn't, frankly, very well suited to. Twice he refused the command of the Army of the Potomac and only took it on the third occasion when he was ordered to do so. The most common comment after one of his engagements was that he had dithered and failed to press home an advantage, committing his troops piecemeal rather than in a concerted assault. After the Battle of the Crater, and a previous disastrous defeat at Fredericksburg, Burnside was finally relieved of his command.

Burnside's contribution to the American Civil War would not seem to amount to much, were it not for one other distinguishing feature. Throughout the conflict he wore a unique arrangement of facial hair, with a thick moustache and bearded cheeks, but a clean-shaven chin, the inverse of another American style, the goatee. Despite his failings as a general, Burnside remained very popular after the war, and both his style of facial hair, and his distinctive soft hat, became known as burnsides. The popularity of the hat soon waned and, as time went on, the association weakened between Burnside and the arrangement of facial hair. At some point in the late nineteenth century the name became transposed as sideburns, which perhaps was considered to make more sense, and so the term was born.

Which English king breathed fire then expired?

On Thursday, 2 August 1100, King William II of England, known as 'Rufus' thanks to his ruddy complexion, was at a hunting lodge in the New Forest, probably near to Brockenhurst. With him was his brother Henry, Robert fitz Haimo and Walter Tirel. For some reason they had not left the lodge that morning to hunt but remained there until after lunch.

William of Malmesbury says in his chronicle that a foreign monk had come to the lodge before sunrise that morning and had spoken to Robert fitz Haimo. The monk had told him of his dream the previous night in which he had seen the king enter a small church and, with his usual disdain, sneer at the congregation. He had then approached the cross and, seizing it, began to gnaw at its arms. The cross had suffered this for a time and had then kicked William to the floor. As the king hit the ground he had belched fire at the cross, the billowing smoke from his mouth reaching so high as to nearly touch the stars.

This may have seemed a touch alarming and fitz Haimo certainly urged the king not to hunt that morning. Such warnings, visions and dreams were common, however, particularly amongst wishful-thinking clerics who wanted to see an end to the reign of the decidedly ungodly William. Knowing this, the king rarely took note of these warnings, so it is more likely that urgent business that morning kept him from the forest, or perhaps just a hangover, for he had indulged more fully than usual at the previous evening's meal. The chronicler Ordericus Vitalis (who liked writing about funny things that happened to kings – see pages 217–19) says that both William and Walter Tirel poured scorn on the warning and, on hearing of the foreign monk's dream, relayed through fitz Haimo, William is reported to have said: *'He is a monk and to get money dreams like a monk.'*

It was late afternoon by the time the hunting party left the lodge. In the woods the party dispersed, as was usual, to their various positions. William stayed close by his friend Walter Tirel, Lord of Poix. In the early-evening light, beaters were set to flush out the deer, which would be chased past fixed positions, known as trysts, from where the hunters would shoot, dismounted, with crossbows or longbows. In two of these positions stood King William and Walter Tirel. The sun was sinking lower and the shadows lengthening, making it harder to aim. To the east the forest lay in deep shadow, whilst to the west the hunters were squinting into the setting sun. Suddenly two stags broke from cover and the cry was raised.

There is some confusion as to what happened next. William of Malmesbury says the king took aim and fired, but the arrow passed over the animal's back, only grazing it. The startled beast darted away but Walter Tirel already had the second animal in his sights and loosed an arrow as it ran between him and the king. Again the arrow failed to hit its mark but sped over the stag's back and on towards the king. William had no time to move and the dart plunged into his chest, piercing his heart. Stunned, he broke off the shaft of the arrow, thereby hastening his own death, and fell to the ground without uttering a single word. Within seconds he was dead.

Who got his nickname for blinding an army?

Basil II, a Byzantine emperor at the turn of the first millennium, did much to restore his empire's fortunes. Bulgaria was a particular thorn in his side as much of the country had slipped from

Byzantine control, something that he took as a personal affront. Initially he attempted to divide and rule, coming up with the splendid wheeze of letting Boris II, the captured Bulgarian emperor, escape and cause trouble. Boris proved a disappointment, however, so Basil decided to try something a little more physical, and he attacked. This tactic had worked rather well for him recently against the Arabs as well as his own rebels, but initially things did not go to plan and his army was ambushed. Basil only escaped thanks to his splendid Viking 'Varangian' bodyguards, who were a present from his new friend Vladimir I, Prince of Kiev.

It was time to give 'divide and rule' another go so he settled on sending his own sister Anna to marry his enemy's brother. Not wishing to waste a perfectly good sister on a barbarian, however, he sent an impostor. She, sadly, was quickly unmasked and the deal was off.

So it was back to fighting again and this time Basil had a lot more luck. On 29 July 1014 the Byzantine and Bulgarian armies met at the Battle of Kleidion, where Basil smashed his enemy, taking 15,000 prisoners. Wishing to make a point to the Bulgarian emperor, who wasn't at the battle, he was then reported to have blinded ninety-nine out of every hundred captives, retaining one eye in one man in a hundred to lead the others home. The point was well made and when the blinded army returned, their king was so shocked that he immediately fainted. Two days later he died of a stroke. This gave Basil his nickname, *Boulgaroktonos* – Basil the Bulgar Slayer.

6

What's in a Name?

Three things I never lends – my 'oss, my wife, and my name.

R. S. Surtees, *Hillingdon Hall* (1845), chapter 33

Who was Gordon Bennett?

James Gordon Bennett Junior was born to the good life, having inherited the *New York Herald* newspaper from his father and founded the *International Herald Tribune*. To say that he was a flamboyant character would be an understatement. To improve the sales of his paper he took to underwriting heroic expeditions and sponsoring epic events. It was Gordon Bennett who paid for Henry Morton Stanley to go to Africa in search of David Livingstone (in return for exclusive coverage) as well as funding George Washington De Long's fatal expedition to the North Pole in 1881. In the sports arena Bennett sponsored 'Gordon Bennett' cups in yacht and motor racing, in addition to the world's oldest race for gas-filled balloons (if we exclude the business in Paris in 1870 – see pages 249–50), the Coupe Aéronautique Gordon Bennett. He also introduced polo to the USA.

Bennett's personal life was no less exciting or unusual. In 1866 he had won the first ever transatlantic yacht race but it was an unfortunate incident in 1877 that perhaps, above all others, turned Bennett's name into an exclamation. In that year he became engaged to the New York socialite and heiress Caroline May, whose parents had gathered together a $20,000 trousseau for her – the largest ever assembled at that time. At a cocktail party at the May mansion, however, Bennett arrived late and very drunk. Mistaking a large fireplace for a urinal, he proceeded to relieve himself, in public, in front of his prospective in-laws and their guests, leaving both the fire and his fiancée's ardour thoroughly doused. Shortly after this, the engagement was cancelled and Bennett found himself on the wrong end of a public horsewhipping, administered by the aggrieved girl's brother. This extraordinary event, startling even by Bennett's standards, turned his name into an expression of surprise – Gordon Bennett!

Shortly after the incident Bennett himself decided to take prolonged leave from New York and headed to Europe to avoid further encounters with vengeful siblings. He would not attempt marriage again until he was seventy-three years old when he wedded the heiress of the Reuter's news agency fortune.

What is bunkum?

We owe the term bunkum, meaning pointless claptrap, to the sterling political efforts of Felix Walker. Walker had fought in the American War of Independence and, after victory over Britain, was desperate to represent the people of his fledgling democracy. In 1816 he was elected to Congress as a Democratic Republican, something that today would be a contradiction in terms. He was not a popular speaker in the house, however, mainly due to his overriding desire to properly represent his constituents as he saw it. In order to make them heard, he spoke at great length in every debate about his constituency, regardless of whether it had anything to do with the business in hand. Every time that congressmen debated taxation, land reform, foreign wars or re-decorating the White House, they also received a lengthy update on the life and times of Felix Walker's constituency. That constituency was Buncombe County, North Carolina, and his 'speeches for Buncombe' soon became a byword for tiresome and irrelevant rubbish. Buncombe was soon corrupted to bunkum and the rest is history.

Who was the original tommy?

The original tommy is thought to have been Thomas Atkins, a private in the 33rd Regiment of Foot during the Netherlands campaign in the French Revolutionary Wars. On 15 September 1794, Atkins was involved in the Battle of Boxtel in which he was horrifically wounded, suffering bayonet and sabre cuts to the head and chest, and a bullet wound to one lung. It was in this terrible state that the regiment's Lieutenant-Colonel Arthur Wellesley, later the Duke of Wellington (see pages 278–9), found him. Atkins would not accept any sympathy, however, and stoically told Wellesley that it was simply 'all in a day's work'. He then promptly dropped dead.

Arthur Wellesley was quite taken with this show of British stiff upper lips and when the army needed a generic soldier's name for the specimen page in the 1815 paybook, he supposedly chose Thomas Atkins. So the term tommy, meaning any British soldier, was born.

Whilst this is the most widely held derivation of tommy, there is one document, a letter sent from Jamaica in 1743 and so pre-dating Thomas Atkins' splendid self-sacrifice at Boxtel, which includes the line, 'ye Marines and Tommy Atkins behaved splendidly.' This might suggest that Tommy Atkins was a generic term for a foot soldier long before the Duke of Wellington got involved. However, no corroborating information for this claim has ever been discovered.

Who is the Bob in 'Bob's your uncle'?

Lord Robert Cecil, 3rd Marquess of Salisbury, was three times Prime Minister and, like many aristocratic politicians of his era, was not afraid of promoting members of his family to positions of power.

The origin of the phrase 'Bob's your uncle' comes from one such promotion when, in 1887, he promoted his nephew Arthur Balfour to the position of Irish Secretary in the hope that Balfour might put down the Irish rebels in the same way that he had suppressed the truculent crofters of Skye when he was at the Scottish Office. This move saw Cecil christened 'Uncle Bob' by some newspapers and so the term 'Bob's your uncle' emerged as a way of describing how simple it was for relatives of the great marquess to get jobs in government. None of this actually bothered the larger-than-life Cecil and in 1895 he appointed another nephew, Balfour's brother, Chief Secretary for Ireland. By 1900, his eldest son, three nephews and a son-in-law were all in government positions.

When he retired, his health damaged by his corpulence and his habit of only taking short rides on a tricycle for exercise, the role of Prime Minister was taken by his nephew Arthur, keeping the government very much in the family.

Who was Uncle Sam?

Uncle Sam is of course the personification of the United States but he is at least in part based on a real person, Samuel Wilson. Wilson was the son of Scottish émigrés to the US who arrived just before the time of the War of Independence. In 1789, Samuel and his brother set up shop in Troy, New York, in the meat packing business and seem to have managed to procure a number of government contracts to provide food for the army. During the war of 1812, Samuel sent meat across the country, always patriotically stamping the containers 'US' to indicate that it was government property. Amongst the troops the story passed around that the initials on the barrels and packets were actually the meat packer's own and stood for 'Uncle Sam'. And so the legend was born. Regardless of just how much truth there is to the story, the 87th US Congress resolved on 15 September 1961 that Samuel Wilson be saluted as the originator of America's national symbol 'Uncle Sam'.

Who was the first nosy parker?

The original Nosy Parker was, according to Corpus Christi College, Cambridge, their former master and archbishop of Canterbury, Matthew Parker. Parker had been chaplain to Henry VIII and Anne Boleyn, and had hence taught the future Queen Elizabeth. On her accession to the throne she rewarded him with the post of archbishop of Canterbury, with responsibility for trying to create some sort of settlement between the new Anglican Church and the old Catholic faith. Frankly, this was a pretty tricky job, what with a small number of Catholics at one extreme plotting to kill Elizabeth and the ultra-Protestant 'precisians' at the other, who wouldn't have minded getting rid of every Catholic in the realm. Parker attacked this problem by trying to find a reasonable, logical basis for the new Anglican faith. Between 1563 and 1568 he produced a new version of the Bible, which remained the official text until James I's Authorised Version. He also took Cranmer's slightly rambling forty-two doctrines of the Church of England and turned them into the much neater thirty-nine Articles of Religion, which still form the basis of Anglican doctrine to this day.

Furthermore Parker wanted to prove that the origins of the Church in England were independent of Rome, as this would provide a neat justification for the English Reformation: the Church hadn't suddenly declared itself independent; it always had been autonomous and was just throwing off an imposed foreign influence. And it was in going about trying to demonstrate this that Parker became 'Nosy Parker'.

He managed to persuade the Privy Council to issue him with a warrant to 'make a general search after all such records and muniments as related to these Realms, and which upon the dissolution of the monasteries had fallen into private hands'.

And there were an awful lot of these records lying around. Every monastery had once had a library and muniment room where it kept the deeds and charters that granted it its lands and privileges. When the monasteries had been dissolved these had generally come on the open market, some being sold, some lost and some just bundled up and thrown in a cupboard. Mixed up with the legal documents, however, were other works – indeed, some of the most important works of history and literature that England possesses. They included illuminated manuscripts, original chronicles, heroic poetry, mediaeval laws – the whole literary corpus from the Anglo-Saxon Chronicle to Zosimus.

In searching for his proof of an independent English Church, Parker came across all this material and realised that perhaps the nation's greatest treasure was teetering on the brink of destruction.

He therefore assiduously searched for and acquired every document, charter, chronicle and poem he could find, gaining him the title 'Nosy Parker'.

On his death he left to his old college one of the greatest manuscript libraries in the world and, in doing so, preserved a thousand years of British history and literature that might otherwise have been lost. Not that the nation was terribly grateful. He died in 1575 and was buried at Lambeth but during the Civil War his remains were exhumed and thrown on a dung heap.

Who were the original Tories?

The term Tory, which is still used within the Conservative Party itself, might prove less popular if its origins were more widely known. The original Tories were not English politicians but Irish rebels, mainly those dispossessed by the English in the seventeenth century, who made a living as outlaws, preying both on the English settlers and on the soldiers sent to protect them. The term probably came from the Middle Irish *tóraidhe*, meaning an outlaw.

An early mention of these Tories comes in a note of 12 July 1732, which records that eight officers *'riding upon the Highway [in Ireland], were murder'd by those bloody Highway Rogues called the Tories'*, whilst the Irish Act of 1707 was expressly for *'the more effectual suppression of tories, robbers, and rapparees'*. The term was soon expanded to include the Scottish bandits or 'moss-troopers' active during the years of the Commonwealth and later also applied to bandits in British India.

The political use of the term began in 1679–80 as an insult applied by the exclusioners, who wished to exclude James II from the throne (because he was a Catholic), to those who wanted him as their monarch. The Tories in turn referred to the exclusioners as 'whigs', which was a term variously applied in the North of England and Scotland to country bumpkins and extreme Presbyterians. They also called them 'fanaticks' but 'whig' seemed to stick. So both the major English political parties derived their common names from Irish and Scottish taunts thrown at them by the opposition. Eventually, in the 1880s, the term 'whig' was superseded by 'liberal', which is perhaps kinder. The Conservative Party has not so easily shaken off the label 'Tory', however.

Who was the earliest maverick?

We owe the term maverick to a Texan rancher and land specu-lator, Samuel Augustus Maverick. Maverick was a well-educated but volatile character who lived in volatile times. After Yale and law school, he moved to Texas, having had to leave South Carolina rather sharpish following a duel with someone who had criticised his father. Texas in the mid-1830s was a lively place, as at the time it was trying to break away from Mexico. Having been captured by the Mexicans, he was set free on condition that he return to the US, something he failed to do, joining the Texan army instead. This led to his fighting at the siege of the Alamo, although he left in time to sign the Texan Declaration of Independence before Santa Anna's famous attack.

But it wasn't the Alamo or Texan independence that put the word maverick in the dictionary, but his cattle. Maverick was an astute businessman who, having moved his family to Texas, had set about building up large landholdings, which exceeded 300,000 acres by the time of his death in 1870. In 1844 he had moved to Decrows Point on Matagorda Bay where he had bought a herd of cattle to graze his land. When his family left that ranch in 1847 the herd was put in the care of some of Maverick's slaves who, his biographer says, failed to brand each season's new-born calves. In the open wilderness of Texas it was every cattle owner's duty to brand their animals so that they could be recognised during round-ups and so that disputes could be avoided. Unbranded animals were like uninsured cars – a potentially costly nuisance, which could be difficult to trace. But around Decrows Point everyone knew who owned the unbranded animals – they were

Maverick cattle, and so the term was born. But even Samuel Augustus Maverick didn't remain a maverick all his life. Following complaints, he returned to his ranch in 1854, rounded up and branded all his cattle before driving them to another of his ranches and selling them.

Who was 'isolated from his kind as if he were a leper of old'?

There are very few polite terms in the English language that owe their origins to estate agents but 'boycotting' is one of them. Charles Cunningham Boycott was a land agent for Lord Erne's 12,000 acres in County Mayo in the 1880s. During this period the Irish Land League was pressing for reform, in particular an end to evictions and a reduction in rent, including a 25 per cent reduction on Lord Erne's estates. Needless to say, Erne and his agent Boycott were unhappy about this and initially refused, bringing the riposte from one of the leaders of the Irish Land League, Charles Parnell, that tenants should respond to a landlord's refusal by 'isolating him from his kind as if he were a leper of old'.

So that's exactly what they did to Boycott. No one would work on the estate's potato harvest; no one would talk to him or sit next to him in church; and the shops refused to serve him. In the end he had to have provisions sent by special steamer to avoid starving. His treatment caused outrage in England and indignation amongst pro-British groups in Ireland. In the end fifty Ulstermen (later known as 'the Emergency men') marched to Lord Erne's estate to dig potatoes for Boycott, for which they required the protection of around 900 soldiers. For the Land League this was seen as a victory as the government was forced to employ nearly 1,000 men to bring in the harvest from just one farm.

Boycott continued to have trouble, being spat at in the street, receiving death threats and even having his effigy hanged and burnt in front of him. Perhaps not surprisingly, in 1886 he left

Ireland for a quieter job in Suffolk, but he does not seem to have harboured a grudge. Despite the ostracism and the threats, he returned to Ireland nearly every year for his summer holiday.

Who formed the first lynch mob?

Several theories have been put forward for the origin of the term lynching but it seems most probably to come from Captain William Lynch, a Virginian planter and local Justice. During the American War of Independence, Virginia was a dangerous place for independent-minded settlers to live. Following a strike by Welsh miners the rumour began spreading of a pro-British uprising against the settlers of south-western Virginia and in response William Lynch, together with other prominent Justices and military officers, began rounding up suspects and subjecting them to ad hoc trials at which they sat in judgment without reference to any other authority. Those found guilty of treachery were either whipped or conscripted into the revolutionary army. Two years later, on 24 December 1782, the General Assembly of Virginia passed an Act that named Lynch and three other leading members of these irregular courts, and retrospectively legitimised their actions in what became known as Lynch's Law. Within Lynch's lifetime, the term 'lynch law' was already in use although, interestingly, neither Lynch nor his compatriots ever executed an individual and the term lynching, to mean an extra-legal hanging, was used only after his death.

7

Animal Magic

Man is the Only Animal that Blushes. Or needs to.

Mark Twain, *Following the Equator* (1897), chapter 27

What caused the Indian Mutiny?

Little things can start wars. It is not that they are of themselves usually enough to fight about but they are the last straw in a long line of grievances. The Indian Mutiny, also known as the Indian rebellion of 1857, or the First War of Indian Independence (depending which side you're cheering for), was kicked off by greasy paper.

The trigger, if you'll pardon the pun, was a gun – the 1853-pattern Enfield rifled musket to be precise. This was the high-tech weapon of its day, replacing the ancient British Army Land Pattern Musket (or 'Brown Bess') and the Baker rifle. Not only was the barrel rifled, increasing accuracy, but the cartridge was ignited not by a flintlock mechanism but by a percussion cap. Some things were still the same, however. To load the gun, a paper cartridge containing the gunpowder (which was greased to keep the powder dry) was taken from the belt; the top was bitten off, the powder poured down the barrel, the bullet (a ball) added and the paper screwed up and pushed down the barrel as wadding. A percussion cap was then placed in the firing mechanism, and *bang*!

The problem came with the greased paper on the cartridges. Amongst the sepoys – native Indian troops working for the British East India Company – the rumour ran through the ranks that the grease used on the cartridges was made from cow or pig fat. To the sepoys, all Hindu or Muslim, the idea of having pig or cow fat in their mouths when they bit off the end of the paper cartridge was unthinkable. Their British commanders, not understanding the importance of the issue, thought this was all a bit of a storm in a teacup and suggested that they grease their own cartridges with beeswax or vegetable oil. This only further inflamed the situation as the sepoys took this as an admission that they *had* been using pig and cow fat. At a time when some elements of the East India Company were actively evangelising and trying to convert sepoys to Christianity, this smacked of a conspiracy.

Small acts of mutiny and minor cases of arson began breaking out amongst the Indian regiments. As news of the supposed nature of the greased cartridges spread, some units refused to use them. In return they were punished with unusual severity, the troopers of the 3rd Light Cavalry at Meerut being stripped of their uniforms in public and then sentenced to ten years' hard labour. Things now started to get rather nasty. There were, of course, a lot of other deep-seated resentments amongst the Indian population which now bubbled to the surface. The last of the Mughal dynasty, who had been sidelined by the British, took the opportunity to declare himself Emperor of all India and the small acts of defiance that had begun the mutiny were transformed into an all-out attempt to expel the invaders. Before long the British were besieging Delhi and the Indians were besieging the British back in Lucknow. Terrible atrocities ensued on both sides but in the end Britain's overpowering military might and a lack of cohesion amongst their enemy granted them a bloody victory. But India would not now be ruled by a company. The East India Company had failed and in its place the British Raj was born.

Who was the real Moby Dick?

Mocha Dick was a real-life albino sperm whale that lived near the island of Mocha, off Chile's southern coast, several decades before Melville wrote his book *Moby Dick*. Mocha Dick, like the whale in Melville's story, had escaped countless times from the attacks of whalers, whom he would often attack with premediated ferocity. Consequently he was reported to have dozens of harpoons bristling in his back. He was described as *'the stout gentleman of the latitudes, the prodigious terror whale of the Pacific, the redoubtable white sperm whale that fought and won a hundred sea battles against overwhelming odds'*. He was probably finally killed in the 1830s although there is a report of a Swedish whaler taking an albino whale that may have been Mocha Dick in 1859. No one knows what prompted Melville to change the name Mocha to Moby, but the sightings of the albino Mocha

Dick, as recorded in the *Knickerbocker Magazine* in 1839, and the stories of the sinking of the whaling ship *Essex* in the offshore ground by a (different) rogue whale in 1820, seem to have combined in his imagination to form Captain Ahab's nemesis.

How many eggs did Queen Elizabeth I use in a year?

Elizabeth's court was certainly not extravagant by the standards of her father Henry VIII but the system that fed and watered courtiers was wide open to abuse, making her yearly shopping bill truly horrific. The problem was the practice known as 'bouge of court' – the right of the queen's staff, as well as the nobles visiting her court, to receive food and lodging at the court's (usually actually the people's) expense. In a busy court it was tricky for the officers of the Board of Greencloth, which managed this, to keep track of who was supposed to be there; it was common for people with no dining rights to just hang around in busy areas in the hope that someone would feed them – and perhaps even give them a bed for the night. Even those with the right to eat at court could abuse the system. Some individuals managed to get themselves entered several times on the relevant lists, claiming several spare dinners (which could be sold on at the palace gates). Senior servants, such as ladies-in-waiting, also received enormous food allowances, partly due to their status and partly to feed their own staff. Much of this was also sold 'out the back' when no one was looking. In one year, probably 1591, the shopping list for this culinary juggernaut included: 1,240 oxen, 8,200 sheep, 2,330 deer, 760 calves, 1,870 pigs, 53 wild boar – and 40 million eggs.

What do you get if you cross a politician with an amphibian?

Elbridge Gerry was one of the signatories of the American Declaration of Independence but has gone down in history as the originator of the term gerrymandering, meaning to unfairly alter electoral boundaries to improve your party's chance of election. Gerry, who pronounced his name with a hard G, was Governor of Massachusetts in 1812 (the same year that Uncle Sam was making his name in New York – see page 76) when he promoted the creation of new electoral districts that seemed to favour his Democratic Republican Party over the Federalists. Indeed, when maps were produced of the new districts they were quickly seized upon by the press and caricatured for their tortuous shape. In particular one district in Essex County was so sinuous and winding that it was said to look like a salamander. This, combined with Gerry's name, gave the world 'gerrymandering'. The game was now up for Gerry and he lost the 1812 election. Fortunately his friends in the White House came to his aid and James Madison made him vice-president, a post he held until his death.

What was the Battle of the Herrings?

The Battle of the Herrings took place on 12 February 1429 when Sir John Fastolf (who is one of the models for Shakespeare's Falstaff) was on a mercy mission to relieve the English besiegers of Orléans. With Lent fast approaching, the English army was in danger of starving, not because there was any real food shortage but because eating meat was banned during that season. An army marches on its stomach, as Napoleon once said, and if the siege was to be maintained the soldiers would have to have another source of protein. That was why Sir John and his men were valiantly battling towards Orléans with a supply column of herrings.

Just outside Rouvray the herrings found themselves in trouble, however. To the south-west a much larger combined French and Scottish army had appeared and it began a ferocious cannon bombardment that cut a swathe through the English soldiers and their fish whilst staying out of range of the English archers. Just as all seemed lost the French allies from Scotland made an error and John Stewart of Darnley managed to seize defeat from the

88

jaws of victory. Ignoring orders from his French superiors, he told his men to dismount and attack the herring carts but as soon as they were in range of the English longbowmen they were, not surprisingly, mown down. Desperate to regain the initiative, the French commander then sent in his men-at-arms to support them and they too were felled, much as they had been at Agincourt. Fastolf, seeing an opening, then sent his small band of men-at-arms into the fray and put the French and Scots into full retreat. Now unopposed, he marched on to the outskirts of Orléans where it was fish suppers all round.

This peculiar scrap between the English, Scots and French over a few barrels of herrings had unexpected ramifications. In the short term, the French army, which was meant to be raising the siege instead of attacking herring carts, was routed. It was also on that same day that another French leader was begging the high command for a chance to attack the English at Orléans. They had until this point been reluctant as this particular commander was a bit unusual. Now with news of the defeat at the Battle of the Herrings drifting into camp, they decided to let this individual have a go. So Joan of Arc got her chance to raise the siege of Orléans, which she did, in the process becoming one of France's greatest heroines (of which more on pages 241–3).

What was unusual about Thomas Hobson's stable?

Thomas Hobson lived from about 1545 to 1631 and was the university carrier in Cambridge. In this role he served the university for over sixty years, making the regular coach – well, cart – journey between Cambridge and the Bull Inn in London, as well as keeping a livery stable opposite St Catherine's College where he rented out horses to locals and students.

The term 'Hobson's choice', which means an apparent choice where in fact there is none, comes from his method of allocating these horses. Many stables allowed the hirer to choose which horse they wanted but this could lead to the overuse of particularly fine or fast horses, which might shorten their useful lives. Hobson allowed his customers to choose whichever horse they wanted, provided it was the one nearest the stable door. In this manner he rotated his stock and prevented his best animals from being over-exploited.

After his death on 1 January 1631 at the age of eighty-six, a number of satirical poems began to appear about Hobson, including two by John Milton. His first, 'On the University Carrier who sickn'd in the time of his vacancy, being forbid to go to *London*, by reason of the Plague', jokingly imagines that the ancient Hobson would have continued to drive between London and Cambridge for ever had he not been temporarily banned from making the journey due to the plague in London. Being as a result at a loose end with nothing to do, it suggests, he promptly died.

Hobson was a shrewd businessman and 'Hobson's choice' helped him to amass a considerable fortune, including the site of the priory of Anglesey, assorted manors and numerous other properties in Cambridge and beyond. His daughters could therefore afford to marry well, one to a gentleman and the other to a baronet, although Hobson wryly noted that the marriage portions he had to pay for such grand matches left him 'whereby my estate is much lesse than heretofore it was'. He did, however, have enough to leave money in his will to improve the water conduit into Cambridge, which still exists today and now bears his name.

How did a spider bring down a king?

It would be fair to say that Lola Montez was not universally loved in Bavaria. By the time she arrived there in 1846, she had already had what most would consider a lifetime of adventure and she was only twenty-five years old. Born Elizabeth Gilbert in Sligo in Ireland, she had lost her father in India, been sent back home, eloped, returned to India, left her husband, had an adulterous affair, been divorced and started a new career pretending to be a Spanish dancer – Lola Montez.

As Lola she had received a mixed reception. No one thought very much of her dancing but she was undoubtedly beautiful and her trademark dance – the tarantula, in which she swirled around pretending to pursue and stamp on a spider – revealed a certain passion. To the men in the audience it also revealed that she rarely wore underwear, a fact that may have altered their opinion of the dance. However, to a combination of horror, moral indignation and rapturous adulation, she toured Europe, having a brief fling with the composer Liszt, meeting Wagner and dancing privately for the Tsar Nicholas I along the way. She also made her mark off the stage, showing her fiery temper by taking a whip to those who crossed her and even managing to get expelled from Baden-Baden for carrying a dagger in her garter. So, after a spell as a *demi-mondaine* in Paris (until her lover was shot dead in a duel), she found herself in Munich, dancing before the sixty-year-old King Ludwig I of Bavaria.

Ludwig was definitely in the pro-Montez camp. Indeed, he became infatuated with her. He gave her property and jewels, and promised to make her a countess. She in return teased him, promising ever more exotic favours in the future. Her promotion of herself and her friends, and her attempts to ruin those she considered her enemies, gradually made her unpopular with the Bavarian people. Amongst the Jesuits, who had a way with words, she became known as 'the Apocalyptic Whore', and when Ludwig insisted that she be granted citizenship so that he could make good his promise to make her a countess, his entire cabinet resigned. In an attempt to shore up her position Montez even went so far as to form a pro-Montez bodyguard for herself from the students of the university. However, when they clashed with locals and she was saved from assassination only by the timely intervention of the army, she realised that it was time to leave and escaped to Switzerland. Ludwig, caught in an impossible situation, was forced to abdicate in favour of his son (the elder brother of the instrument-swallowing Alexandra – see pages 191–2). Montez wrote asking him to join her in Switzerland but after he learnt how he had been used by her, he broke off contact. Montez lived for another thirteen adventure-filled years, including spells dancing in Australia and the California gold-rush fields. She died in 1861, only thirty-nine years old.

Who were the victims of the War of the Currents?

The War of the Currents was fought in the late nineteenth and early twentieth centuries between the companies of George Westinghouse Junior and Thomas Edison. In the race to provide America with electric lighting, two methods of transmission had been proposed, the 110-volt direct current model of Edison, and Westinghouse's alternating current, which used 3,000 volts. Westinghouse's AC system had the advantage of losing less power in transmission, as transformers could be used to step up the voltage for distribution and then bring it back down for public consumption, but Edison believed that this high-voltage transmission was dangerous.

Already losing the War of the Currents due to the failure of his DC system to deliver power over distances greater than about a mile without significant voltage drop, Edison set about a publicity campaign to persuade the public that AC was too dangerous to adopt. To do this he presided over a number of public electrocutions of stray cats and dogs until in 1903 the chance came to make a really big statement. That year Topsy, a circus elephant that had killed three people, was ordered to be put down. The American Society for the Prevention of Cruelty to Animals considered hanging to be too cruel and so Edison offered to electrocute the beast. The *Commercial Advertiser* of New York carried the story on Monday, 5 January 1903.

> Topsy, the ill-tempered Coney Island elephant, was put to death in Luna Park, Coney Island, yesterday afternoon. The execution was witnessed by 1,500 or more curious persons, who went down to the island to see the end of the huge beast, to whom they had fed peanuts and cakes in summers that are gone. In order to make Topsy's execution quick and sure 460 grams of cyanide of potas-

sium were fed to her in carrots. Then a hawser was put around her neck and one end attached to a donkey engine and the other to a post. Next wooden sandals lined with copper were attached to her feet. These electrodes were connected by copper wire with the Edison electric light plant and a current of 6,600 volts was sent through her body. The big beast died without a trumpet or a groan.

Edison filmed the event and even went as far as trying to persuade people to refer to electrocution as being 'Westinghoused' but, due to the physical limitations of the DC system, the War of the Currents was in fact already lost and Westinghouse was triumphant.

However, one macabre side-effect of the War of the Currents means that it is still claiming victims to this day. In his desire to discredit the AC system, Edison employed Harold P. Brown to develop the electric chair – an AC-based execution system for criminals, which he hoped would not only satisfy the American public's desire for a more humane form of execution but also discredit Westinghouse to boot.

It was first used on William Kemmler in 1890, utilising one of Westinghouse's own generators, which Edison had bought by subterfuge, supposedly for use in a university. The execution was botched and the initial 1,000-volt charge failed to kill Kemmler. He was then shocked again, this time with 2,000 volts, which caused blood vessels in his arms to burst and his body to catch fire. The whole event took eight minutes and was described by one witness as 'far worse than hanging'. Westinghouse is reported to have commented: 'They would have done better using an axe.' Despite this, both the electric chair and the AC system remained in use, much to Edison's annoyance.

How did Dracula get his name?

Dracula got his name from a mythical beast, or rather his father's mythical beast. The man on whom at least part of the legend of Dracula is based is Vlad the Impaler, a fifteenth-century ruler of

Wallachia (now a province of Romania). But the title originally belonged to his father, Vlad II, who was a vassal of the Hungarian Empire, responsible for protecting the trade routes from the south into Transylvania and beyond.

At the time when Vlad II was on the throne, Europe was threatened from the south by the expansion of the Ottoman Empire. Vlad therefore decided to curry favour with the Holy Roman Emperor in the hope of receiving help during any Ottoman invasion of his lands. To do this, Vlad took the oath of the Order of the Dragon in 1431 by which he promised to protect the emperor's family in return for the emperor's goodwill. Vlad was rather pleased about his induction into a high chivalric order and became known as Vlad the Dragon, or in his own language Vlad Dracul.

As is often the way, things did not go to plan for Vlad. When the Ottomans threatened, Hungary (which was part of the Holy Roman Empire) ordered Vlad to obey the Oath of the Dragon he had taken and join the crusade against the Turks. Vlad refused so, after the Christian army was destroyed, the Hungarians repaid the compliment by arranging to murder him and his eldest son (who was blinded with hot iron stakes and then buried alive). They then replaced them with their own nominee. Young Vlad was rather cross about this and decided to back the Ottomans, who invaded Wallachia and installed him as puppet ruler. The Hungarians certainly weren't having such nonsense, however, and promptly reinvaded to remove him. Vlad now wisely ran away to Moldavia but when a new sultan came to the Ottoman throne, whom he hated, he took a chance and fled to the Hungarian court, of all places. Astonishingly, the king was terribly impressed with Vlad's knowledge of things Ottoman and decided to pardon him. Reinstalled on the throne of Wallachia, he proudly took the title that his father had once held from the Hungarian court, calling himself Dracula – the son of the Dragon.

Who fought the Dog Tax War?

Just when you thought there simply couldn't be any more stupid wars, along comes the Dog Tax War. The name is a bit misleading as it wasn't really a war at all but more of a nasty colonial spat between the European settlers of New Zealand (not the New Zealand that Willem Janszoon discovered – see pages 205–6) and the native Maori people. It was, however, caused by a dog tax.

The Maori people had not had a good nineteenth century. In 1840, just before the beginnings of large-scale European settlement, they were a populous, independent nation, but by the outbreak of the Dog Tax War in 1889 they owned just 10 per cent of the least fertile areas of their land and their population had fallen by 90 per cent, mainly due to diseases introduced by the settlers. In this situation, strongly anti-settler groups had grown up amongst the Maori, as perhaps you might expect, and they were looking for an excuse to expel the Europeans.

In 1889 the white-led Hokianga County Council on North Island obliged when it imposed a tax of two shillings and sixpence on dog owners for every dog they owned. Not surprisingly, some people objected, notably the Maori people of the Waima area who refused to pay and were promptly arrested. Matters now began to get a bit heated as the Maori independence movement, the Pai Marire, got involved. When the only police officer for the region arrived in Waima on 28 April he found a well-armed group, refusing to pay their dog tax and threatening to advance on the administrative capital, Rawene. As the war party marched off he sent a message to Rawene, advising that all women and children be evacuated for fear of a massacre. Soon the entire town was empty. Meanwhile six policemen from Auckland had arrived to defend the town and had set up a cannon on the quay. Just what they expected to do with one cannon is unclear but when the angry Maori mob arrived, they wisely ran away.

At this point it looked as if a war might well be in the offing, were it not for the quick thinking of a local hotel owner (and the only remaining European in the whole town), Bob Cochrane. He opened his bar, invited the war party in and, rather than pointing cannons at them, offered them a beer and a chat. This calmed things down a bit. The war party (which only numbered about twenty people in the first place) then went home.

By now the government had had time to overreact and sent a force of some 120 heavily armed soldiers and policemen, plus a warship, to the area. Fearing an all-out firefight, the local member of the House of Representatives, Hone Heke, sent a telegram to the Maori leader, Hone Toia, advising him to disband his men and seek redress through parliament. This he did, but he and fifteen others were later arrested. In court Hone Toia pleaded not guilty to conspiring to levy war but guilty of conspiring to prevent the collection of taxes. He was sentenced to eighteen months' hard labour and, to add insult to injury, all his group had to pay their dog tax.

8

Bedhopping

I have never yet seen anyone whose desire to build up his moral power was as strong as sexual desire.

Confucius (K'ung Fu-tzu), *Analects*, chapter 9, v. 17, trans. Arthur Waley

Who wasn't amused by a sex scandal?

Dilke was, in many ways, the Profumo of the nineteenth century. By 1885, and still only forty-one years old, Dilke looked like becoming a major player in British politics. Gladstone had nominated him as his successor to lead the Liberal Party and even his political opposite, Disraeli, admitted that he was one of the most useful men in politics.

It was at this point, on the brink of a glorious career, that Charles Dilke's life fell apart for reasons that even today are not entirely clear. The immediate and obvious cause was that great political leveller – a sex scandal. Dilke, the wealthy proprietor of a number of magazines (including *Notes and Queries*), like many Victorian public figures, did not lead a completely spotless private life. He had conducted affairs with several women, including his sister-in-law's mother, and so was known to be at least occasionally unfaithful. But the 1885 accusation came from an unexpected quarter. In that year Virginia Crawford, the sister of his brother's wife, announced to her husband that she had been 'ruined' by Dilke, who had seduced her when she was nineteen and newly married. She claimed that the affair had continued for two and a half years in which time Dilke had taught her 'every French vice' and even persuaded her to indulge in a threesome with the maid. Mr Crawford promptly sued for divorce, citing Dilke as co-respondent.

Society was both scandalised and titillated, and the press soon got their teeth into 'three-in-a-bed Dilke', whose case wasn't helped by the fact that whilst he claimed never to have seduced Virginia, he happily admitted that at the same time he *was* having an affair with her mother. All the same, the whole thing did look like a bit of a fit-up and Dilke managed to persuade the jury in the trial that he was entirely innocent. The judge did, however, grant Crawford his divorce, which left the press wondering how Virginia could be found guilty of having an adulterous affair with Dilke but not Dilke with Virginia. Dilke then suicidally had the case reopened in an attempt to clear his name and through bad legal advice found himself on the wrong end of a series of damning cross-examinations, which, whilst not in any way proving the affair, effectively destroyed his public standing. When it was time for Gladstone to draw up the list for his third cabinet, he wrote against Dilke's name just one word: 'Unavailable'.

Dilke spent the next decade trying to prove his innocence but the damage was done. He would never reach high office and, without a young successor, the Liberal Party foundered and collapsed. So was it true? A commission set up ten years after the case found that Mrs Crawford had probably made the whole thing up. The question was, why? It has been suggested that Dilke may have had an affair with Virginia before her marriage and refused to marry her himself. When she later needed a divorce (having contracted syphilis from another lover, which she couldn't hide from her husband), she decided to end her marriage and avenge herself on Dilke in the same breath. Whilst her story was unlikely, Dilke was certainly no saint and there were plenty of people happy to see him fall, not least Queen Victoria, who despised him for having accused her of dereliction of duty and proposing in the House of Commons that Britain become a republic (the last time that such a suggestion has ever been made in the House). Indeed, even Victoria's most famous comment is a reference to Dilke. When she overheard her courtier Alick York repeating the 'three-in-a-bed' scandal, she supposedly commented, 'We are not amused.'

How did Charles the Mad stop his wife having an affair?

Isabeau of Bavaria has gone down in history as a misguided nympho-maniac who signed away her son's inheritance. She was the daughter of Thaddea Visconti and Stephen III of Bavaria, and she married the unpromisingly monikered French king Charles the Mad (see page 225) in 1385 at one of the unhappiest periods in French history.

She had few abilities as a leader, and suffered from being both female and foreign at a time when such things didn't give you much authority at the French court. This proved problematic, particularly during Charles's bouts of insanity. She further compromised her position by becoming the mistress of Louis of Orléans, whilst her sexual appetite and financial incontinence made her extremely unpopular, particularly in Paris. Eventually the king, who had developed a persecution complex fixated on his wife, disbanded her court at the Hôtel Barbette, which was well known for its extravagance and promiscuity.

In 1417, the queen was banished, allegedly due to the behaviour of her ladies-in-waiting, but actually because the king believed her to have been having an affair with her *grand maître d'hôtel*, Louis de Bosredon. Louis was arrested and imprisoned. Later he was sewn into a leather sack that bore the legend, *Laissiez passer la justice du roy* ('May the king's justice be served') and thrown into the Seine. Isabeau's banishment may also have had much to do with her unpopularity at court, brought about by her rapacious behaviour, particularly her channelling of state funds to her Bavarian family.

After the defeat in 1415 of the French forces at Agincourt, Isabeau's last 'disgrace' was to agree to the Treaty of Troyes, although in fairness she had little choice about it, which dispossessed her son (later Charles VII) in favour of the heirs of Henry V of England and his new wife, Catherine (her own daughter).

Who was as happy as the Dey was long?

Caroline of Brunswick-Wolfenbüttel was the wife of the Prince Regent (later King) George IV, but their marriage was a decidedly unhappy one. He suspected her of not being a virgin on their marriage and also accused her of being 'unhygienic'. For her part she thought him a profligate adulterer, which he was. Having only ever shared the same bed three times, they separated and she eventually moved abroad where, it was believed, she had numerous affairs. On George's accession to the throne she was recalled for the sake of appearances but the couple could no longer bear each other's company. When she appeared at the coronation in Westminster Abbey, the king ordered the doors to be slammed in her face.

The king then began divorce proceedings under the Pains and Penalties Bill of 1820, which was created to strip her of the title queen and annul her marriage, but this involved airing a lot of dirty linen in public. Caroline's numerous affairs were recounted in parliament in lurid detail, including a rather exotic liaison with the Dey of Algiers, which led to Chief Justice Lord Norbury quipping that Caroline was 'as happy as the Dey was long'. Despite the humour, however, the effect of the revelations was actually to create a groundswell of sympathy for the queen as her 'crimes' seemed modest by comparison to her husband's profligate adultery. In the end the Bill was thrown out but Caroline would not live to enjoy it. She died three weeks after the coronation.

Who preferred adultery to a pint of beer?

Nancy, Lady Astor, was the first woman to actually take up her seat in parliament and she quickly became known for her outspoken views, particularly on the subject of alcohol, which she was very much against. Opposing her on this crusade was the majority of the British male establishment, naturally enough, led by none other than Winston Churchill, who famously liked a drink, preferably champagne, at any time of day. Lady Astor, an American by birth, was not easily overawed by the looming form of a slightly inebriated establishment, however, and her quick wit could put even Churchill in his place. Perhaps her most famous put-down to the great man came after she invited him to a costume ball and he asked her what sort of disguise she would recommend for him. She replied: 'Why don't you come sober, Prime Minister?' Churchill got his own back with an even more famous exchange, when Lady Astor told him, 'If you were my husband I'd put arsenic in your coffee,' to which he replied, 'Madam, if I were your husband I'd drink it.'

The last laugh on the subject of temperance must go to the outspoken Labour MP Jack Jones, the man who had single-handedly ended the House of Commons tradition of quoting in Latin by shouting, 'And that is the winner of the two-thirty' at the top of his voice every time someone attempted it. When Lady Astor buttonholed him on the subject of the demon drink, she declared to him, 'I would rather commit adultery than drink a pint of beer.' Jones thought for a moment and then replied, 'Who wouldn't?'

Who said 'cock-a-doodle-doo' to a bishop?

Charles Beresford was something of a Victorian action man, maintaining parallel careers in the navy and the Houses of Parliament, which saw him fighting in Egypt and Sudan when not speaking in the Commons in favour of expanding the navy. He was also a great self-publicist, known to the newspapers as Charlie B, the embodiment of the John Bull spirit (in fact, he used to travel everywhere with his bulldog to reinforce this image). Popular both with the ladies and in royal circles, he became aide-de-camp to the Prince of Wales (later Edward VII) and in this capacity met the Countess of Warwick, Frances Evelyn Greville, known as Daisy to her friends. Daisy was the Prince of Wales's mistress at the time but she seems to have fallen genuinely in love with Beresford. The difficulty was that she was not discreet. Indeed, as the wife of Lord Brooke, she was known as 'the babbling Brooke' and provided the inspiration for the song 'Daisy, Daisy'. Her feelings for Beresford soon became well known to the prince, straining relations between the future king and his aide for the rest of their lives.

However, when it comes to indiscretion, it was Charles Beresford who must take the prize. At a house party shortly after their affair began, Beresford crept late one night into what he thought was Daisy's bedroom and leapt on to the bed with a cry of 'cock-a-doodle-doo!' After some frantic scrabbling around, a lamp was lit and Beresford found himself lying between the bishop of Chester and his wife, having broken into the wrong room. After this, it proved hard to keep the affair secret.

Which MP said his sister was a prostitute?

Henry Du Pré Labouchere was one of the most prominent radical politicians in England in the late nineteenth century although his cynicism and dissolute habits meant that few in government took him as seriously as perhaps they should. It was Labouchere who invented the term Grand Old Man (GOM) for Gladstone (see pages 270–1), and who set up and ran the radical magazine *Truth*, a sort of forerunner of *Private Eye*, whose fearless exposure of corruption led to an almost continuous series of libel cases, most of which he won. His dry wit and radical stance did not make him popular, however, and high office eluded him. Indeed, Queen Victoria personally ordered his exclusion from government at one point on the grounds that the proprietor of a scurrilous magazine such as *Truth* ought not to hold a Crown office. In the diplomatic corps he fared equally badly. During a reception at Baden-Baden the Foreign Secretary (Lord John Russell) offered him a new posting to Buenos Aires. When Labouchere replied that he'd be delighted to accept, provided he could carry out his duties from Baden-Baden, the humourless Foreign Secretary dismissed him from the service.

Such quips, which won him instant fame but few powerful friends, had a long history with Labouchere, going back to his days at Cambridge University, where he managed to run up debts of £6,000 in just two years (and that at 1850s prices). One of the ways that he spent his money was on the town's courtesans, all of whom, as an undergraduate, he was banned from mixing with under university law. It was whilst he was walking through town with one such woman that a university proctor, one of those charged with upholding university regulations, approached him and demanded to know the identity of the woman on his arm. Labouchere politely introduced her as his sister. An apoplectic proctor countered that she was actually well known to be one of the most notorious prostitutes in the city, to which Labouchere replied, 'I know that, sir, but is it kind to throw my family misfortune in my face?'

How did Old Rowley get his name?

Old Rowley was a nickname of King Charles II, which came about as a product of the two great loves in his life, watching horse racing and siring (illegitimate) children. Horse racing had been banned by Cromwell under the protectorate but Charles reintroduced it, adding royal patronage to what would become 'the sport of kings'. Charles's first experience of horse racing was probably at Epsom Downs in 1661 but it was Newmarket in Cambridgeshire that particularly benefited from his support. From 1666 he would regularly attend meetings there, actually riding on some occasions. In 1671 he even managed to win the 'Town Plate' trophy that he had instituted. Amongst the many horses that Charles personally owned was a stallion called Old Rowley, known not so much for his racing as for the very large number of foals he had sired. This chimed rather well with Charles's own activities in the field, he famously having acknowledged fourteen illegitimate children by nine mistresses. There were possibly others as there were certainly at least another seven mistresses. Unfortunately for Charles, however, he had no legitimate heirs. Nevertheless, he might certainly be called the legitimate father of British horse racing and to celebrate his, and his horses', achievements, one of the two courses at Newmarket is known as 'the Rowley Mile'.

Who is the only member of the royal family to be sued for adultery?

Prince Henry Frederick, Duke of Cumberland (1745–90), the fourth son of Frederick Prince of Wales, was intended for a steady and none-too-public life in the navy. To this end he enrolled as a midshipman in 1768 and, as is sometimes the way with princes, had managed to make it to rear admiral just a year later.

Henry's real interests were very much on land, however, beginning and ending in the person of Harriet, Lady Grosvenor, wife of the 1st Baron Grosvenor. Their relationship began in the spring of 1769 and their habit of being seen openly together soon caused a minor scandal as well as infuriating her husband. Events reached a head around 2 a.m. on the morning of 22 December 1769 when Grosvenor's servants burst into a room at the White Hart Inn in St Albans and found Henry and Lady Grosvenor in bed together. Usually a prince might expect to walk away from such a scene in return for a favour or two granted to the husband or his family, but Grosvenor was incensed and chose to pursue Henry in the courts. On 5 July 1770 the prince was tried for 'criminal conversation' with Lady Grosvenor and found guilty, having to pay his lover's husband £10,000 in compensation – money he didn't have and which he had to borrow from his brother the king. The public took badly to what they saw as the state coffers paying out adultery fines for the royal family and the duke was pilloried in the press. Even the private correspondence of the two lovers managed to find its way into popular pamphlets where Henry was further ridiculed for his appalling English grammar.

Did George I go to bed with an elephant?

The arrival of the House of Hanover at the accession of George I brought to England a fascinating selection of foreign court creatures for the British aristocracy to observe, and none was more fascinating than Sophia Charlotte von Kielmansegg, Countess of Darlington. She was nominally the daughter of the Baron von Platen and his wife but was actually the illegitimate daughter of Duke Ernst August of Brunswick and Lüneburg and hence George I's half-sister. When he became king of Great Britain she followed him to England with her husband, who was made Master of Horse and started life as a courtier. She certainly made an impression on the English court. The young Horace Walpole described meeting her thus:

> Lady Darlington, whom I saw at my mother's in my infancy, and whom I remember by being terrified at her enormous figure, was as corpulent and ample as the duchess was long and emaciated. Two fierce black eyes, large and rolling beneath two lofty arched eyebrows, two acres of cheeks spread with crimson, an ocean of neck that overflowed and was not distinguished from the lower parts of her body, and no part restrained by stays – no wonder that a child dreaded such an ogress, and that the mob of London were highly diverted at the importation of so uncommon a seraglio!

From the above description it's perhaps not surprising that the London crowd soon had a nickname for the countess – the Elephant – as well as a rumour to attach to her. Her closeness to George I, and her insistence on openly competing with his mistresses (particularly the very thin Melusine von der Schulenburg, known as 'the Maypole') for his attention, led to the belief that she was having an affair with the king, even though she was his half-sister. In many minds this was perhaps just how the exotic German court behaved. The king's confectioner even went so far as to make public 'indecent suggestions' about the two, for which he promptly received his cards. Certainly Walpole believed that they had been lovers although this was probably more to do with the failure of the British aristocracy to understand how the Hanoverian court worked, and who had influence and why, than any proof he might have been privy to. The king's mother had written in 1701 to confide her 'certain knowledge' that the two were not having an affair and there is no conclusive evidence that at any later date George ever slept with his Elephant.

9

Improbable Lives

The worst of madmen is a saint run mad.

Alexander Pope, *Imitations of Horace* (1738), book 1, Epistle 6, 1.27

Where is the place in England nearest to Nazareth?

In 1061, Lady Richeldis de Faverches, a wealthy lady from near Walsingham in Norfolk, claimed she was taken in spirit to Nazareth. This was before Thomas Cook, you understand, so journeys 'in spirit' were often all that was available, particularly in the travel agencies of Walsingham.

Well, whilst Lady Richeldis was there, she bumped into the mother of Jesus who had a great idea about how to liven things up back in Norfolk, which was a bit flat in every sense of the word. She suggested that the good lady might like to build a replica of the house in Nazareth where she, Mary, was brought up and where she received the Annunciation of Christ.

It was a rather odd idea by all accounts but Lady Richeldis was game and decided to give it a go. When she got back home she immediately constructed a house that measured twenty-three feet six inches by twelve feet ten inches, according to a plan given her by Mary. It always pays to listen to the ideas of the Holy Family and, sure enough, the fame of this house soon spread, so much so, in fact, that in 1150 a group of Augustinian canons decided to cash in and built a priory beside it. Soon pilgrims were flocking there from all over England (and farther afield), leaving precious gifts at the house, which now turned a tidy profit.

They could not have anticipated that Henry VIII would one day cast his beady eyes on their splendid wealth. In 1534, Walsingham became one of the first religious houses to sign the Oath of Supremacy, recognising Henry VIII as head of the Church in England. In 1538, the repo men arrived and the house was stripped of its valuables, its statue of the Virgin was taken to London to be burnt, and for the next three centuries its buildings were used as farm sheds.

There is, however, a happy ending. In 1897, Pope Leo XIII refounded the ancient shrine and pilgrimages were permitted to resume. In 1981, construction began on the Chapel of Reconciliation, a cooperative effort between Catholics and

Anglicans, who had decided to let bygones be bygones, and the feast of Our Lady of Walsingham was finally reinstated in 2000.

Why didn't St Wilborada take her own advice?

St Wilborada has the distinction of being the first woman formally canonised by the Vatican (in 1047, by Clement II), thus marking her out from the 'pre-congregation' group of saints (as those who come before are known), many of whom are frankly fictional. As an anchoress she became renowned for her gift of prophecy – something that enabled her to warn the monks of St Gall of an impending Hungarian invasion. However, this was where being an anchoress had drawbacks. Having been walled into a small cell, she was unable to take heed of her own advice and run for the hills, and hence was martyred by the Hungarians when they arrived.

What was unusual about St Solange's head?

St Solange was a ninth-century shepherdess who took a vow of chastity – greatly to the annoyance of Bernard, Count of Poitiers, who rather fancied her. She remained true to her vow, however, and rebuffed all his advances until he became so frustrated that he decided to murder her by cutting her head off. But if Bernard thought that that was the end of the story, he was sadly mistaken. St Solange promptly picked up her head and marched to the nearest village where she preached to the people. This must have surprised the villagers somewhat. History, or rather hagiography, does not record whether she also took the opportunity to 'point the finger' at Count Bernard.

What was St Eulalia's ambition?

St Eulalia was a consecrated virgin in the late third century who had a rather unusual ambition. If you ask the average teenager what they want to be when they grow up, you'll probably get the usual range of answers from Stoic philosopher to acrobat, but Eulalia's ambition was to be dead.

All her life what she'd really wanted to be was a martyr, which must have left her school careers adviser with a lot of explaining to do. Some children are in such a hurry to grow up, which is a shame because being grown up is rubbish, but Eulalia was no exception. Keen to get on with her chosen career, she went before the tribunal of the Roman emperor Diocletian of her own free will and confessed her Christianity.

Diocletian, who disliked Christians almost as much as his predecessor Decius (see pages 118–20), was only too happy to fix it for her to achieve her life's ambition and he arranged for her to be tortured and thrown naked into the streets. At this point the miracles start happening and God, seeing his virgin servant exposed in this way, made it snow – which is good going for that part of Spain – and so covered her modesty. Just how thankful a naked and tortured girl was to be covered in ice-cold snow is not recorded but then God moves in mysterious ways.

Anyway, the Roman authorities were a bit miffed by all this, as they always were when God started teasing them, so they decided to warm the poor girl up by burning her alive. Having burnt her to death (and hence granted her her wish for martyrdom), they threw her ashes into a field and guess what? God again made it snow over them, forming a burial pall.

What happened to Sir Alured's wife when he swore?

Rumwold is a rather peculiar saint as he only lived for three days although in that short time he did his parents proud. The son of the Christian queen St Cyneburga, and the pagan King Aldfrith of Northumbria, during his short life he apparently repeatedly shouted, 'I am a Christian,' which was a little precocious, and asked for baptism (which he received from Bishop Wilderin) and holy communion. Immediately after baptism, he made a confession of faith and then set about preaching a sermon on the Holy

Trinity, reciting scripture and the Athanasian Creed as part of his proofs. He completed this performance by predicting his death, and outlining his desired burial arrangements.

A statue of Rumwold at Boxley Abbey could supposedly be moved only by people who lived pure lives. Purity could apparently be measured by your gift to the abbey since, if it was sufficient, one of the monks would operate a ratchet mechanism that helped move the statue. This scam was exposed and the statue was burnt during the Reformation.

Sir Alured was chastised by the saint for swearing on his wedding day in 1282. Alured repented and cleaned up his language. However, at a royal feast some time later, a cold dessert made his tooth ache, which caused him to curse with gusto. The tiny but vengeful Rumwold suddenly appeared in a window, and Sir Alured's young bride disappeared in a puff of perfume, leaving behind only her clothes.

What is Emperor Karl I's surprising title?

Emperor Karl I, of the Austro-Hungarian Empire, has the official title 'Blessed', having been beatified by the Catholic Church on 3 October 2004 by Pope John Paul II, leaving him now just a step away from full sainthood. He has one attested miracle to his name – the curing of varicose veins in a Brazilian nun in 1960 – with other claims pending. One more proven miracle is needed before he can be canonised.

Some people think that making one of the figureheads of the First World War a saint is not quite cricket. After all, there are still arguments as to whether he authorised the use of mustard gas on the Western Front. He also made two attempts to return to power after the end of the war, which seemed to many a little insensitive. Karl did, however, take seriously Pope Benedict XV's Peace Note of 1 August 1917, making him the only belligerent leader to do so. Germany ignored the peace plan, as did the Allied powers who had, in the secret Treaty of London in 1915, agreed to ignore papal interference in the war as part of their bid to persuade Italy to join the Allies.

Who saved a monastery with a fat mouse?

St Cadoc had a lively childhood as the son of the Welsh king St Gwynllyw, who was really more of a bandit than a king. Indeed, his mother, St Gladys, only arrived at court after his dad stole her from a neighbouring chief.

Young Cadoc was educated by an Irish monk who was given the job after demanding that Gwynllyw returned the cow he had stolen from him. The thieving chieftain clearly thought this sort of chutzpah in the face of a notorious bandit showed some gumption so he handed over his son forthwith.

Like the lives of all good pre-congregation saints, there's very little known about that of St Cadoc but many a story is told . . .

Once he was chased through a wood by an armed swineherd from an enemy tribe, probably for having said something rude about pigs. Having decided to duck behind a tree to avoid said fiery peasant, he accidentally disturbed an old grey wild boar that made three great leaps at him, then disappeared. Cadoc took this as a sign – not to drink less but to found the great church and monastery at Llancarvan.

Legend also says that he once saved his brother monks in a famine by tying a white thread to the foot of a fat mouse that he'd noticed lumbering around the monastery. He then followed the thread to an abandoned, but well-stocked, underground granary.

Another time he and his brothers went out to meet a band of thieves, chanting and playing harps. This so surprised the highwaymen that they turned and fled.

Sadly this monastic variety show didn't have such a splendid effect when he tried it on the pagan Saxons in southern England. He was martyred by them while serving at mass around AD 580 near Weedon in Northamptonshire.

Who made her name by giving away other people's milk?

Brigid was the daughter of Dubtach, the pagan Scottish king of Leinster, by Brocca, a Christian slave of his who had been baptised by St Patrick. Just before Brigid was born, Dubtach decided to sell her mother to a local druid. Brigid grew up in the druid's family until she was old enough to return to her legal owner and father – Dubtach. This rather neat legal wrinkle meant that Dubtach didn't have to pay for her upbringing, of course. But if the king thought he'd got a good deal, he had another think coming. As soon as she returned to work for him, she started giving away all his things to the poor – which made him rather cross. She even gave his favourite sword to a leper, saying that through this poor unfortunate she was giving it to God because of its great value. At this point he decided to grant her her freedom before she bankrupted him.

Brigid then returned to her mother Brocca (who was working for the druid, if you remember) and took over the dairy there. Despite the fact that she gave away nearly all of the produce, the dairy flourished and the druid was so pleased that he freed Mum too. Mother and daughter then went back to Dubtach, who probably wasn't all that pleased to see them, so he decided to marry Brigid off to a local bard. Brigid refused, however, and prayed that God would make her ugly so that no suitor would want her, and God obliged. She then decided to take her vows and, at the moment that she dedicated herself to God, her looks were restored.

From then on her life settled down to the usual round of founding convents, even inventing the rather saucy 'double monastery' – with houses for both nuns and monks. Brigid died on 1 February 523 of natural causes and is buried in Downpatrick. All except her head, that is, which somehow found its way to Lisbon in Portugal.

She is the patron saint of bastards.

How did St Kevin get the land to found his monastery?

According to his frankly highly unreliable hagiography, St Kevin was sent for by the sixth-century pagan King O'Toole of Glendalough who had a problem. Being rather lonely, as pagan kings often are, he had become overly fond of his pet goose, but the poor bird was by then on its last legs. King O'Toole, aware of the saint's astonishing powers, asked Kevin whether he could make his goose young again. The wily Kevin agreed, if in return the king would give him all the land that the goose flew over as soon as he'd rejuvenated it. This seemed like a good deal to King O'Toole as his geriatric goose could barely walk, let alone fly, and so he agreed. With that, Kevin touched the goose and it immediately grew young again. It then proceeded to take wing and fly over the whole of the Glendalough valley. The king was a little miffed but he was as good as his word and handed over the valley, where Kevin founded the monastery of Glendalough.

Despite this rather exotic tale, and others that include him being fed by an otter, letting a cow lick his clothing in return for producing fifty times the normal amount of milk, and standing still for several weeks whilst a blackbird incubated its egg on his outstretched arm, Kevin is not a pre-congregation saint but was canonised only in 1903. He is the patron saint of blackbirds.

How did St Collen defeat the fairies?

Few hagiographies are more detached from likely historical events than that of St Collen but his story is worth retelling if only as a reminder of what once did pass for history. The story goes that Collen was walking along one day, daydreaming about that time he'd killed a giantess, when a talking peacock came up to him, which was something of a surprise.

The peacock then asked Collen if he'd care to have dinner with the king of the fairies but three times the saint refused. The peacock was very persistent, however, in the way that peacocks are, and eventually he agreed.

Collen duly rolled up at the king's place in his Sunday best and was initially rather impressed. The king of the fairies seemed to live in a huge castle, with lots of servants, and Collen was shown into a room where the king, like the ghost of Christmas Past, sat surrounded by an enormous quantity of food. Collen wisely surmised that this was all a bit fishy so he reminded the king about the fate of the godless and then started sprinkling holy water around as if it was going out of fashion. Instantly the castle, the food and the king evaporated and all that was left was a demonic bird, which flew away, never to be seen again.

Another version of the story has it that Collen was living in a cave near Glastonbury when he was asked to mediate in the age-old May Day dispute between Gwynn ap Nudd, Lord of the Underworld, and Gwyther, Lord of Summer, for the hand of the fair Creiddylad, the Maiden of Spring. The Lord of the Underworld was very insistent in his suit but the friends of the Lord of Summer pointed out, quite rightly, that the year above-ground would drag somewhat if Spring went off with him. At this point St Collen arrived and told them both that he would settle their dispute but they would have to wait until the day he chose. They agreed, at which he chose Doomsday, which was a neat trick. There followed a liberal dousing with holy water and, as before, all the pixies and fairies of the ancient gods disappeared.

What couldn't St Venantius do?

St Venantius of Camerino lived during the persecution of Christians by the Roman emperor Decius (around AD 250), which should have been a good time for anyone looking for martyrdom, but Venantius found it surprisingly difficult.

Having learnt that he was about to be arrested as a Christian, Venantius immediately presented himself to the governor of

Camerino, Antiochus, and somewhat provocatively announced to him that the lives of the pagan gods were filled with every kind of crime and that there was only one God. This rather annoyed Antiochus, who tried to persuade him otherwise, but the young man wouldn't move. To try to encourage him, Antiochus ordered him to be scourged, but he was miraculously saved by an angel. Necessity being the mother of invention, Antiochus decided to try a different tack and burnt him with torches before suspending him over a low fire in the hope that the smoke might suffocate him. Once again an angel came to the rescue, however, stamping the fire out and setting Venantius free.

Antiochus now summoned Venantius again but, unable to make him renounce his faith, the governor cast him into prison with an apostate soldier, who strove in vain to tempt him. Antiochus, furious, then ordered Venantius's teeth and jaws to be broken and had him thrown into a furnace, from which the angel once again delivered him. The saint was then sent to a city magistrate to be condemned, but after hearing his defence of Christianity, this judge fell headlong from his seat and expired, saying, 'The God of Venantius is the true God; let us destroy our idols.'

Antiochus was now rather irritated so he ordered Venantius to be thrown to the lions at once. Frankly he should have guessed what would happen next. These wild animals, forgetting their natural ferocity, crouched at the feet of the saint like kittens. Antiochus, not a man to give up easily, ordered Venantius to be dragged through a heap of brambles and thorns until he expired. After a few hours of this, they decided to drag him over rocks and stones as well for good measure. This had very little effect on the saint but it did make the soldiers dragging him very thirsty. Aware of their suffering, the martyr knelt at a stone, made the sign of the cross on it and a jet of cool water burst forth from within for the soldiers to drink. They were all so impressed by this that some of them decided to convert and have a go at becoming martyrs themselves.

Antiochus was now absolutely beside himself. Not only had all

Venantius's wounds healed, but now his best executioners were all going around looking dewy-eyed and wanting to be saved. There was only one thing to do – he had the whole lot beheaded. That seemed to do the trick.

10

I Say!

'Then you should say what you mean,' the March Hare
went on.

'I do,' Alice hastily replied; 'at least – at least I mean
what I say – that's the same thing, you know.'

'Not the same thing a bit!' said the Hatter. 'You might
just as well say that "I see what I eat" is the same thing as
"I eat what I see"!'

Lewis Carroll, *Alice's Adventures in Wonderland* (1865),
chapter 7

What did Stalin call Lenin's wife?

By December 1922 the relationship between Lenin and Stalin had been sour for some time, with Lenin finding himself unable to rein in Stalin's drive towards absolute power. It was, however, a phone conversation about Lenin's wife that proved to be the last straw. Nadezhda Krupskaya had been a key member of the early Russian Communist Party, as well as a loyal wife and political companion to Lenin. One thing she certainly was not was unfaithful, so when Stalin, in a phone conversation with Lenin, referred to her as 'a syphilitic whore' Lenin was reasonably justified in being irked. That Stalin felt free to make such a comment speaks volumes for his increasing power and Lenin's increasing impotence. Indeed, Lenin died just over a year later, leaving Krupskaya to continue to do battle with Stalin as she vehemently opposed the decision to have her husband embalmed and put on display. Supposedly this very public argument led Stalin to darkly comment, 'Comrade Lenin may be in need of a new widow.'

What did one newspaper consider 'slipshod' and 'puerile'?

The *Chicago Times* was commenting on a speech given on 19 November 1863, during the dedication of a war cemetery at Gettysburg in Pennsylvania following a very bloody battle there in the American Civil War some four months previously. The main speaker at the event had been Edward Everett, who gave a 13,607-word speech that had taken him two full hours to deliver. After that the President, Abraham Lincoln, had agreed to say 'a few words', 272 of them in fact. The *Chicago Times* considered the speech 'slipshod' and 'puerile'. Not everyone since has agreed with the paper, however, and the Gettysburg Address has been called *'the world's foremost statement of freedom and democracy and the sacrifices required to achieve and defend them'* by James M. MacPherson, the Professor Emeritus of US History at Princeton University.

What, according to Disraeli, was the difference between a misfortune and a calamity?

Late nineteenth-century Prime Ministers Benjamin Disraeli (for whose last laugh see pages 128–9) and William Gladstone (see pages 270–1) never really got on and there are numerous recorded jibes by each at the other. Most famously, Disraeli was, according to Wilfred Meynell's 1903 biography, once asked what he thought was the difference between a misfortune and a calamity, as the terms were employed in the politics of the day. He thought for a moment and then replied: *'If Gladstone fell into the Thames, that would be a misfortune; and if anybody pulled him out, that, I suppose, would be a calamity.'* Fortunately for Gladstone such a misfortune never took place although there seems no reason to doubt the seaworthiness of a man who once wrote, *'My name may have buoyancy enough to float upon the sea of time.'*

Who was dubbed Lord Cupid?

The British nineteenth-century Prime Minister, Henry Temple, 3rd Viscount Palmerston, had something of a reputation as a ladies' man. He had first come to parliament as an MP for Newport on the Isle of Wight, a 'pocket borough' (the next best thing to a rotten borough – see pages 273–4) in the gift of Sir Leonard Holmes, who granted him the seat provided he promised never to go there. London life suited Palmerston and he soon began affairs with ladies at Almack's Assembly Rooms, then the first London club to admit women. Having seduced Lady Jersey and Her Serene Highness Dorothea von Lieven, wife of the Russian ambassador to Great Britain (and perhaps the most politically influential woman in the world), in 1810 he fell in love with Emily, Lady Cowper. Sadly for Palmerston she too was married but that didn't prevent their conducting a rather public affair. Her brother, Lord Melbourne, described Emily as 'a devoted mother, and excellent wife – but not chaste'.

After her husband's death in 1839 she and Palmerston finally married. He was by then fifty-five years old but his amorous reputation was still intact and his eye was still roving, leading *The Times* to dub him 'Lord Cupid'. Nor did this reputation seem to diminish with age. Indeed, it was twenty-four years later, in 1863, that a Mrs O'Kane visited Palmerston at the House of Commons when he was Prime Minister and later claimed that the two had committed adultery there. Her husband, a journalist, immediately sued for divorce, citing Palmerston as co-respondent and claiming the huge sum of £20,000 in damages. The case was dismissed but the newspapers, marvelling in the apparent fact that a Prime Minister at the age of seventy-eight was still capable of adultery, wrote, *'She was certainly Kane, but was he Abel?'* The public seemed to think that he was and, far from damaging his career, the sprightly septuagenarian's antics increased his popularity. He died still in office in 1865, aged eighty-one.

How did Frederick the Great deal with a deserter?

Frederick II of Prussia was a somewhat enlightened monarch, which is perhaps all the more surprising, considering that his father was a dour disciplinarian with an unhealthy fascination for the army who had tried his son for treason when he had run away, and forced him to watch the decapitation of his best friend. Despite this, and a marriage that had driven him to contemplate suicide, when in 1740 Frederick became king of the fragmented territories known as Prussia, he was already regarded as a civilised, well-educated and progressive ruler. He was also not averse to a fight, however, and became renowned as the greatest tactical genius of his day (indeed, according to Napoleon, of any day).

Frederick was not always successful in war and at the disastrous Battle of Kunersdorf (in what is today Poland) during the Seven Years War, his 50,000-strong army was routed by a combined Austrian and Russian force of just under 60,000. By the evening 6,000 of his men were dead, 13,000 were wounded and another

23,000 had been scattered, either unable or unwilling to regroup. After the battle one such deserter was caught and hauled before Frederick, who asked him why he had run away. The soldier, convinced he would die for the crime, told Frederick, 'Because things were going so badly for your Majesty.' Frederick beckoned him closer and whispered, 'I suggest that you wait for a week. Then, if things are still going badly, we'll desert together.'

Which general was accused of eating his men?

Adolphus Washington Greely had served in the volunteer infantry in the US Civil War and shortly after joined the regular army. Whilst in the cavalry he heard of an army expedition to the Arctic planned for the first International Polar Year (1882–3) and he applied to command it. Given a team of twenty-five men, he was allotted the task of setting up a base on Ellesmere Island from which he was to make a series of expeditions north to take geophysical and meteorological measurements. Greeley arrived in 1881, established a camp at Fort Conger and began his year's work. The weather in 1882 in the far north proved extreme, however, and the relief ships sent in that year and the next both failed to reach his base. In August 1883, Greely and his men began heading south on their own but could not get further than Cape Sabine. Here they were forced to winter and here they were finally picked up by a relief expedition in June 1884. The conditions that they had endured had been terrible and nineteen of the men had died, either from starvation, hypothermia or drowning, including one whom Greely had ordered shot. Of the six survivors, one died before reaching home and the remaining five arrived back in the US to rumours that in that last desperate winter they had resorted to cannibalism and murder.

Greely's career survived nonetheless and in June 1886 he was promoted to brigadier general and Chief of the Signal Corps on the express orders of President Grover Cleveland. This, and the rumours surrounding Greely's Arctic expedition, prompted

General Weston to incredulously quip: *'General? But he never commanded more than ten men in his life – and he ate three of them.'*

What did Leopold II say when accused of 'fornication'?

Leopold II is a largely forgotten but darkly fascinating product of that short golden period between the last years of the nineteenth century and the outbreak of the First World War, known as 'La Belle Époque'. There were two distinct sides to Leopold's character. In terms of his public work he is probably best remembered for his rather personal view of colonialism. As a cousin of Queen Victoria he was all in favour of building a Belgian empire, which, he believed, would be a sign of his country's greatness. As his people and government were really not interested, he decided to build his own personal empire. With the help of the famous explorer Henry Morton Stanley – the man who had been sent to find Livingstone (see page 73) – he managed to found a colony in the Congo. At the Berlin Conference of 1884–5 he persuaded the world powers to grant him that land – a country over seventy times larger than Belgium – as his private kingdom, controlled by his own private army.

What actually happened next is a matter of some dispute but all sources agree that his rule of the country, which he used simply as a source of rubber and ivory, was a disaster. The enslavement of the local population and the outrageous human rights abuses shocked even the other European imperialists of the day. Even the Blessed Austro-Hungarian emperor (see page 114) thought he was 'a thoroughly bad man'. Eventually the Belgian government forced him to hand over his private kingdom to the state. Investigations then revealed that slavery, mass killings and execution squads were common in the country, and Belgian rule became the epitome of imperialist abuse. The Belgian Congo was chosen by Joseph Conrad as the setting for his novel *Heart of Darkness,* which in turn was the basis for the film *Apocalypse Now!*

But there was also another side to Leopold. He loved European high society, adored the company of the most beautiful Parisian courtesans and insisted on living like a king, which of course he was. His frequent love affairs with 'unsuitable' ladies often made him the butt of jokes. His infatuation with the French dancer Cléo de Mérode got him the nickname 'Cleopold', whilst his deathbed marriage to Caroline Lacroix, a notorious courtesan and his long-term lover, caused a scandal at home. He did not always take these criticisms lying down, however, and was known for the occasional barbed response. When a priest told him in admonitory tones that he had heard that the king engaged in fornication, he replied: *'Well, well, well, haven't people got vulgar minds? I was told the same story about you the other day, but I refused to believe it ...'* Despite these sporadic quips, it seems that the Belgians didn't think much of him and they booed his funeral cortège.

What new name was given the river Pissa?

When the burghers of Gumbinnen (now Gusev in the Russian Federation) applied to the Prussian king Frederick William IV for the right to change the name of their local river, the Pissa, to something a little more salubrious, he was reported to have written on the application, 'Granted, recommend Urinoco.'

Why wouldn't the dying Disraeli see Queen Victoria?

Benjamin Disraeli, Earl of Beaconsfield, was Victoria's favourite Prime Minister perhaps because, as he put it, *'Gladstone treats the Queen like a public department; I treat her like a woman.'* It is therefore perhaps not surprising that Victoria was anxious when Disraeli's health began declining in the spring of 1881, which was, incidentally, the year of the gunfight at the OK Corral (see page 213). As well as sending him flowers and a letter – the last he would ever receive from her – she enquired via a courtier whether she should visit him. Disraeli, for all his fondness of the woman he called 'the Faery', had not lost his sense of humour or his awareness of the queen's overriding obsession with her dead husband. He replied to the offer: *'No, it is better not. She would only ask me to take a message to Albert.'*

Who wanted to see Baron Holland dead?

George Augustus Selwyn was a famed eighteenth-century wit and politician whose academic career had ended when he was seen mocking the act of holy communion in a pub in Oxford. Undeterred, he began a life in politics, helped by the fact that he could, by inheritance, nominate two MPs, for one of which he nominated himself. When he became MP for Gloucester, he simply auctioned off the rights to his other seat to whoever happened to be the incoming administration. In his forty-four years in parliament he never bothered to speak.

Selwyn's real love, however, was executions, which he attended whenever possible, even travelling to Paris in 1757 to witness the unusual sight of a dismemberment. It was this interest that led to the macabre quip of Henry Fox, 1st Baron Holland. Selwyn had enquired after the health of the seriously ill baron and left his calling card. When his servant brought the card up to him, Lord Holland said: *'If I am alive I shall be delighted to see him, and if I am dead he will be delighted to see me.'*

11

Ouch!

It is almost a definition of a gentleman to say that he is one who never inflicts pain.

John Henry Newman, *The Idea of a University* (1852)

Which Foreign Secretary killed himself with a letter-opener?

Poor old Viscount Castlereagh was a much maligned man. A great diplomat, he was instrumental in negotiating both the Treaty of Paris, which brought peace with France in 1814, and the Congress of Vienna, proposing the Congress System by which European powers met every two years or so to work out their differences politically, rather than simply resorting to killing each other. He also brought about the Act of Union with Ireland.

None of this made him very popular at home, however, and his support in parliament for the repressive Home Secretary Lord Sidmouth (who had congratulated the troops responsible for the Peterloo Massacre) led Shelley to write in 'The Masque of Anarchy':

> I met Murder on the way –
> He had a mask like Castlereagh –
> Very smooth he looked, yet grim;
> Seven bloodhounds followed him:
>
> All were fat; and well they might
> Be in admirable plight,
> For one by one, and two by two,
> He tossed them human hearts to chew
> Which from his wide cloak he drew.

This rather got to Castlereagh, who became increasingly paranoid – perhaps with good reason. On 9 August 1822 he asked for an audience with the king in which he revealed that he believed that, following an 'incident' with a male transvestite, he was being blackmailed and 'accused of the same crime as the Bishop of Clogher'. The former bishop had been caught in the back room of the White Lion pub in Haymarket with his trousers down accompanied by a young grenadier guardsman. A contemporary poem, not quite in Shelley's league, ran:

> The Devil to prove the Church was a farce
> Went out to fish for a Bugger.
> He baited his hook with a Soldier's arse
> And pulled up the Bishop of Clogher.

King George IV advised Castlereagh that he should probably see a doctor. So Castlereagh retired to North Cray Place in Kent where his deteriorating condition led his doctor to remove the pistols he usually carried (ever since there had been an attempt to assassinate the cabinet) and his razors. Despite these precautions, on 12 August he went into his dressing room and cut his throat with a letter opener. An inquest concluded that he was not in his right mind so he was spared the ignominy of having a stake driven through his heart (see pages 41–2) and instead lies next to William Pitt in Westminster Abbey.

After the tragedy, most people were kinder to Castlereagh, with the exception of Lord Byron, who wrote:

> Posterity will ne'er survey
> A nobler grave than this:
> Here lie the bones of Castlereagh:
> Stop, traveller, and piss.

Which seems rather harsh. And for those of you wondering what happened to the Bishop of Clogher, he was defrocked and ran away to Scotland, where he worked as a butler under an assumed name.

What was the 'extraordinary question'?

The extraordinary question in question was actually a euphemism for a form of water torture, also known as the 'water cure'. The idea was to induce in the victim the sense that they were drowning. This was done quite simply by putting a clip on the victim's nose, a funnel or tube in their mouth and then pouring gallons of water (or sometimes urine) down their throat. In order not to suffocate, the subject would have to swallow the enormous quantity of liquid, leading to water intoxification and stomach cramps. When the prisoner was 'full' or unconscious, they would be beaten until they were sick and then the process was repeated.

The 'cure' was popular in seventeenth- and eighteenth-century France where it came in two varieties, the 'ordinary question', which consisted of just eight pints of water, and the 'extraordinary question', which consisted of sixteen pints. It was also used by the USA in the Philippines–American War of 1899–1902.

Which king died from a splinter?

Henry II of France did not come from a lucky family. He and his elder brother had spent three years of their childhood together in a Spanish cell after their art-loving father Francis I (see pages 61–2) lost the Battle of Pavia to the Spanish and offered his boys as hostages in return for his own release. Later, Henry had only just become heir to the throne when his brother suddenly died after drinking a cup of water following a tennis match, something which, even then, was considered a little suspicious.

Henry's downfall came not via the machinations of his enemies, however, but during a celebration of his diplomatic skills. After the signing of the Treaty of Cateau-Cambrésis, between France, Spain and England in 1559, and celebrating the marriage of his daughter to the king of Spain, he decided to partake of a congratulatory joust, a favourite hobby of his, at the Place des Vosges in Paris. His opponent was one of his Scottish guards, Gabriel, Comte de Montgoméry, Seigneur de Lorges. The two men rode rapidly towards each other and clashed lances. The Comte de Montgoméry's lance shattered on impact, which was not particularly unusual in itself. It was only when the king reached the end of the tilting yard and turned back that the crowd realised something was very wrong. The heralds rushed to Henry's aid. The king had been wearing the protective armour usual for jousting, which covered the whole body and head, so he should have been well protected, were it not for a freak accident. What the heralds found was that a splinter of wood from the lance, two feet long, had somehow managed to shoot through the small slit in the visor of Henry's helmet, piercing his eye and brain, and exiting through his ear.

It took nine days for Henry to die from this terrible brain injury, during which his jealous wife, Catherine de Medici, deprived him of the company of his long-term mistress, Diane de Poitiers. The unfortunate de Montgoméry was pardoned of any wrong by Henry on his deathbed but still found himself in disgrace after the king's death. He later converted to Protestantism, the religion that Henry had spent his life trying to suppress, and he was one of the few to escape the St Bartholomew's Day massacre of Protestants orchestrated by Catherine de Medici. On his return to France from exile in England he was captured and beheaded.

How do you play mediaeval football?

The most characteristic English outdoor game of the mediaeval and Tudor periods, especially favoured by the working classes, was football. Mediaeval football was traditionally violent, loud, and dangerous – to bystanders as well as to players. The puritanical writer Philip Stubbes, who took against just about every form of recreation and pastime in his 1583 rant, The Anatomie of Abuses', describes the game thus: 'Football playing . . . may rather be called a friendly kind of fight, than a play, or recreation; A bloody and murdering practice, than a fellowly sport or pastime.'

Football was a general term for a game involving a ball (usually a farm animal's bladder), two teams of indeterminate size and two 'goals', which could be several miles apart. Soccer (association football) is a nineteenth-century attempt to codify these games. Most football games in the sixteenth centuty would have involved two villages in what amounted to a running battle in which the ball was kicked, carried, hidden – whatever – between agreed 'goals', which might be village churches, trees, anything at all. There were not usually rules governing how you got the ball, so punching, kicking, tripping and gouging were all fine (although stabbing was frowned upon). Teams could consist of simply whoever turned up – whether ten people or a hundred – and players would come and go as the game might last for hours or even days. By 1600, with the introduction of the Reformation of Manners, these games were progressively proscribed as they encouraged drunkenness and riots, and were often associated with the old (and now prohibited) Catholic festivals. However, that didn't mean that people stopped playing them altogether. The most violent versions of football were known as 'camp-ball' in England, 'hurling' in Cornwall, or *cnapan* in Wales. In these games, a ball or other object was conveyed over open country to opposing goals by any means possible – even horsemen might be involved. These games frequently led to serious injuries and death.

Football was exclusively a male sport, but there were games with some violent content that might be played by both sexes. These might seem a little ludicrous but try them before you condemn them. In Hot Cockles, one player hid his head in another's lap while the others slapped him on the rear. If he could guess who had slapped him last, the two traded places. Blindman's Buff, also known as Hoodman Blind, was a similar game in which a blindfolded player tried to catch the others while they dealt him 'buffs' (blows). If he could identify the person he caught, they would trade places. In both of these games, men and women might play together, although they were more commonly played by boys and girls.

Similar to football in concept, if not equipment, was the game of bandy-ball, the ancestor of modern field hockey. The object of the game was to drive a small, hard ball through the opponents' goal with hooked clubs (almost identical to field hockey sticks).

Stoolball (which is still played in Hampshire to this day) was an ancestor of cricket and baseball, in which a stool was set on its side and players tried to hit the seat with a ball. In this game, women were expected to hike up their long skirts and play with the men. In the game of trap or trapball, the ball was placed on a device for casting it up in the air to be hit with a stick.

What did the Empress Irene, Ivan the Terrible, Süleyman the Magnificent and Constantine the Great have in common?

They all endangered their own family line by killing or attempting to kill their own eldest sons.

The Byzantine Empress Irene, who usually styled herself 'Emperor', such was her control over the empire, rubbed along perfectly happily with her son whilst he was a child but when he attempted to seize the throne for himself in AD 797 she captured him and had his eyes gouged out. Some sources say he died of his wounds shortly after, others that he survived his mother by a few years but in a terribly mutilated state. Either way, the family quickly fell from power.

Ivan the Terrible killed his son in 1581 after a family tiff. Ivan had beaten his son's wife for wearing immodest clothing, causing her to miscarry. Infuriated, the son had got into a heated argument with his father over this. At some point the argument got out of hand and Ivan struck his son on the head with his iron staff, killing him, albeit accidentally. On Ivan's death the Russian throne was inherited by his other son, Feodor I, known as Feodor the Bellringer, who was very devout but weak and probably mentally retarded. As he had no heir, Ivan's family line died out.

Süleyman the Magnificent's heir, Mustafa, had the disadvantage of not being the son of his favourite wife, Hurrem Sultan. As it was the custom on the succession of a new sultan for him to have his brothers strangled, Hurrem went about protecting her sons by starting a whispering campaign against Mustafa. Despite Mustafa's being easily the most talented and widely respected of Süleyman's sons, Süleyman came to believe the worst of him thanks to his wife's propaganda. Having been accused of treachery,

Mustafa was invited by the sultan into his tent to defend himself. When he entered the tent, he was seized and murdered. Süleyman was then succeeded by one of Hurrem's sons, Selim, known as Selim the Sot, under whom the empire began to decay.

Constantine the Great's eldest son, Crispus, also fell prey to court machinations. His stepmother Fausta feared that Crispus would inherit the empire before her own three sons by Constantine and so she told the emperor that his son had propositioned her and then tried to rape her. On the basis of this, Constantine had his eldest son tried and executed in AD 326. Some months later he seems to have learnt that the incestuous affair was an invention of his wife's and he ordered her executed, too. According to one source, this was done by drowning her in a scalding-hot bath.

What were soldiers in the First World War advised to leave at home?

At the outbreak of war there were virtually no dental facilities in the British Army and not a single dentist accompanied the British Expeditionary Force to France. Indeed, it was only because the British commander at the first Battle of the Aisne, Sir John French, got toothache and demanded a British dentist that any were sent at all.

Twelve dental surgeons were drafted in November 1914 but an Inspecting Dental Officer was not appointed until 1916. Until then dentistry on the front line was entirely haphazard, being carried out by anyone prepared to have a go. It was therefore considered preferable to receive dental treatment *before* leaving for the front, the most usual treatment being complete extraction. The author Hector Hugh Munro, known by his pen name Saki, enlisted on the opening day of the war and immediately had all his front teeth taken out before being sent to France. From February 1915 men could be passed fit for duty 'subject to dental treatment'. Men who had had all their teeth extracted would be held back from the draft until their gums had healed and they could be fitted with dentures.

Who made anal surgery fashionable?

Louis XIV lived his life in public, in a manner that emphasised his magnificence and also required the constant attendance of his nobles, thereby preventing them from sloping off and plotting behind his back. His palace at Versailles was designed to reflect this novel way of life – a huge, sumptuous mansion filled with public spaces (even the world's first shopping mall) where the king and his courtiers' daily lives could be minutely observed.

Nor was Louis at all shy about this public living. From the moment he woke up until last thing at night, he would entertain guests and see petitioners as he ate or dressed – even whilst on the lavatory. He also liked to talk publicly about his various health problems, including the number and type of enemas he'd had and their unpleasant results. In January 1686 he reported a more painful problem – an anal fistula (an unnatural tunnelling into soft tissue from the anus). Initially his doctors suggested a poultice but when this didn't work they suggested surgery, which of course at that date would have to be achieved without anaesthetic.

Louis was naturally a little unwilling and asked around court for other suggestions whilst decrees were sent out into the countryside, inviting other sufferers to come forward as guinea pigs so that various treatments (usually taking mineral waters) could be tried on them. As none of these treatments worked and the fistula continued to grow, eventually a Parisian surgeon was sent for. Nevertheless before the king would submit to the procedure, some of the 'guinea pigs' were operated on first just so that the surgeon could have a bit of practice. Then, on 18 November 1686 the king went under the knife in the presence of his entire medical staff, his ministers and his mistress. And astonishingly, as John Evelyn wrote in his diary entry for 5 January 1687: *'The French K. [is] now sayd to be healed or rather patch'd up of the fistula in Ano, for which he had ben severall times cutt.'* The operations were a great success and Louis was delighted with the result, as I imagine anyone would be who had formerly had an anal fistula. The surgeon was given a large estate and that same day the king was back at work.

But a life lived so much in public has some strange side-effects. As he was constantly surrounded by pandering courtiers who all looked to Louis for preferment and profit, anything they could find to have in common with him might prove a useful lever. And so over the next few months a craze for anal fistula surgery swept Versailles as thirty courtiers presented themselves as suffering from the same problem as the king, all of whom now demanded painful anal surgery. It is to the great credit of the now wealthy surgeon that he refused to operate in every case as none of the courtiers had had a fistula in the first place.

Who tried to seal a soul in a barrel?

Frederick II, Emperor of the Holy Roman Empire, managed something of a sacrilegious hat-trick by getting himself excommunicated from the Catholic Church three times during his rule: for perjury, blasphemy and heresy. He was thus considered by many to be the Antichrist. To his supporters, however, Frederick was 'Stupor Mundi' – the Wonder of the World, the 'Emperor of the Last Days' or the 'Warrior Saviour' of the Sybelline Oracles. Indeed, his death in 1250 marked the birth of the legend of a king who would sleep for a thousand years and reawaken when his people needed him. It was this that gave Hitler the idea for his thousand-year Reich.

Frederick was in many ways a man born before his time and his wide scientific interests created suspicion in a deeply religious country. He was brought up in Sicily, the great-grandson of the very sophisticated but slightly gullible Queen Adelaide, who had had an unfortunate run-in with an insolvent crusader (see pages 228–30). The island was at the time the most cosmopolitan place in the Mediterranean, and the only kingdom where Arab, Jewish and Christian scholars and artists freely mingled. Frederick therefore grew up with a fascination with science that was completely out of keeping with mediaeval Christian thought, and he had a dislike of dogma that led him to delight in blaspheming in front of Christians and Muslims alike.

Perhaps the most famous story about him is peculiar in that whilst it sounds like anti-Frederick propaganda (of which there was an awful lot as he spent much of his life defying or actively attacking the papacy), it also sounds like just the sort of thing he might do. The story goes that Frederick was concerned about the nature of the soul, which in Christian theology was said to leave the body at the moment of death. To prove whether or not this was the case, he took a condemned man and sealed him in a barrel. He then waited for him to die, reasoning that when he did so, his soul would leave his body but find itself trapped in the barrel. Frederick could then open the barrel at his leisure and, if the Christian theory were true, he would see the soul fly out. Needless to say, it didn't.

Where is John Brown's body?

The 'Bleeding Kansas' crisis was the prelude to the US Civil War and its most famous participant was John Brown of 'John Brown's body' fame. Pro- and anti-slavery sentiment came to a head in the US in the 1850s in the newly created states of Kansas and Nebraska. It had been decided that the inhabitants of these new states should vote on whether they would allow slavery or not in the new territories, but it was rather assumed that Nebraska would be settled by 'free-state' anti-slavery northerners and Kansas would become a 'southern' slave state. Whilst this was true in Nebraska, in Kansas there was going to be a fight.

Both pro-slavery southerners and northern abolitionists headed for Kansas, with the intention of ensuring that the vote went their way, with both sides quite prepared to use intimidation and violence if necessary. Foremost amongst the abolitionists heading for Kansas in October 1855 was John Brown, a man who remains one of the most controversial characters in US history. To some he is the icon of anti-slavery and the founder of the Civil Rights Movement, whilst to others he is little more than a terrorist. It is certainly true that he was quite prepared to use physical force to make his point.

The fighting in Bleeding Kansas was not on the scale of the American Civil War as a whole but it was brutal nonetheless. Following the attack on the free-state stronghold of Lawrence during which homes and businesses were ransacked by a gang of southerners, Brown prepared a retaliation that became known as the Pottawatomie Massacre. On 23 May 1856 he led a group of abolitionists, including four of his sons, into Kansas territory to the pro-slavery settlement of Pottawatomie Creek. Here they dragged five men from their homes and hacked them to death with broadswords. Some historians have claimed this as the opening action of the US Civil War.

Fighting in Bleeding Kansas continued into 1858, although Brown headed back east in 1856 to raise more money. In total about fifty-five people were killed. Brown's own death came after his most famous exploit, the raid on Harper's Ferry. In 1859, Brown attempted to seize the Federal armoury at Harper's Ferry in what is now west Virginia with the intention of arming southern slaves. Seven people were killed by Brown's men in the raid, including, rather ironically, a freed slave, and the project came to nothing as all the raiders were captured within a few days. Brown was also taken, tried and convicted of treason. Despite a plea for pardon from Victor Hugo, who sent an open letter in which he predicted civil war in the US if the execution went ahead, John Brown was hanged on 2 December 1859 in front of 2,000 soldiers, including the future Confederate general and friendly-fire victim Thomas 'Stonewall' Jackson (see page 8) and presidential assassin John Wilkes Booth. His body was dumped in a coffin with the noose still around his neck. He was buried at the John Brown farm, North Elba, New York.

12

Magic

For I have sworn thee fair and thought thee bright,
who art as black as hell, as dark as night.

William Shakespeare, Sonnet 147

Why did Dick Whittington need a magical cat?

The extraordinary rise to prominence of Dick Whittington at a time when the idea of social or financial improvement was entirely novel has led to his becoming perhaps the only hard-nosed businessman ever to make the transition to well-loved pantomime character. The tale of Dick Whittington is one of the great success stories of a new era of social mobility that grew out of the devastation of the Black Death and so remarkable was his particular case that it was given magical elements to help it.

Richard Whittington was not from the poorest class; indeed, his father was a Gloucestershire knight, but as the third son he had little chance of inheriting much land on his father's estate. Without land (plus the social status and money that it brought) the only other option open to Richard was to go to town and 'make his fortune'. Before the Black Death the idea of simply moving away may have seemed dangerous, if not impossible, to many in the country, but with the aid of the City guilds Richard would do just that and become an enormous success. Apprenticed in London, he went on to become one of the leading lights of the Mercers' Guild, which represented the cloth dealers. Cornering the extremely lucrative silk and velvet market, he rapidly rose to prominence, selling to the aristocracy, who thanks to the sumptuary laws were, at least in theory, the only people who could wear his goods. He went on to deal with the king himself, first selling Richard II two gold cloths for £11 in 1389 in his first taste of what went on to become a hugely profitable trade. When Richard II was deposed ten years later he owed Whittington £1,000, which the mercer immediately recouped by continuing the trade with the king's successor, Henry IV.

As he was three times master of the Guild and four times Mayor of London, the trade in luxury cloth and wool made him one of the richest merchants of his day. So great was his wealth in fact that it became necessary to invent a reason for his success in a world where aspiration was a wholly new concept – hence the birth of the legend of his magical cat. To a mediaeval mindset – in which everyone was born into a station in life and died in that same station, where everybody had their set place – magic still seemed the only possible way that Dick Whittington could have been so successful. So Dick didn't need a magical cat, but those hearing of his perfectly genuine rise to fame and fortune needed him to have one.

Richard Whittington was grateful for the support that the Mercers' Guild had given him and, on his death, he pointedly left his huge estate (he died without heirs) not to the Church as his ancestors might have done, but to the Guild. At the time that estate was valued at £5,000, well in excess of £5 million in today's terms. The Mercers in return kept the name of Whittington alive, building almshouses, endowing the first Guildhall Library in London, funding a college of priests, making numerous bequests for church and hospital building, funding the rebuilding of Newgate gaol, and even commissioning a public lavatory. Even today the Mercers' Guild still runs the almshouses that bear Whittington's name.

Who first fell prey to the Curse of Tecumseh?

William Henry Harrison probably deserved his turn as President. His father Benjamin had been one of the signatories of the Declaration of Independence and a governor of Virginia, and William himself was a hero to many white settlers, thanks to his victories in the Indian wars and the war of 1812. In 1836 he'd run for President and been defeated, but in 1840 he was returned with a landslide, mainly thanks to his military reputation. By this time he was sixty-eight (and the oldest President before Ronald Reagan), which led to doubts about his capability, culminating in his being called 'Granny Harrison'. To scotch rumours that he was too old and weak to run the country, he refused to wear an overcoat whilst he took the Oath of Office despite its being a bitterly cold March day. To ram the point home he then gave the longest inaugural address in US presidential history, which took him nearly two hours to read, before riding through the streets of Washington to meet the people. The end result was that Harrison caught a cold. With his hectic social and political schedule there was no time for him to rest, however, and the cold rapidly developed into pleurisy and pneumonia. He died just thirty days, eleven hours and thirty minutes after taking office, making his the shortest presidency ever.

His alarmingly brief tenure gave birth to the myth of the presidential 'Curse of Tecumseh'. Tecumseh had been a leader of the Shawnee who had been defeated by Harrison at the Battle of Tippecanoe (the battle that had made Harrison's name) and was later killed fighting alongside the British in the war of 1812. It was said that he had placed a curse on Harrison, stating that every US President elected in a year ending in zero (i.e. every twenty years) would die in office. This proved true, not just for Harrison but for every President since, until the presidency of Ronald Reagan, who managed to sidestep the curse.

Who controlled a king with magical rings?

Being the mistress to a mediaeval king had its benefits but it was also an excellent way to make enemies. Alice Perrers, the mistress of the aged Edward III, seems to have been particularly good at annoying people. Thomas Walsingham, a chronicler, was clearly not a fan:

> She was a shameless, impudent harlot, and of low birth, for she was the daughter of a thatcher from the town of Henny, elevated by fortune. She was not attractive or beautiful, but knew how to compensate for these defects with the seductiveness of her voice. Blind fortune elevated this woman to such heights and promoted her to a greater intimacy with the king than was proper, since she had been the maidservant and mistress of a man of Lombardy, and accustomed to carry water on her own shoulders from the

mill-stream for the everyday needs of that household. And while the queen was still alive, the king loved this woman more than he loved the queen.

In a world where titles and ranks were inherited, the growing influence of a woman who was apparently not of noble rank was resented by many and the enormous control that she wielded over an increasingly senile king terrified them. Somehow it had to be explained and preferably in a way that damned the upstart mistress in the process. Surely the only answer was magic?

In 1376, Edward's last year, the anti-Perrers faction finally gained the upper hand and Alice was formally charged by the Commons with having gained the king's affections, procured his madness and enervated his strength through magical arts. She was said to have employed a Dominican friar who, according to Walsingham, used wax images, powerful herbs and incantations similar to those used by the great Egyptian sorcerer, King Nectanebus. The friar was also accused of giving Alice magical rings of remembrance and forgetfulness, like those that Moses made, for the king to wear. This, then, was the cause of the king's senility and the source of Alice's power over him.

Of course Thomas Walsingham was a little biased. He was a monk at St Albans, the abbey that had got Alice's father outlawed (and incidentally he was a Hertfordshire knight, not a thatcher), so there was little love lost between them. There is also no evidence in the court records for that year that a charge of sorcery was brought against Alice, nor even that the magical Dominican friar was apprehended at her manor in Fulham, as Walsingham gleefully tells us. What was the case, however, was that the Good Parliament of that year ordered Alice on pain of banishment to stop using her influence at court to settle disputes. It also discovered, rather embarrassingly for Alice, that she was already married to one Sir William Windsor.

Edward III, now happily beyond reason, didn't seem too bothered and a pardon was soon issued. Alice returned to his side where she stayed until his death, at which moment, Walsingham can't help but add, she seized the rings from his dying fingers and ran away. Alice really was in trouble then – not because of the ring incident, which probably never happened – but because everyone with a grievance against her was invited to London to press their case, now that the king could not protect her. She was tried again and found guilty of having illegally used her influence with the king, which in all fairness was true. Her possessions were seized and she was banished. She died around twenty-three years later, embittered and still fighting to have her fortune restored.

What is the use of 'inheritance powder'?

'Inheritance powder' lay at the heart of the Affair of the Poisons – the greatest scandal to hit the court of Louis XIV of France, mainly because it implicated a number of his mistresses, not just in attempted murder but in satanic rituals with a good dose of naked black masses and witchcraft thrown in.

In a country where titles and money came from owning land, inheritance was often a sticky issue, particularly as it was rather tricky to work out *when* one might inherit. To help with this, a thriving trade in 'inheritance powders' had grown up – 'inheritance powder' being a somewhat polite term for poison. This forceful method of helping along legacies had come to the public's attention in 1676 during the trial of Marie Madeleine Gobelin d'Aubray, Marquise de Brinvilliers, who along with her lover had poisoned her father, brother and two sisters to ensure she inherited the estate. For this she was tortured with the 'extraordinary question' (see pages 134–5), decapitated and her body burnt to ashes.

Her sensational trial brought to light a number of other mysterious deaths that looked as if they might be poisonings, making the king in particular nervous. He asked his Chief of Police, Gabriel Nicolas de la Reynie, to investigate although by the time he'd finished his inquiries he probably wished he had let well alone.

The usual Parisian alchemists, abortionists, fortune-tellers and quacks were rounded up, revealing a thriving trade in poisons, potions and spells, all designed to help the upwardly mobile to 'get on'. So concerned did la Reynie become that he re-established the Chambre Ardente – the 'burning chamber' – a secret court that answered directly and solely to the king.

Its investigations brought to light the case of one Catherine Deshayes Monvoisin, known as 'La Voisin'. Amongst her clients were names that shocked the investigators, including the Marquise de Montespan, Louis's mistress and the mother of seven of his children.

Slowly the story emerged that de Montespan had not only worked her way into the king's affections through magic, but had obtained spells to do away with Mademoiselle de la Vallière, another of the king's mistresses. More serious charges followed: it appeared that for several years Madame de Montespan had added aphrodisiacs, without his knowledge, to the king's food and drink, and had tried to kill her newest rival, Mademoiselle de Fontanges, by impregnating either her clothes or her gloves with poisons.

The third charge was made by an accomplice of La Voisin's, an old abbé called Etienne Guibourg who apparently liked to prac-tise the black mass on the body of a naked woman. He said that in the 1670s when de Montespan was competing with la Vallière, he had bought a still-born child for an écu in order to celebrate a black mass in the presence of Madame de Montespan. During the first mass the baby's throat was pierced with a knife and the blood was caught in the chalice to celebrate the mass. At the second mass the baby's heart and entrails were consecrated in order to make 'powders' for Madame de Montespan. In these ceremonies, de Montespan's naked body was used as the altar.

Whilst royal anal fistulas were everybody's business (see pages 140–1), obviously the mother of the Sun King's children using her naked body for black masses and poisoning her rivals was not the sort of PR that the French Crown needed. In fairness to Madame de Montespan the accusations against her were unsubstantiated but in an atmosphere of increasing suspicion Louis began appointing food tasters and his relationship with de Montespan waned. There would be no scandal in her lifetime, however. La Reynie's findings were sent to Louis who ordered them sealed in a chest. This he then burnt in 1708, unaware that la Reynie's own notes were stored separately in the police archive. It is thanks to these surviving copies that de Montespan's role in the Affair of the Poisons is known today.

When was the last prosecution in the UK under the Witchcraft Act?

The story of Britain's last trial for witchcraft is not some dark mediaeval tale of burnings at the stake (although there are only two attested cases of witches ever being burnt at the stake in Britain). It is a war story and, most extraordinarily, the war in question is the Second World War.

In the autumn of 1940, Hitler ordered the saturation bombing of major British cities. Amid the rubble and confusion of the London Blitz a middle-aged woman began to gain a reputation for helping bewildered Londoners keep in touch. But the people she was helping them keep in touch with were unusual. They were dead.

Helen Duncan was a spiritualist gifted, so her supporters said, with the ability to contact the departed. In a time when tragedy and death touched many families in Britain, hundreds sought her services, hoping to find comfort in a final meeting with their deceased loved ones.

Soon she was in great demand – and not just by her bereaved clients. The police were also taking an interest. By the beginning of 1944, with the invasion of Europe imminent, the Allied governments were worried about security and that brought them to Helen Duncan's door.

Helen had been conducting seances for the relatives of those killed in the war who wanted to know more about their loved ones' deaths than the information in the bald telegrams that first brought the news. But spiritualists claimed that she was doing more than this. It was alleged that on one particular evening in 1943 the spirit of a sailor had come into the room, wearing a cap from the ship HMS *Barham*. This would not be particularly unusual save for the fact that the government was keeping its sinking secret and didn't announce the disaster for another three months. And this was just one of several cases where Helen Duncan claimed to know about deaths long before the government officially announced them.

For Helen Duncan's followers it was just more proof that she really could look into the spirit world but for the government and the police the only way that she could know about the *Barham* was if she was a spy, or if she'd just guessed and was spreading dangerous rumours. So on 19 January 1944 they arrested her.

But proving Helen Duncan to be a spy was difficult. She had no access to secret documents, no 'friends in high places'. Unable to prove espionage, the government now took an extraordinary step. She would not admit to being a traitor, but she would admit to talking to spirits, so Helen Duncan was charged and convicted under the 1735 Witchcraft Act and spent eight months in prison. When she emerged, the war was in its final phase and she no longer presented a threat.

Helen Duncan died in 1956 shortly after the police raided another of her seances, taking the stigma of her witchcraft conviction to her grave. Churchill was furious that she was hounded by the police and accused of 'pretending to raise the spirits of the dead' but he was overruled by his intelligence officers. She died as the last person in Britain ever to be convicted under witchcraft legislation.

Who tried to make a king die from sadness?

The story of Henry V's brother should be enough to deter anyone from trying this at home. Humphrey, Duke of Gloucester, and his second wife Eleanor had every reason to want to know what the future held. With Henry dead and his sickly son Henry VI on the throne, Humphrey was only a step away from the crown itself.

As discovering the future through horoscopes was not unknown or even illegal at the time, Humphrey actively recruited and protected fortune-tellers. But being so close to the king made fortune-telling a dangerous game. Whilst Humphrey might be untouchable, his enemies knew that his second wife was not. And so began the biggest witchcraft scandal in English history.

In 1441, Eleanor was accused of witchcraft in which she was said to have been aided by Margery Jourdemayne, the 'witch of Eye', and various members of her household. It was claimed that Eleanor had won Humphrey (who had divorced his first wife to marry her) '*by such medicines and drinks as the said witch made*'. There were also whispers that she was attempting to kill the king and, in a mood of apprehension following the stunning successes of Joan of Arc (see pages 88–9 and 241–3), the charge seemed plausible.

According to a contemporary chronicle, the charges against Eleanor came after a spell of very bad weather had endangered Henry VI's life on a trip to London on 15 July 1441. Following the charge of treason against her, two clerics were arrested, Roger Bolingbroke and Thomas Southwell, the charge being that they had attempted to destroy the king by necromancy. Southwell was further accused of having said a mass in a forbidden place using certain instruments on which Bolingbroke had practised '*his said craft of necromancy against the faith and good belief*'. The plot (if it existed) was known about before the king's visit to London, and Bolingbroke and Southwell were probably first tried by an ecclesiastical inquisition. On Sunday, 23 July, Bolingbroke was displayed on a high stage at St Paul's Cross in the midst of his magical paraphernalia. After a sermon he was forced to do penance, abjuring the items he had used, in the presence of the archbishop of Canterbury and numerous nobles. Only after this was he examined by the King's Council.

At the King's Council (probably following torture), Bolingbroke admitted to using necromancy at the instigation of Eleanor, who had asked to know *what should fall [become] of her, and to what estate she should come*. Although this was not strictly illegal, for a woman who would be queen if the frail Henry VI died, it was foolish if not treasonable. She was also suspected of having acted on this divination and attempted by witchcraft to shorten the king's life.

Eleanor was summoned to appear before the archbishop and other clerics to answer charges of *necromancy, of witchcraft or sorcery, of heresy, and of treason*. She pleaded not guilty to the twenty-eight charges levelled against her.

The trial was adjourned until the autumn and Eleanor was ordered to be sent to Leeds Castle for safe keeping. She attempted to escape by river but was caught. Her ecclesiastical trial was resumed on 19 October when Bolingbroke, Southwell and Margery Jourdemayne all testified against her. It was claimed that she used Bolingbroke to contact demons and other malign spirits and, with Southwell, used horoscopes to predict the death of the king. Most damningly, it was said that the information so gained was passed amongst some of the nobles so that they would withdraw their support for Henry and thus, in his sorrow, he would die more quickly.

Accounts vary as to whether Eleanor refuted all the charges but she seems to have put herself at the mercy of the court. Fortunately for her, she got off lightly, having only to perform a penance. Margery Jourdemayne, however, was burnt to death in Smithfield that same day. Southwell, who was due to be arraigned, escaped execution by dying at the Tower during the previous night, thus fulfilling his own prophecy that he would die in bed and not at the hands of justice.

On 9 November, Eleanor began her penance, walking barefoot with tapers to several London churches. She was also formally divorced from her husband as, it was said, she had only gained his affections by sorcery, and was stripped of her title. On the day of her final penance, 18 November, Bolingbroke, Sir John Hom and William Wodham (a squire) were condemned at the Guildhall for treason and sentenced to death. Hom and Wodham were pardoned by the king but Bolingbroke was found guilty and the sentence was carried out. He was taken *'from the Tower of London unto Tyburn; and there he was hanged and let down half alive, and his bowels taken out and burned, and his head smitten off and set on London Bridge, and his body quartered and sent to certain towns of England, that is to say, Oxford, Cambridge, York and Hereford'*.

The main chronicle of the events ends as it began, with a great storm for which Eleanor was given the 'credit'. She was kept a ward of court in Westminster until 24 January 1442, then moved to confinements progressively farther from London, finally ending her days on the Isle of Man.

How did a dead man create fog?

Friar Bungay was a weather witch who, it was said, was in the pay of the Yorkist Edward IV in his fight against the Lancastrian Henry VI. In 1470 it was claimed by the Lancastrians that the bad weather in the Channel, which had prevented Queen Margaret, Henry VI's wife, from joining her husband, *'was done by some sorcery or witchcraft of one named at that days Bungay or such other'*. Friar Bungay's most famous action, however, was claimed to be at the Battle of Barnet in 1471 when a mist came down over the battlefield that confused the Lancastrian troops, leading to a Yorkist victory.

All of this is quite impressive for two reasons. First, the fog at Barnet seems to have caused both sides equal problems, as you might expect. Second, the man given the credit for the incantations that brought it down had already been dead for 188 years.

Friar Bungay was certainly a real man but he had lived in the late thirteenth century and spent his time studying theology, rather than meteorology and necromancy, at Oxford and Cambridge.

Bungay was a considerable man of letters and a contemporary of that other great mediaeval scientist, Roger Bacon, although we don't know whether the two ever met. His wide-ranging interests in science, mathematics and religion do not seem to have got him into any trouble in his day; indeed, it seems that after his death his reputation for wisdom led people to pray for his help. By the time of the Wars of the Roses, however, both his and Roger Bacon's great learning, something that was always considered a bit suspicious to the mediaeval mind, had transformed them in the popular imagination from academics to sorcerers. What might have started as prayers offered up to a great mind from a previous century soon became chronicled as invocations to a necromancer. Before long chroniclers were writing about Friar Bungay as a living sorcerer, a man returned from the dead and the shadowy figure behind Edward IV's throne. This only goes to show that a little learning is a dangerous thing.

Which part of Britain is under an archbishop's curse?

In 1525, Archbishop Dunbar of Glasgow issued an official 'monition of cursing' on Carlisle in an attempt to rid it of the Border Reivers whose illegal activities made it a centre for lawlessness and everything that Dunbar considered 'evil'. It is an extraordinary curse – the longest known official English curse in existence and certainly the most comprehensive. In the Scottish dialect of the day, the archbishop started off by cursing the hair on their heads and then worked his way down:

> I curse thair heid and all the haris of thair heid; I curse thair face, thair ene, thair mouth, thair neise, thair tongue, thair teeth, thair crag, thair shoulderis, thair breist, thair hert, thair stomok, thair bak, thair wame, thair armes, thair leggis, thair handis, thair feit, and everilk part of thair body, frae the top of thair heid to the soill of thair feet, befoir and behind, within and without.

But in case simply cursing every part of their body wasn't enough, he went on to curse their movements and postures before cursing all their possessions as well, right down to their cabbage patches.

I curse thaim gangand [going], and I curse thaim rydland [riding]; I curse thaim standand, and I curse thaim sittand; I curse thaim etand, I curse thaim drinkand; I curse thaim walkand, I curse thaim sleepand; I curse thaim risand, I curse thaim lyand; I curse thaim at hame, I curse thaim fra hame; I curse thaim within the house, I curse thaim without the house; I curse thair wiffis, thair barnis, and thair servandis participand with thaim in thair deides. I wary thair cornys, thair catales, thair woll, thair scheip, thair horse, thair swyne, thair geise, thair hennes, and all thair quyk gude [livestock]. I wary their hallis, thair chalmeris [rooms], thair kechingis, thair stanillis, thair barnys, thair biris [cowsheds], thair bernyardis, thair cailyardis [cabbage patches], thair plewis, thair harrowis, and the gudis and housis that is necessair for thair sustentatioun and weilfair.

The 1,500-word curse still seems to hold people in its thrall today. In March 2005 a city councillor went so far as to suggest that this curse might be the reason for a string of bad luck in the city, which included some of the worst floods in living memory, factory closures, a murder and the relegation of Carlisle United football team. In particular the councillor took against a four-teen-ton granite artwork commissioned by the council for the millennium celebrations on which is written the curse in its entirety. He formally proposed to the council that the artwork be either broken up or moved beyond the city limits, provoking the artist to compare him to the Taliban and their destruction of the Buddhas of Bamiyan. A council meeting on 8 March rejected the proposal.

Who was rescued by the Queen of Elfland?

The life of James IV of Scotland is quite well documented. It's what happened after his death that is something of a mystery.

Elves only ever pop up in historical narratives at times when no one is really all that certain what's going on and this was the case with James IV of Scotland. James was killed by the English at the disastrous Battle of Flodden Field, having invaded England in support of his French allies whilst Henry VIII was away on the continent.

Flodden was a massacre and after the battle it proved difficult to identify which body was James's. Eventually a likely candidate was found but this presented a new problem. James had died whilst under sentence of excommunication, having broken the Treaty of Eternal Peace with England. This had been brokered by the Borgia pope, Alexander VI, who agreed to excommunicate anyone who violated its terms.

James's body, therefore, could not be given Christian burial rites so it was taken to Berwick and embalmed, then sealed in lead and sent to Richmond Palace while everyone decided what to do with it. On his return from France, Henry VIII suggested that the body be buried in St Paul's but the pope refused to countenance this, so it was moved to the monastery at Sheen in Surrey and left there. In 1538 the problematic issue of the body resurfaced when the monastery was dissolved. James's remains were taken off show and put in an old lumber room. And that was the last place that James IV was ever seen.

There are three stories as to what happened next. One states that the body remained in the lumber room until the early years of the reign of Elizabeth I, at which time a glazier working in the partly demolished building reported the smell of embalming spices. A delegation duly arrived and inspected the remains but no further action was taken. Feeling now at liberty to do as he wished, the glazier then severed the head and took it home to show the family. Clearly they weren't too impressed so he took the head to the church of St Michael's, Wood Street, in the City of London, where he had it coffined and buried.

Whilst there is still a tradition that James's head is in St Michael's, according to the second story his body (with or without the head) rests in an unmarked grave in the grounds of Sheen monastery, although there is no documentary evidence for this.

Bearing that in mind, the third option, favoured in Scotland at the time of Flodden, is perhaps no less dubious. This states that James IV wasn't killed at all but was rescued by the Queen of Elfland and is even now waiting patiently for the day of his triumphant return.

13

Where in the World?

If some countries have too much history, we have too much geography.

William Lyon Mackenzie King (Canadian Prime Minister)

Which city is named after Dismal Jimmy?

One American city, originally the home of the native Lenape people, began to be colonised by the Dutch around 1624 when thirty Walloon families made their homes on the banks of the Hudson River. A year later, the settlement of New Amsterdam was founded on the island of Manhattan and the following year the land was officially purchased for the bargain price of sixty guilders' worth of goods.

So the settlement slowly grew until in 1664 it reached the attention of King Charles II back in England. He thought, as a prelude to the Second Anglo-Dutch War, that it might be best to annex the territory and attach it to the other English possessions in North America. A fleet was duly dispatched and control of the settlement was surrendered by the Dutch to the British after the usual combination of threats and assurances had been received. Of course it looked a bit odd that this latest British colony was called New Amsterdam, so a name change was required. As the brother of the king, James, Duke of York, was then Lord High Admiral and as such vaguely in charge of these operations, his name was put forward.

There were two views of James (the future King James II). As a director of the Royal African Company he was very keen to see Dutch sea power destroyed as this could make him a lot of money. He was thus very popular with those angling for another war with the Netherlands and he welcomed any chance to get hold of new territories.

The other view was summed up by Charles II's mistress Nell Gwyn, who referred to him – the antithesis of his flamboyant brother – as 'Dismal Jimmy'. Considering his later disastrous rule as James II and his removal from power in the Glorious Revolution, perhaps Nell was the better judge but in the 1660s the pro-Yorkists had the upper hand and so both the province and the city were named New York in James's honour. For the hat-trick the former Fort Orange was renamed Albany after James's other title, Duke of Albany, and to this day that remains the name of the state capital. So delighted was James that he arranged for his brother to grant him the whole of New England in a charter of 1676, thus ensuring that the name stuck.

What country's name is an acronym?

Pakistan is one of the few countries whose name is an acronym. It was coined by Choudhary Rahmat Ali, a Muslim Indian nationalist and Cambridge academic who had first voiced his idea for a separate Muslim nation in India in his 1933 pamphlet 'Now or Never'. According to his friends (who disagree on the subject) he either came up with the idea whilst walking along the banks of the Thames, or whilst riding on the top of a double-decker bus. In either case, in 'Now or Never' he suggests a name for this new nation, based on letters from what he calls the 'five northern units of India', namely punjab, the North-West Frontier Province (afghan Province), kashmir, sind and baluchistan. Together this made 'Paksstan'. By the end of the year, and with the addition of a letter 'i' to make it easier to say, the word Pakistan was already in wide use.

Ali later claimed the derivation was from panjab, afghania (North-West Frontier Province), kashmir, iran, sind (including Kach and Kathiawar), tukharistan, Afghanistan, and Baluchistan, but whichever is true the name of the nation Pakistan had been born. Usefully it also meant 'land of the pure' in Sindhi, Urdu and Persian. Choudhary Rahmat Ali, who had spent most of his life in England, finally arrived in the new country he had named in 1948. However, his criticism – that the Pakistan so newly brought into existence was a smaller and feebler version of the grand plan that he had outlined in his pamphlet – made him enemies, as did his threats to form a national Liberation Movement that might undermine the gains so recently made. He was therefore refused a passport and ordered out of the country. He died back in Cambridge in 1951.

Which Indian princess is buried at the English seaside?

Her real name was Matoaka, a princess of the Powhatan Indians, but those who knew her well had a pet name for her. To them she was called 'frolicsome' or, in the language of her people, Pocahontas. The story of how Pocahontas befriended the first Virginian settlers in the early days of the seventeenth century is known to every schoolchild. As legend has it, the noble princess brought about peace between the English settlers and the Native Americans, sealing the pact with her own marriage.

But the story so well known in everything from textbooks to Disney cartoons ends before Pocahontas's greatest voyage had even begun. Pocahontas was not to live happily ever after, nor was she even to find rest in her own land and with the people she had done so much to preserve.

Her final journey took her to a much stranger place, across the ocean with her beloved husband, John Rolfe, to England and the court of James I. Pocahontas caused a sensation and seems to have thrived at court – even taking the name 'Lady Rebecca'. One thing she couldn't cope with, however, or even understand, was that this was a world not only full of new people but new diseases, to which she had no resistance.

It was as her ship left London to take her home in triumph that she showed the first symptoms of smallpox, a disease unknown in America. At Gravesend she was taken ashore, too weak for the long voyage ahead, and there she died. She was buried in the local church on 17 March 1617.

There is still a church and churchyard at Gravesend, and many a tourist comes to pay their respects to Pocahontas – after all, Americans don't have many princesses – but sadly no one is quite sure precisely where she is.

We do know that she was buried in a vault under the chancel of the church, but that church burnt down in 1727. When the church was rebuilt, her vault was disturbed so she was reburied in the graveyard but the exact location has been lost. The last major search for Pocahontas took place in 1927 when a number of graves were exhumed. It was thought then that by measuring the skulls scientists could tell which one was hers but, not surprisingly, they couldn't.

This fruitless exercise just left the vicar of the time with a lot of bodies to rebury. As a result the church has discouraged further attempts ever since at locating her for fear of disturbing other graves.

Which London street is named after a famous turncoat?

Perhaps appropriately for a street inhabited entirely by politicians, Downing Street is named after one of England's most famous turncoats, a man described by diarist Samuel Pepys as 'a perfidious rogue'.

George Downing had been born in Ireland and studied in America (he was the second-ranking member of Harvard's first ever graduating class) before returning to England during the Civil War. Having been brought up in the anti-Royalist environment of the New World, he took wholeheartedly to Cromwell and, after stints as a preacher in the New Model Army, was appointed Scoutmaster General in 1650 (a job that at the time had nothing to do with woggles). In this role he maintained a network of spies that would form the basis of his later diplomatic career.

During the Commonwealth, Downing was made a teller of the receipts in the exchequer, and served in parliaments for Edinburgh and Carlisle. In return he was one of the most vociferous voices in trying to persuade Cromwell to take the title of king, something that Cromwell refused. Downing's diplomatic and spying skills saw him appointed to The Hague in 1657, mainly to negotiate with other Protestant powers and help track down Royalist exiles whom he termed 'phanatiques'. However, this got him conveniently out of the way during the interregnum after Cromwell's death and the failure of the Lord Protector's son to take power.

Still in position in The Hague on the return of Charles II, Downing managed to persuade the king that although he had been infected with anti-Royalist sentiment whilst in America, he had now seen the error of his ways. He also handed over secret government documents, demonstrating at a stroke his usefulness to the new king. As a result he was confirmed in his diplomatic position, knighted and regranted his tellership of the exchequer. Downing was also given a valuable piece of land in London that adjoined St James's Park, which would later be developed as Downing Street.

Downing now quickly turned on his old Commonwealth associates and arranged for the arrest and deportation of three of the signatories to Charles I's death warrant, who were then in hiding in Holland. This included his old friend John Okey whose chaplain he had been during the Civil War. Okey later famously forgave his 'chaplaine who pursued my life to the Death' in his final gallows speech. The king was delighted to see the fall of his father's enemies and, in 1663, Downing was created a baronet. His later career involved further stretches in Holland as well as serving back at home as an MP for Morpeth. More valuable offices followed until the other great diarist of the era, John Evelyn, could write: *'From a pedagogue and fanatic preacher not worth a groat he has become excessive rich.'*

Downing died in Cambridgeshire in 1684. In New England a 'George Downing' became the term for someone who betrayed their trust.

How many graves does Eva Perón have?

Eva Perón's turbulent career brought her as many enemies as it did friends. As the wife of Argentina's President, Juan Perón, she was adored by the poor for her work in founding hospitals, schools and orphanages. To Argentina's women she was an icon of freedom, ensuring that they got the vote in 1949. But to her country's elite she was the greatest threat to their traditional privileges.

Her nomination as vice-president in 1951 could have made her the most powerful woman of her era, had not fate intervened. On 26 July 1952, Eva Perón died of cancer. She was thirty-three years old.

She was buried in Buenos Aires, her tomb becoming a shrine for the poor and disenfranchised. Her followers even petitioned the pope to grant her sainthood. But the political situation was deteriorating. Just three years later her husband was forced to flee to Madrid. His power had gone and so had her body.

Desperate to prevent her tomb becoming a political rallying point for the opposition, the new government's first act had been to dispatch one Colonel Cabanillas on a secret mission to steal Eva's body. Her mortal remains were taken from Bueños Aires and shipped to Italy, where the colonel arranged for her burial outside Milan. And here Eva rested for sixteen years.

But if Eva's body was at rest, her memory certainly wasn't. In 1971, in the face of growing unrest at home, Argentina's military government finally told her widower where she was and arranged to hand over her body to him in Madrid, where he arranged for her third burial. He would not be staying long in Madrid himself, however. Inspired by Eva's tragic tale, Juan Perón was swept back to Argentina and power, dying in office in 1974.

But Juan Perón was not to sleep alone. Next to the president's body in the crypt of the presidential palace, another tomb was prepared, another body sent for and the man they sent to get it was, of course, Colonel Cabanillas – Eva's ghoulish chaperone.

The arrival of Eva Perón's body in Buenos Aires brought jubilation. But fate had one final cruel trick in store. When the ever-turbulent politics of that country saw another military government come to power, poor restless Eva was again exhumed from her husband's side and secretly placed in her family's vault in Recoleta cemetery. As far as anyone knows she is still there, in her fifth grave.

Where was described as 'the Dunghill of the Universe'?

Port Royal in Jamaica is now a fishing village with a population of about 2,000 and frankly it no longer really deserves the name 'the Dunghill of the Universe', although there are, in all honesty, nicer places on Jamaica to spend a holiday. However, 350 years ago the place was a little different and those who didn't refer to it as the Dunghill of the Universe often used its other nickname – the Sodom of the Indies.

Port Royal was founded as a sort of consolation prize by the British. An expedition in 1655 to wrest Hispañola from the Spanish had gone badly and the retreating British force had decided instead to take the nearest and largest undefended island. This happened to be Jamaica, and here on the Palisadoes Spit, just outside what is now Kingston, they founded a town that they called Point Cagway. When news came of the restoration of Charles II, this town was grandly renamed Port Royal.

Port Royal was a first-class port, with a huge deep-water harbour, which led directly to its notoriety. Lying on the Spanish treasure route between Panama and Spain, it quickly attracted the most notorious pirates in the Caribbean. Initially the British were none too bothered about this as the pirates did a good job of harrying Spanish trade without the cost and inconvenience of Britain having to keep a navy fleet in the region to do the job itself. But a town full of rich pirates letting their hair down soon acquires a certain reputation and Port Royal rapidly gained the worst. With a tavern or alehouse for every ten inhabitants, and the streets full of men whose pockets had been filled with the proceeds of piracy and slavery, it was said to be the most lawless place on the planet. Charles Leslie, in his *New History of Jamaica*, published in 1740, described the scene: '*Wine and women drained their wealth to such a degree that ... some of them became reduced to beggary. They have been known to spend 2 or 3,000 pieces of eight in one night; and one gave a strumpet 500 to see her naked. They used to buy a pipe of wine, place it in the street, and oblige everyone that passed to drink.*'

Things in Port Royal began to calm down after 1674 when one of the most notorious Caribbean pirates, Captain Morgan, returned to the island as lieutenant governor and, with all the zeal of a poacher turned gamekeeper, went about catching and hanging many of his former shipmates. This must have had quite a profound effect on Port Royal's nightlife as it was estimated that half the population made their living from piracy. The real death knell of the city was not a change in government policy, however, but, much to the delight of religious commentators, the hand of God. On Tuesday, 7 June 1692, a series of earthquakes hit the area and the sand spit on which the city was built liquefied. Two-thirds of the town slowly slipped beneath the waves, never to be seen again. Attempts were made to rebuild it but further earthquakes and a devastating fire eventually led to its abandonment in favour of a new settlement at Kingston.

Who is buried in the sea off Marseilles?

D. H. Lawrence died peacefully in his sleep on 2 March 1930 at the Villa Robermond, in Vence, France, and was buried in the local cemetery, attended by a group of ten mourners including his wife Frieda (who was a distant relative of the Red Baron) and Aldous Huxley. The obituary notice in the *Daily Telegraph* of 4 March 1930 ended with these rather harsh words: 'It is with justice that his books were forbidden by the censors. The man was sick, his brain affected.'

But it was not just Lawrence's memory that was to suffer such indignity. One year later, his wife Frieda left France to return to the ranch in Taos, Mexico, that Lawrence had bought for them in exchange for the sale of the manuscript of *Sons and Lovers*. But she was not alone. With her came Angelo Ravagli, with whom she had previously had an affair and who now abandoned his own wife and three children to join her.

Five years later Frieda decided to bring Lawrence's remains home to Taos too and she charged Ravagli with the job of arranging the exhumation and cremation of the body, as well as the passage of the ashes back to Mexico. On 14 May 1935 a wooden box, holding a sealed zinc container in which were Lawrence's ashes, was delivered, together with the transatlantic transport authorisation, to Ravagli, now in New York. Frieda asked that Ravagli transfer the ashes to a vase that she had purchased especially for the purpose and personally bring them back to Mexico.

According to the archives of the D. H. Lawrence ranch in Mexico, that is exactly what happened. Lawrence's ashes were then mixed into a concrete slab that now stands in a little shrine on the site.

But D. H. Lawrence is, in fact, not there at all. According to the Baron de Haulleville, who was Ravagli's guest at Taos, one evening after Ravagli had polished off the better part of a bottle of bourbon, he made an admission. Not wishing to suffer the trouble and expense of bringing Lawrence home, and perhaps feeling just a tiny bit jealous, he had opened the zinc container somewhere between Marseilles and Villefranche and had dumped the writer's ashes in the sea. When in New York he had filled the vase with ashes from a fire and taken that back to Mexico.

Frieda eventually married Ravagli but died shortly thereafter. Ravagli promptly sold Lawrence's manuscripts and paintings, which he had inherited from Frieda, along with the ranch, and moved back to Italy where his wife was still, surprisingly, waiting for him.

How did Prussia Cove in Cornwall get its name?

Prussia Cove is particularly linked to a local sailor, John Carter. He and his extended family were smugglers on the Penwith coast in the late eighteenth and early nineteenth centuries. According to the nineteenth-century historian, Sabine Baring-Gould, Carter had been given the nickname 'the king of Prussia' when just a boy, possibly due to his admiration for his illustrious contemporary,

Frederick the Great of Prussia (see pages 192–3 for another fan).
It is from this 'king of Prussia' that the cove gets its name.

John Carter managed to balance being a devout Methodist and
honest merchant with being the most notorious smuggler on the
Cornish coast. Many legends have grown up around his exploits
although it is difficult at this distance in time to know how much
is true. We know that Carter and his family lived at Portleah, later
renamed Prussia Cove, a small inlet in Mounts Bay that was well
screened from prying eyes by both land and sea, allowing luxury
goods to be landed from the continent without the payment of
customs. According to *The Cornishman* magazine of 1899, the
inlet was

> so sheltered and secluded that it is impossible to see what boats
> are in the little harbour until one literally leans over the edge of
> the cliff above; a harbour cut out of the solid rock and a roadway
> with wheel-tracks, partly cut and partly worn, climbing up the
> face of the cliff on either side of the cove, caves and the remains
> of caves everywhere, some of them with their mouths built up
> which are reputed to be connected with the house above by secret
> passages – these are still existing trademarks left by one of the
> most enterprising smuggling gangs that Cornwall has ever known.

Most of the stories of the Carters come from the rambling
autobiography written by John's brother Harry after he'd decided
to give up smuggling and become a Methodist preacher. Although
they certainly contain exaggerations, there may be elements of
truth in some of them. The most famous related to the king of
Prussia's honesty. After an unsuccessful smuggling trip, the customs
house in Penzance had John's cargo of tea under lock and key.
John went to visit his associates one night and told them that he
was planning to break into the customs house and get it back.
They thought him mad but he told them that he had promised
to deliver the tea by a certain date and was a man of his word.
Therefore he simply had to break in and get it. Sure enough,
Carter did break in and recovered his cargo. When the excise man

returned to find the store ransacked, he was reported to have said: *'John Carter has been here, and we know it because he is an upright man, and has taken away nothing which was not his own.'*

Despite this 'honest roguishness', which included Carter forbidding anyone swearing on his ships (perhaps a unique occurrence in British maritime history), he was involved in a dangerous and sometimes fatal game. Before he went straight, his brother Harry had his nose split and lost two pieces of skull to the sword of a customs man. Carter also travelled well equipped to defend himself. His two ships carried twenty guns and nineteen guns respectively and he was even known to open fire on a customs cutter from a cannon battery on the cliffs above his house.

But John apparently did not die from his trade, although the fate of the king of Prussia is unclear. In 1803 his house was auctioned, at the same time that a copper mine opened on the cliffs above the cove. Possibly, the arrival of coal shipments at the cove to fire the mine's pumping engine had made operations there a little too public. By 1807, John Carter had disappeared from the records, perhaps, like his brother, turning over a new leaf, and is never heard of again.

Where is Theodore, king of Corsica, buried?

Theodore Stefan von Neuhoff, Baron von Neuhoff, king of Corsica, is buried in an unmarked grave in the churchyard of St Anne's in Soho, London, and the story of how he got there is a strange one. Quite where Theodore's family picked up the title Baron von Neuhoff is uncertain but even before he became a king he certainly liked to live like one. In the Bavarian army he ran up huge gambling debts that forced him to desert, fleeing to his sister's house in Paris, and then, after an unfortunate incident in which he tried to kill his brother-in-law in an argument, to London.

He next joined the staff of the Swedish minister in the Netherlands but when his boss was executed he popped up in Spain, where he married 'Lady Sarsfield', the daughter of a Jacobite peer at the Spanish court. When the marriage didn't work out, he abandoned her, pregnant, at the Escorial. One report says that he took the precaution of stealing her jewels before he left.

He then appeared again at his sister's house in Paris, but soon absconded again, this time with 200,000 livres of his brother-in-law's money. Not surprisingly, perhaps, his next few years were spent travelling around a lot, often using a pseudonym. During this time, however, he certainly became acquainted with the rebel leaders in Corsica who were trying to throw off Genoese rule and in 1736 he saw his chance. Sailing from Tunis on a British ship (whose captain thought he was on official business), he landed on Corsica with a rather unimpressive army made up of a handful of freed slaves, a Sicilian doctor and a couple of fraudulent monks who claimed to have invented a 'universal medicine'. With considerable chutzpah, Theodore wrote to the rebel leader, offering himself as king of Corsica and, astonishingly, was accepted.

On 14 April 1736, Theodore was crowned hereditary king of Corsica. Sadly for him, the Genoese did not simply pack up and go home, nor were the rebels who had installed him as their king too happy when it became clear that he couldn't provide the weapons and military support for them that he had promised to help them fight Genoa's claim to the island. As he had done little more than issue possibly the era's most poorly produced coinage and made a lot of people nobles, it was time for Theodore to leave. On 4 November he announced a regency, effectively returning power into the hands of the rebel leaders, and once again he ran away.

More travelling followed as the spurned king of Corsica moved around the courts of Europe looking for support in his bid to regain the throne. Whilst several half-hearted expeditions were arranged, however, one of which didn't even have sufficient courage to land on the island, it became clear that no European power was going to support this adventurer in a war against Genoa and France (which now had a 5,000-strong expeditionary force on the island).

Eventually Theodore found himself back in London where he now called himself Baron Stein and here he was introduced to 'society' by the Hanoverian minister, Baron Münchhausen, which seems pleasingly appropriate. With London's predilection for gambling, Theodore was arrested within a year for debt and imprisoned.

There, the king of Corsica became something of a celebrity, entertaining a string of visitors whom he would enrol into the 'Order of Deliverance' as a thank-you. Eventually interest waned and no one was prepared to provide the money necessary to discharge his debt, something that Horace Walpole put down to Theodore's completely untrustworthy nature. A subscription was raised but it was not enough and even a benefit play, starring Garrick as King Lear (appropriate for a distressed royal), failed to produce the necessary sum. Finally Walpole, who was used to dealing with awkward kings and elephants (see pages 106–7), did help to get Theodore out of gaol in 1755, after he had spent six years in confinement. Under the terms of the Insolvency Act he was required to sign over all his assets to his creditors, which he listed simply as 'the kingdom of Corsica'.

Theodore was now ill and, after just a few days lodging with a tailor in Soho, he died. A little later Horace Walpole had an inscription placed on the church wall at St Anne's, which he composed himself. It reads:

NEAR THIS PLACE IS INTERRED
THEODORE, KING OF CORSICA
WHO DIED IN THIS PARISH DEC. 11 1756
IMMEDIATELY AFTER LEAVING THE KING'S BENCH PRISON
BY THE BENEFIT OF THE ACT OF INSOLVENCY,
IN CONSEQUENCE OF WHICH
HE REGISTERED THE KINGDOM OF CORSICA
FOR THE USE OF HIS CREDITORS.

Where did the terms 'left wing' and 'right wing' originate?

The political terms left and right wing derive very simply from a seating plan. In the run-up to the French revolution, France was said to politically consist of three parts – the First Estate (which was the Catholic clergy, about 100,000 strong), the Second Estate (which comprised the 400,000-strong nobility) and the Third Estate (the bourgeoisie and peasantry, amounting to some 25 million souls). Due to the worsening financial crisis in 1789, the king, Louis XVI, was forced to call a meeting of the representatives of these three groups, known as the Estates General – something that French kings avoided if at all possible. At this gathering, the chair for the president of the assembly was placed in the middle, with the Second Estate, the conservative nobility, to the right of it and the Third Estate, the radical bourgeoisie and peasantry, to the left. The term became popular in English thanks to Thomas Carlyle's epic history, *The French Revolution*, which, as we all know, he had to write twice (see pages 7–8).

Where is JFK's coffin?

Despite the sound of this question, this is not a conspiracy theory but an unusual incident that only goes to show that even the modern world has its relics.

Following the assassination of John F. Kennedy in Dallas on 22 November 1963, the world watched as his bronze coffin was taken from the hospital to the airport, loaded on to *Airforce One* and flown back to Washington. But by the time the funeral took place, this casket had magically transformed into a mahogany coffin, adding plenty of weight to conspiracy theories.

According to papers released in 1999, the reason for the switch was more prosaic, however. During transport the coffin had been damaged and one of the handles had come loose, so JFK's body had been moved into a new and more fitting casket for the state funeral. This left the government with a problem – what to do with the first coffin? Initially, as the country reeled from the assassination, it was locked in the basement of the National Archives in the hope that everyone would forget about it, but this situation became untenable when the owner of the funeral parlour that had made the coffin offered $100,000 for the return of what was now an American icon.

In early 1966, the FBI and the Kennedy family finally agreed a plan and early on the morning of 18 February, the coffin was removed from the National Archive and driven to Andrews Airforce Base. Here it was drilled full of holes and filled with sandbags before being packed into a wooden crate (also drilled with holes) and loaded on to an airforce transport plane.

Several hours later, and over a hundred miles out to sea, the coffin of John F. Kennedy was pushed out of the cargo bay of the C11 and arced down on a parachute towards the Atlantic waters below. The place chosen was a disposal ground for the US military, well away from trawling and diving areas where the coffin might be disturbed. Here it now rests in just under three kilometres of water.

14

Unsound Minds

As an experience, madness is terrific . . .

Virginia Woolf, letter to Ethel Smyth, 22 June 1930

What do French lawyers and rats have in common?

Bartholomew Chassenée was a famous sixteenth-century French jurist and, rather surprisingly, the rats were his clients. Prosecutions of animals were not as rare as you might reasonably expect in mediaeval and post-mediaeval Europe. The rats in Chassenée's case had been put on trial in the ecclesiastical courts for having 'feloniously eaten up and wantonly destroyed' a crop of barley. Set against the might of the French judicial system, you might imagine that the rats would have come off worst (let's face it, they did in Russia – see pages 192–3), particularly as they didn't show up for their trial. But never let it be said that such trials were unfair. The brilliant Chassenée, who was appointed as their counsel, argued that his clients probably didn't receive their summons since they had no fixed abode but moved from village to village. And even if they had received it and managed to read it, they were almost certainly far too frightened to come to the court in the town as that was where the cats lived. As cats ate rats, that meant that appearing in court put them in mortal danger – and that meant they could refuse the summons under French law. Chassenée went on to say that if the townsfolk could guarantee to keep their cats indoors and hence guarantee the safety of his clients, then they would answer the summons. As they were unable to do this, the judge dropped the case and the rats went free.

This was not an isolated case, however. In E. P. Evans's 1906 book, *The Criminal Prosecution and Capital Punishment of Animals*, he lists numerous legal cases brought against a range of animals. In 1494 a pig that clearly couldn't secure as good an attorney as Chassenée was tried and hanged near Clermont for having 'strangled and defaced a child in its cradle'. In 1519 some mice in Stelvio in the western Tyrol were convicted of damaging crops and ordered to leave – with the exception of expectant mothers and babies, who could not reasonably be made to leave in their current condition and were allowed to stay until they were fit enough to move on. A case against some flies in fourteenth-century Mayence rather backfired when their counsel managed to secure them a piece on land on which to retire. A group of lucky weevils at St Julien pulled off the same trick in 1587 when they were granted an estate some distance from the town in return for promising not to attack the local vineyards. In fact so confident were the weevils that they (or rather their human counsel) rejected the initial land offered as it wasn't good enough for them and secured a better plot instead. Less lucky animals included a sparrow accused of chattering in church and a cockerel convicted of laying an egg.

And before you put this down to some continental madness, in Britain a case was brought in AD 946 against a wooden statue that fell on a woman, killing her, and let's not forget the infamous 1535 Nottingham haystack trial.

Who defeated Napoleon on paper?

When Gustav IV Adolphus came to the throne of Sweden in 1792, most people thought that the country finally had a sensible, sober and devout king, and that they could put behind them all that nasty business with the assassination of his father (whose death was the subject of Verdi's opera *Un Ballo in Maschera*). They were wrong. Gustav turned out to be a touch fanatical about his religion, so much so that his arranged marriage to Catherine the Great's granddaughter had to be called off immediately as he absolutely refused to allow her to worship in the Russian Orthodox faith.

Fortunately he shared with the Russian Tsar Paul I an obsessive hatred of the French Republic, which prevented an immediate breach between the two nations, but that too was about to get him into hot water. In 1805 he enthusiastically signed up to the third coalition against Napoleon and, despite his lack of any military experience, offered to personally lead his troops into battle. Although he was dissuaded from this, his campaign went badly and the French occupied a part of his territory. Russia then promptly made peace with France and invaded another part of

Sweden's lands whilst Denmark, not wishing to miss out on the fun, also declared war on the beleaguered Gustav.

With European powers freely seizing chunks of his country, Gustav now lost what little control he had. On 13 March 1809 a group of army conspirators broke into the king's apartment and removed not only the king but all the royal family to Gripsholm Castle where they were kept in captivity. Just over two weeks later, Gustav abdicated to save the throne for his son. However, the Riksdag declared that the whole family had already forfeited the throne and handed it to his uncle, who became Charles XIII.

Gustav retired to Germany and then St Gallen in Switzerland where he lived under the name Colonel Gustafsson. By now his opinion of Napoleon was even lower than that of Beethoven (see pages 19–20). Gustav had become convinced that Napoleon was actually the Beast of the Apocalypse, although as a private individual he had lost the power to destroy him. Instead, he spent his days drawing symbolic pictures of himself defeating his nemesis and wondering whether things might have been different if he had been allowed to lead his army into battle personally.

Who liked kissing her dead husband's feet?

History has not been kind to Joanna of Castile. Despite being queen of Castile and mother to two Holy Roman Emperors, two queens of Portugal, a queen of France, a queen of Hungary and a queen of Denmark, she is known today simply as 'Joanna the Mad'.

The cause of Joanna's madness is disputed, not least by those who claim she wasn't mad at all but simply a pawn in a male game of power politics. However, she certainly displayed some unusual behaviour and the events of her life were, frankly, enough to drive anyone mad. Joanna was the daughter of Ferdinand and Isabella, the first joint rulers of a united Spain. In 1496 she was married to the dashing son of the Holy Roman Emperor, a lad whom history has more kindly granted the title 'Philip the

Handsome'. It appears that he lived up to his name and Joanna fell deeply in love with him, to the point of obsession, beating her hands against the walls of her room when he refused to share a bed with her and attacking with scissors women at court whom she considered rivals for his affections. To be fair to her, her jealousy was not entirely misplaced. Philip was somewhat less than faithful and to avoid his wife's tantrums kept her a virtual prisoner.

If it was not a particularly happy life for the emotionally unstable Joanna, it was about to get much worse. In 1502, after the death of her brother, sister and her sister's child she became the heir to the throne of Spain. The powerbrokers of Europe therefore began to take a renewed interest in her – even her husband, who was hoping for a job as king of Spain. Sadly for him, and tragically for Joanna, Philip died in 1506, apparently of typhus, whilst only twenty-eight years old. Joanna took the death of her philandering, power-obsessed husband very badly and this seems to have hastened her mental decline. On the slow journey through Spain to his final resting place in Granada, she took to opening the coffin and caressing his body. In the first few days after his death no one really thought this unusual but after several months the regular opening of the coffin so that she could kiss his feet became a bit of a pungent ordeal – for everyone except Joanna.

With Joanna in such a vulnerable condition, her father Ferdinand took the opportunity to exploit her weakness and have himself declared co-regent of Castile (the title that his late wife had held). Meanwhile Joanna was becoming increasingly protective of her dead husband's body, refusing to allow it to rest in nunneries or be approached by women in case they became aroused by his rapidly decaying corpse. It was reported at the time that she had heard what sounds like a precursor to the story of Sleeping Beauty or Snow White – a legend of a fair prince who came back to life fourteen years after his apparent death – and so she resolved to wait by his coffin. However, she was not living in a fairy tale (although there's a fair chance that, like Snow White, Philip had been poisoned) and he remained resolutely dead.

Depending on whose side of the story you want to believe, her father either realised that Joanna was too ill to rule or he seized the opportunity to persuade the world that she was mad so that he could take control. Either way, he sent Joanna to the castle of Tordesillas where she was effectively imprisoned, the isolation only increasing her mental instability. Here she remained, until a revolt briefly freed her, but she failed to take advantage of her liberty. Her son, now king, suppressed the rebellion and had his mother locked in a single windowless room in the castle where she was held until her death some thirty-five years later. If she hadn't been mad when she married Philip, by the end of this life of cruel persecution she certainly was. Before she died it was said that she had become so terrified of people that she would run up the curtains of her cell like a cat when someone approached.

Who never came back from a swim with his psychiatrist?

King Ludwig II has gone down in history variously as the 'Mad king', 'the Swan king' and, perhaps most kindly, 'the Dream king'. It is telling that his peasants, who adored him, called him the king of the Alps, whilst his uncle, who usurped his throne, referred to him as simply 'mad', which in all fairness he was.

Ludwig ascended the throne of Bavaria in 1864 at the age of eighteen, following the death of his father, Maximilian II. He was considered a quiet boy, rather naive and in many ways too immature to rule. Whilst he loved the idea of kingship, he hated the rituals and responsibilities that came with it and found public appearances distressing, often cancelling them at the last minute or simply refusing to appear.

The young Ludwig did have two great loves, however – the music of Richard Wagner, of whom he was a great patron, and the tales of Germany's romantic and chivalrous past. After 1868 it became easier for Ludwig to indulge these loves as the death of his grandfather left him with a much larger portion of the Civil List.

He immediately started preparing plans for a series of great buildings. As a child his wooden building blocks had been his favourite toy and now as king he could realise in stone the romantic fairy-tale models of his childhood. Of his three great palaces, the first to be started, in 1869, was Neuschwanstein. The initial designs for the castle were drawn up not by an architect but by Christian Jank, the set designer of the Bavarian Royal Court Theatre, and their wild romanticism appealed instantly to Ludwig. His architect, Eduard Riedel, was instructed to render this dream world in stone, and Ludwig wrote excitedly to Wagner, telling him that the new castle would be a shrine to *Lohengrin*, *Tannhäuser*, *Parsifal* and the knights of German chivalry. He also hinted that the one man he wanted to share this place with was Wagner himself.

Even the Franco-Prussian War did not interfere with the work as Ludwig did, after all, take little interest in affairs of state. Fantastical, elaborate and exotic, the castle boasted electric light, an indoor winter garden with five hummingbirds and a fully functioning moon. The throne room, largely based on Ludwig's own designs, was modelled on a Byzantine basilica. At one end white marble steps rose into an apse where the throne that Ludwig would never live to see was due to rest.

Neuschwanstein displays the romanticism and eccentricity of its creator, but even while it was still under construction, doubts were being cast on the king's sanity. Ludwig began to retreat farther from public life, refusing audiences and avoiding the responsibilities of government. Chronically shy, he objected even to the servants who served his meals, and had a table installed that could be lowered through the floor so that each course could be laid upon it before being hoisted back into his private room where no one could see him eating. It is also reported that, despite dining alone, Ludwig would have the table set for four guests so that he did not feel lonely. He often fantasised that these invisible guests were the Bourbon kings of France, whom he greatly admired, and he was sometimes heard chatting to the long-dead Louis XVI.

One of his grooms reported that at night he would often go to the riding school and there make pretend journeys. He would calculate exactly the distance between two towns and then ride around the arena until he had covered that distance, stopping halfway for a picnic lunch. His love of horses was well known; indeed, he invited his favourite grey mare, Cosa Rosa, to dine with him. After they had consumed the soup, fish, main course and dessert, the ungrateful horse proceeded to smash the hugely costly dinner service, much to Ludwig's amusement.

Gradually Ludwig's behaviour became more eccentric and his expenditure on his palaces, which as well as Neuschwanstein included a near copy of Versailles, began to bankrupt the state. There were other, wilder schemes for which architects provided plans, knowing that the money would never become available to see them made reality. Eventually, Ludwig's uncle took the situation into his own hands. A delegation was sent out from Munich to Neuschwanstein in 1886 to declare the king insane and institute a Regency in his uncle's name. With the aid of Dr Gudden, an asylum owner, and various asylum warders, the king was taken to the castle at Berg on Lake Starnberg where he was to be held in restraint. He was by now in a highly excitable state and often talked to the few staff who remained loyal to him of suicide.

On the evening of Whit Sunday, 1886, the king persuaded Dr Gudden to accompany him on a walk in the gardens of the Berg. Gudden grudgingly agreed to go and the two headed off for the shores of the lake. When, several hours later, they had not returned the alarm was raised. Around midnight two objects were sighted in the shallows of the lake: the bodies of the king and Gudden.

Ludwig had often said that drowning was a good death as it did not disfigure the body, but whether or not his death was suicide will perhaps never be known. His legacy is his castles, which bankrupted his kingdom, but which since have become some of the most visited tourist attractions in Europe. Ironically, the last words of the Dream king as he left Neuschwanstein – his dream castle – for the last time were, *'Preserve this room as a sanctuary; don't let it be profaned by the inquisitive, for in it have passed the bitterest hours of my life.'*

Who was Lulach the Idiot?

Lulach is not a man who's often spoken of today and yet he holds an important place in the history of Scotland, partly as the first king for whom we have any coronation information, but more importantly because he inherited the throne from his stepfather Macbeth.

Discovering the real story of Lulach is tricky as very little contemporary material survives from the eleventh-century Scotland in which they lived. This, of course, was a great benefit to Shakespeare when he came to write *Macbeth* as he could make most of it up. We know that Lulach's mum was Gruoch and his father was Gille Coemgáin, the king of Moray, but when Gille Coemgáin died, Macbeth married his widow and adopted their son Lulach. This sounds rather generous but there's a reasonable chance that Gille Coemgáin, who was reported to have been burnt to death along with fifty of his followers, had been killed by Macbeth in the first place. Macbeth certainly became the next king of Moray. Life on the throne wasn't easy, however, and there were lots of people who wanted to seize his kingdom, whilst he equally did his best to seize theirs. In 1040 this struggle came to a head when King Duncan I of Scotland campaigned against Macbeth and was killed by him in battle, leaving Macbeth as king of Scotland and his stepson Lulach as heir to the throne.

Duncan's family were none too happy about this and they fought to regain the throne. On 27 July 1054, King Duncan's son, Malcolm III Canmore, backed by a large Northumbrian army, met Macbeth in battle at Dunsinane in Perthshire, a battle that Macbeth lost but survived. As a result, he was forced to give Malcolm land and influence, whilst Malcolm used the following three years to build up his power base before attacking Macbeth again. This time, at Lumphanan in Mar, he finally killed his old enemy.

It's at this point that Lulach takes centre stage. This is surprising for two reasons. First, we might expect that Malcolm might claim the kingship of Scotland, having killed the king who had killed his father. Second, the early sources on Lulach generally refer to him as 'Lulach the Idiot', which does not make him sound like an ideal alternative to the brave, popular and well-armed Malcolm. Recently historians have suggested that the reason that Lulach became king at this point was that he had secretly sided with Malcolm. After all, as we have seen Macbeth had probably killed Lulach's father, so Lulach was put on the throne to help maintain the status quo amid all this blood-letting. But if Malcolm and Lulach had once been allies, it wasn't to last long. Malcolm was rather enjoying the blood-letting and on 17 March 1058 he murdered Lulach at Essie in Strathbogie. How exactly he did this is unrecorded but the sources say it was 'by treachery'.

What did Alexandra of Bavaria believe she had swallowed?

Even the most staunch royalist would probably concede that the nineteenth-century Bavarian royal family had occasional mental health issues. Most famously the reclusive and paranoid Ludwig II (see pages 187–90) had insisted on building fairy-tale castles that had nearly bankrupted the state and led to his own deposition, but a history of madness ran deeper within the family. Ludwig's father, Maximilian II, was one of nine children who were all destined for the great royal houses of Europe. He would rule Bavaria, his little brother Otto would go on to become king of Greece, whilst their sisters Mathilde, Adelgunde and Hildegarde would marry a grand duke, a duke and an archduke respectively.

Then there was Alexandra Amalie, who was born in Aschaffenburg in 1826 in the Pompejanum – a peculiar replica of the house of Castor and Pollux at Pompeii. Her father had commissioned it as a country retreat and it was perhaps an early intimation of the family's unusual architectural preferences. She was the eighth of the nine children but whilst her brothers and sisters were tentatively stepping on to the world stage, Alexandra was not. Despite her slim figure and good looks (if we believe her portrait at least), her father did not want to bring Alexandra out in public. Initially this was due to the fact that she refused to wear any colour other than white. This is not of course in itself unique nor necessarily mad, but when the princess also began walking awkwardly, as though she was having difficulty negotiating around objects, it was considered wise to make an investigation. In the process Alexandra revealed that she had suffered an accident as a young child that had so upset her that she had kept it secret. The reason for her strange gait, she told her doctors, was that she had swallowed a grand piano (although one source claims that it was actually a glass sofa – not that that makes any more sense really). The inconvenience of walking around with such a large piece of furniture inside her was hence the explanation for her peculiar movements. Perhaps not surprisingly, Alexandra went on to become the only one of her brothers and sisters who reached adulthood not to marry. She died, aged forty-eight, in Munich on 8 May 1875.

Who court-martialled a rat?

Tsar Peter III has had a difficult press, mainly because most of what we know about him was written by those who not only deposed him after his six-month reign but killed him. They included his wife, Catherine the Great (although no one really knows whether she approved of the murder part of the plan).

According to the French historian Claude-Carloman de Rulhière, whom Catherine certainly didn't like and whose work she tried to suppress, Peter was a childish figure, obsessed with matters military, who would prostrate himself before a portrait of Frederick the Great of Prussia, exclaiming, 'My brother, we will conquer the universe together.' The closest he got to mobilisation, however, was building cardboard fortresses and peopling them with toy soldiers. This is a perfectly reasonable thing for a ten-year-old prince to do, but more unusual in a tsar in his thirties.

On one occasion, the tsar discovered that one of his soldier puppets had been nibbled by a traitorous rat and, having caught the offending creature, had the animal court-martialled. The nibbled puppet proved to be a smoking gun, as it were, and the rat was found guilty and sentenced to death. Peter then built a tiny gibbet with his own hands and hanged the wretched rodent.

Peter's own end wasn't much better. On 29 June 1762, whilst he was at the Oranienbaum palace, his wife Catherine drove to St Petersburg where she was proclaimed empress. Peter was separated from his favourite things, which included his mistress, his violin and a pet monkey, and was sent to the royal estate at Ropsha. After he penned a grovelling letter to his wife, the monkey and violin were returned but the mistress was already on her way to Siberia. Shortly afterwards, he was murdered. Catherine gave the estate to her lover, Count Orlov (see pages 8–9 for what Orlov gave Catherine in exchange), and decreed, 'Ropsha is not to be mentioned again.' And that was the end of the matter.

Who exchanged a gilded cage for glowing knees?

Some rulers get epithets, and the lucky ones get good epithets like 'Alexander the Great' or 'Süleyman the Magnificent'. One less lucky ruler was Ibrahim the Mad. He was the son of the powerful Valide Sultan Kösem, the wife of Ahmet I (1603–17). When her eldest son, the Sultan Murat, died from alcoholism, Ibrahim – the last of the Osmanli family, which founded the Ottoman Empire – was summoned from the gilded cage where he had been confined for the previous eighteen years (as was customary for unneeded sons). Initially, Kösem thought that Ibrahim was impotent after his long years shut away, so she liberally dosed him with aphrodisiacs and took to buying him the most desirable women she could find in Istanbul's slave market. Soon, however, Ibrahim proved this unnecessary by entering into a reign of unparalleled depravity.

An account of his reign is given by Demetrius Cantemir, a Greek who prospered in the Ottoman Civil Service. He wrote of Ibrahim:

> As Murat was wholly addicted to wine so was Ibrahim to lust. They say he spent all his time in sensual pleasure and when nature was exhausted with the frequent repetition of venereal delights he endeavoured to restore it with potions or commanded a beautiful virgin richly habited to be brought to him by his mother, the Grand Vezir, or some other great man. He covered the walls of his chamber with looking glasses so that his love battles might seem to be enacted in several places at once. He ordered his pillows to be stuffed with rich furs so that the bed designed for the Imperial pleasure might be the more precious. Nay, he put sable skins under him in a notion that his lust might be flamed if his love toil were rendered more difficult by the glowing of his knees.

Eventually the increasingly erratic Ibrahim turned against his own harem, ordering all 280 of them to be sewn into weighted sacks and drowned, supposedly because one of them had seduced an outsider. This excess led to his downfall and he was strangled by the Chief Executioner, Black Ali, in a plot orchestrated by the Grand Mufti.

Who had himself racked?

Christian VII of Denmark should have had an excellent childhood as the son of the rather enlightened Frederick V, whose last words were: *'It is a great consolation to me in my last hour that I have never wilfully offended anyone and that there is not a drop of blood on my hands.'* Sadly, Frederick was also an alcoholic who, although he may not have wilfully offended his son, did leave him in the care of a sadistic tutor who regularly beat his nervous charge, possibly inducing the epileptic fits that would dog him for the rest of his life. Even when he was a child, it was clear that Christian, whilst enjoying periods of clarity, was not quite what Dad had hoped for and he is now generally believed to have suffered from schizophrenia.

The strains of being king of Denmark, king of Norway, Duke of Schleswig and Holstein and George III's brother-in-law to boot whilst aged only seventeen did not help the king's condition and he soon fell under the influence of a young doctor, Friedrich Struensee. He worked his way into the king's affections with a combination of charm and heavy sedation. Although an enlightened chap, Struensee also had an eye to the main chance and, as the king's mental abilities waned, he took over not only the running of the country but also the bed of Christian's queen, Caroline Matilda, much to the disgust of her brother George III. When the queen produced a daughter, Louise Augusta, her likeness to Struensee was so marked that it caused a riot.

Of course none of this made Struensee very popular with the ordinary people of Denmark, particularly as he never bothered to learn a word of their language and, in his reforming zeal, tried to abolish just about every state institution they had ever known. During the period of his absolute power, in which he would issue decrees without even obtaining the king's signature, he was responsible for over 1,000 proclamations at a rate of three a day. Not surprisingly, a plot was eventually hatched to remove him and he was convicted of having usurped royal power. An idea of just how unpopular he had become can be gauged by the manner of his death. His hand was cut off, he was broken on a wheel, beheaded and then quartered.

But it wasn't Struensee who had himself racked. Whilst the world's attention was on the upstart doctor, the king's mental condition continued to deteriorate. He had taken a lover whom he ordered to wear male naval uniform and maintained her publicly until the scandal threatened revolt and she was removed. After that his mental health disintegrated and, following an exciting afternoon watching a prisoner confess under torture, he began to take an unnatural interest in pain. Enjoying watching prisoners tortured was not all that unusual for monarchs but, according to the very sober diaries of his adviser, Elie Salomon François Reverdil, the pain that Christian enjoyed most was his own. So it was Christian who ordered himself racked (and whipped) so that he could discover their unique pleasures for himself. As he now ruled Denmark in name alone, the real power being in the hands of his stepmother, he could devote nearly all his time to self-punishment. After thirty-six agonising years of torture, he finally died in 1808 of a brain aneurysm. He was fifty-nine years old.

What was the Cadaver Synod?

Pope Formosus, whose name means 'good-looking', was certainly not good-looking at the time he appeared before the Cadaver Synod, mainly because he'd been dead for a year. In the troubled politics of ninth-century Europe, Formosus had become caught up in power struggles between various royal families, each of which had their own religious nominee. In 891, after a spell of excommunication and banishment from Rome, he had made a triumphant comeback and got himself elected pope, making plenty of enemies on the way, including his eventual successor. Formosus was a pretty good pope, however (certainly by that day's standards), and thanks to some careful diplomacy he managed to hang on to the papal throne until his death in 896. Pope Stephen VI, who now took over, couldn't wait to take his revenge. In 897, Formosus's body was exhumed, dressed in papal robes and propped up on a throne to answer charges brought by what became known as the Cadaver Synod.

Pope Stephen himself prosecuted, appointing a deacon to speak for Formosus who obviously couldn't really answer for himself, being dead at the time. He was accused of usurping the papal throne, perjury, violating the canons forbidding the translation of bishops (of which he was actually guilty) and of serving as a bishop whilst still a layman. Not surprisingly, the silent Formosus was found guilty. His punishment was to have the three fingers of his right hand (with which he had performed the benediction) torn off whilst all his acts and ordinations were declared null and void. His body was reburied, dug up again and thrown in the Tiber.

Not surprisingly the people of Rome found this a touch peculiar and they took against Stephen. He was deposed and imprisoned and, shortly after, strangled. Pope John IX then nullified the acts of the Cadaver Synod and Formosus's body, which had been fished out of the Tiber, was returned to St Peter's. That wasn't an end to the infighting, however, and in the early tenth century Pope Sergius III reconfirmed the conviction, although he didn't go as far as digging poor old Formosus up again. This caused a problem as it meant that all the priests who had been ordained by Formosus, plus everyone that *they* had ordained since, weren't really priests at all and needed to be reordained. This proved simply too baffling for everyone concerned and the Church decided to ignore Sergius. Nor was Sergius really the sort of pope who should have presumed to cast the first stone. The sixty years of papal rule beginning with his election saw the throne of St Peter controlled by three Roman families and, in particular, by powerful women within those families. It has become known to Church historians as the 'pornocracy'.

15

All at Sea

There's something wrong with our bloody ships today.

David Beatty, British Admiral of the Fleet at the Battle of Jutland, 1916

What was the Floating Republic?

Conditions in the British navy in the late eighteenth century were not very good, partly due to the failure of the Admiralty to keep up to date with the effects of changing technology on the lives of its sailors, and partly due to the fact that none of them had had a pay rise in 139 years. Eventually, in 1797, discontent erupted into outright mutiny, initially at Spithead, where sixteen ships of the Channel Fleet refused to take orders and instead sent delegates to negotiate with the Admiralty. Considering the harsh reputation of the navy of that era, these mutineers made a pretty good case. Even the Admiralty could see that their grievances made sense and, at a time when Britain was at war with revolutionary France, they needed all their fighting men and certainly didn't want any revolutionaries of their own. Admiral Lord Howe therefore negotiated anonymity for the mutineers (so that no one could persecute them later), full pardons, better pay and improved conditions. In return the Channel Fleet went back to work and, with that splendid English talent for understatement, the Spithead Mutiny went down in history as the 'Spithead Breeze'.

At the Nore moorings on the Thames later that year, the outcome was rather different. Inspired by the Spithead Breeze, the crew of the warship *Sandwich* mutinied on 12 May and were rapidly joined by the rest of the fleet riding at anchor with them (in total some twenty-eight vessels). They too elected delegates and drew up a series of demands, which they presented to the Admiralty. The Nore mutineers went a great deal further than their Spithead comrades. As well as pardons, and improved pay and conditions, they wanted changes to the articles of war and proposed introducing corporal punishment for officers they disliked. When their demands were not met, they began blockading the river, preventing merchantmen from reaching the Port of London. To the Admiralty and many in government, this looked too close to being a revolution for comfort. For six weeks the stand-off between the Admiralty and what was becoming known as 'the Floating Republic' continued, as the fleet took pot-shots at its own merchant ships whilst the government lined the shore with troops, preventing food from reaching the mutineers. By 11 June the crews were hungry and nervous. There seemed little chance now that they would achieve their aims and a rumour was going around that a brig had been prepared to take their leaders to revolutionary France, leaving their crews to starve to death. From this point the Floating Republic began to look decidedly leaky and by the end of the month all the ships had surrendered. Their leader, Richard Parker, received neither anonymity nor a pardon and, having been convicted of piracy and treason, was hanged from the yardarm of the *Sandwich*. The other ships' representatives were flogged and either imprisoned or transported.

Why shouldn't you insult a British ensign?

Apart from its being a shade uncivilised, there have been times in the past when insulting a British flag could start a war.

The Second Opium War (1856–60), also known as the Arrow War, was really a continuation of the First Opium War (see pages 239–40) but somehow managed to have an even more ridiculous pretext. When a Qing dynasty official boarded a Chinese ship, the *Arrow*, and arrested some of the Chinese crew on suspicion of smuggling, the British claimed that it was in fact a British-registered ship and that the prisoners should therefore be returned to them. They then claimed that the official had insulted the British ensign being flown on the ship – and what could be more serious than being rude about a flag? War ensued, in which the French, Americans and Russians all joined, hoping to improve their own fortunes in China. It came to an end only after the burning down of the beautiful Imperial Summer Palace by Lord Elgin, whose father had, incidentally, taken the marbles from the Parthenon following the unfortunate partial demolition of the building in 1687 (see pages 214–15). The final treaty (there were a couple of false starts) gave more territory to Britain, granted reparations to Britain and France, allowed the British to take indentured Chinese to America and fully legalised the opium trade.

What did Pedro Cabral discover by accident?

Pedro Álvares Cabral is one of the great unsung heroes of the age of exploration. Given the job of continuing the work of the great Vasco da Gama by Manuel I of Portugal, he set out on 9 March 1500 with a commission to establish trade and Christianity wherever he went, and with the added intention of heading for the rich spice markets of India. In order to avoid the doldrums in the Gulf of Guinea off the west coast of Africa, Cabral tacked far across the Atlantic, in the opposite direction to where he was ultimately heading, in the hope of getting a clear run on the return tack around the Cape of Good Hope at the southernmost tip of Africa.

On 22 April, however, at the end of his first tack, he spotted a mountain, which he called Monte Pascoal. He decided to land near by and claim what appeared to be a largish island in the Atlantic. On 25 April his entire fleet sailed into Porto Seguro where he landed and took possession of the 'island' by erecting a cross and getting a Franciscan friar on his ship to hold a church service. Noting that the island lay on the Portuguese side of the line with which Pope Alexander VI had divvied up the New World between Spain and Portugal, he sent a messenger back home with the news that Manuel I could now add a new land to his kingdom, the 'island of Vera Cruz' – the island of the true cross. Then on 3 May he set off again for India. The journey to India was difficult and he returned to Portugal in 1501 with only four of his initial fleet of thirteen ships. He died there about nineteen years later, never having returned to his 'island' and never having realised that the 'island' that he had claimed for Portugal was Brazil – the largest country in South America.

How did Sark become British?

Sark became British thanks to a very unusual French monastic pirate. We know of Eustache Busquet from some contemporary sources but mainly from a mediaeval romance, which probably means that the tale has been embroidered somewhat. Nevertheless it gives a fascinating insight into the job opportunities available in the late twelfth and early thirteenth centuries for those with the will and lack of moral scruples to seize them.

Eustache was born in 1170 into an important family, training first as a knight and then in Italy as a sailor. More unusually, he next went to Toledo to study necromancy. When he got home he entered a monastery where he remained until his father was murdered. Having tracked down the murderer he challenged him to a judicial duel, which his champion lost. Unable to get restitution of his family's land, he entered the service of the Count of Boulogne where he rose to become seneschal, before being accused of fraud. At this point he made a run for it and became an outlaw, engaging in the usual Robin Hood school of forest banditry. After a while Eustache decided on a change of direction so he bought a ship and became a pirate in the English Channel, mainly attacking English ships until King John (who was a nicer man than many say) hired him. Eustache continued to do much the same thing, but for the British rather than against them, proving that it's always best to keep your enemies close. In the process he captured the island of Sark from the French and set up his HQ there. As his reward he was given lands in Norfolk.

There then followed a *Carry-On*-style series of events where Eustache turned up at the wrong place at the wrong time, at the end of which he was outlawed by just about everyone, which is an occupational hazard when you change sides as frequently as he did. Fortunately at that time a new group of people to defraud hove into view – the English barons, who had risen up against John. Eustache was now on to a nice little earner selling them arms. This made him terribly unpopular with King John who confiscated his English property, so Eustache went back to sea where he virtually controlled the Channel. Abandoning all his English allies (most of whom were now also his enemies, to be fair), he agreed to land the French king and his army on the Isle of Thanet. On the return from this act of treachery, his vessel was captured by four British ships and Eustache was beheaded on the spot.

Which island did Anthony van Diemen discover?

Oddly enough, van Diemen didn't discover Van Diemen's Land although he is often claimed as the 'discoverer' of Ceylon (modern Sri Lanka), to the great surprise of the native peoples of that island who had been living there for around 125,000 years. Van Diemen did establish much of the island as a Dutch colony, however, and in European eyes at that time that was as good as a discovery. As governor-general of the Dutch East Indies, Van Diemen was interested in expanding the Dutch trading empire further, in particular to the mystical continent that was believed to exist far to the south. This had first been spotted by Willem Janszoon in 1606 although he thought that the coast he had actually landed on (which was part of Australia) was a part of New Guinea, which, to add to the confusion, he named New Zealand.

So in August 1642, van Diemen dispatched Abel Tasman to explore further. In November of that year Tasman duly found what he thought was a large land mass, which he named after his boss – Van Diemen's Land – and which he claimed for the Dutch. He didn't ask the native Australians (who had been living there for about as long as the natives of Ceylon) whether they agreed to being 'discovered'. Unfortunately for Tasman, while this was certainly a good-sized island, it wasn't the southern continent that he'd been looking for, although he thought it was, and so his confusing voyage continued. From there he sailed off and discovered the South Island of the real New Zealand, which he called Staten Land on the grounds that he thought it was attached to

Staten Island off the coast of Argentina, which it isn't. Tasman got back to van Diemen's capital at Batavia in June 1643 and told the governor the good news that he'd found his continent and named it after him, leaving van Diemen to die a happy man.

The name did not last, however. The terrible reputation of the subsequent British convict settlements on Van Diemen's Land meant that, when transportation to the island ceased in 1853, it was decided that a change of name was required. In 1856 the locals elected to rename their land after its (European) discoverer – and so Van Dieman's Land became Tasmania.

Who were the Sea Beggars?

The Sea Beggars were a group of pirates who accidentally kicked off the Dutch independence movement. The term 'beggars' had originally been given to a group of Dutch nobles who had petitioned their then masters, Spain, for increased rights. When they had appeared before Margaret, Duchess of Parma, she had apparently been frightened by their numbers but one of her councillors had whispered to her, 'What, madam? Is your highness afraid of these beggars?' Strangely, the Dutch nobles rather liked the insult, saying they would happily become beggars for their country, and so the name stuck.

These first 'beggars' were actually quickly crushed by Spain but when William of Orange set himself against Spanish rule in 1569 he gave letters of marque (a sort of piracy licence for use against a particular country) to a group of seafaring desperadoes who became known as the Sea Beggars. They happily raided Spanish ships, taking their booty across the Channel to England, until 1572 when Queen Elizabeth suddenly banned them. With nowhere to take their loot or repair their ships, the Sea Beggars were in a bit of a bind and they decided that the only thing they could do was to seize a port for themselves. So they attacked Brielle – where the Spanish garrison just so happened to be away – and, to their own great surprise, took it. Elated with their success, they then moved on to Flushing, which they also took, rather to everyone's astonishment. These two events are usually cited as the first engagements in the Dutch War of Independence.

Who sank Vice-Admiral Tryon's flagship?

He did, really. Tryon was a distinguished nineteenth-century naval officer who, in 1891, was put in charge of the British Mediterranean Fleet – the linchpin to the security of Britain's naval empire. Tryon was a somewhat taciturn man who liked to keep his crews on their toes by ordering endless manoeuvres but issuing very few orders (until the last minute) to encourage independent and quick thinking. This was both his strength and his downfall.

On 22 June 1893, eight of his battleships and three light cruisers were on manoeuvres off Tripoli in what is now the Lebanon. With his fleet in two parallel lines ahead, he told his captains that he planned that each ship in each line would turn inwards by 180 degrees and reverse their direction of travel. Then, after a few miles, they would all turn 90 degrees to port and anchor. This seemed reasonable, if somewhat balletic.

The problem was that Tryon had ordered his columns to travel just 1,200 yards apart – far too close for the turning circle of such large warships. Some of the braver officers pointed this out to Tryon, and he agreed to increase the distance to 1,600 yards. However, as the manoeuvres began he ordered the columns to close once again to 1,200 yards and increase their speed to 8.8 knots. At 3 p.m. he raised the signal flag, ordering the two columns to turn in on each other in succession. When his deputy, Rear Admiral Hastings Markham, at the head of the other column, hesitated to confirm this, Tryon issued a public rebuke, raising the signal for the whole fleet to see: 'What are you waiting for?' So Markham turned in, and Tryon turned in, with both ships' crews imagining that Tryon would issue some clever new order at the last minute. He didn't and, with just 1,200 yards between the vessels, each of which had turning circles of at least

800 yards, the inevitable now happened. The ram on the front of Markham's ship crashed into Tryon's flagship, tearing a huge hole below the waterline. The ship flooded before the watertight doors could be sealed and sank in just thirteen minutes. Thankfully all the other ships of the fleet managed to pull out of the manoeuvre before they collided with one another. Tryon was last seen on the bridge of his flagship and was heard to say, 'It's all my fault,' before he, his ship and 358 of his crew went to the bottom.

How is the Flying Dutchman related to Corbie's Aunt?

Italian mariners of the fifteenth and sixteenth centuries believed that St Elmo's Fire, the light sometimes seen dancing around a ship's mast during electrical storms, emanated from the body of Christ, and hence gave it the name Corpo Santo, which became corrupted into English as Corbie's Aunt. Generally the arrival of Corbie's Aunt was seen as a good omen, foretelling the arrival of better weather, but it was believed that if the light fell on the face of an individual on board, they would die within twenty-four hours.

This latter myth may derive from the legend of the Flying Dutchman. The story goes that a Dutch skipper, Captain Vanderdecken, whilst on the voyage home from Batavia, met with a great storm. Fearing for his ship, he swore by *Donner und Blitzen* (not the reindeer) that he would reach the shelter of Table Bay but as the words left his lips his ship foundered. He and his ship became ghosts, condemned for ever to seek but never reach Table Bay. Anyone seeing this spectral ship as they pass the Cape of Good Hope will, it is said, die in a shipwreck.

A German version of the myth has Herr von Falkenberg condemned to sail for ever around the North Sea without helm or helmsman, whilst playing dice with the devil for his soul. Still, at least it wasn't Kerplunk.

Both myths may ultimately derive from the Norse saga in which

Stöte steals a ring from the gods and is later found as a skeleton draped in a robe of fire aboard a black ghost ship.

What was wrong with Captain Bligh?

William Bligh is a case in point of how real life is usually much more complicated and much less cut and dried than in the movies.

To begin with, Captain Bligh wasn't even a captain during the famous 1789 *Bounty* voyage but only a commanding lieutenant. There was also no such ship as HMS *Bounty*, as the *Bounty* was an armed auxiliary vessel and thus should be referred to as HMAV *Bounty* (His Majesty's Armed Vessel *Bounty*). Nor did Bligh have a bad reputation amongst the men. The mutinous Fletcher Christian had sailed with him twice before without reporting any problems and had been promoted to sailing master during the *Bounty* voyage with the rank of acting lieutenant, so he had every reason to be grateful to Bligh.

Bligh was also lenient. When three crewmen went AWOL in Tahiti (and who can blame them), they were recaptured but Bligh ordered them flogged in place of the usual penalty of hanging. An analysis of ships' logs shows that flogging on board the *Bounty* was well below the average Royal Navy level. When the crew did mutiny, it's also worth noting that only a quarter of them opposed their captain.

Having said that, Bligh did find himself mixed up in two further mutinies, first the Nore mutiny (also known as the Floating Republic, see pages 201–2) in 1797 when he was expelled from his ship *The Director* by the crew, and then when governor of New South Wales during the Rum Punch Rebellion. During this tussle with the New South Wales Corps of the army (basically over who ran the colony), Bligh was arrested and imprisoned for a year. It was the only time that the military have ever successfully taken over the Australian government. When he finally returned to Britain, he was promoted first to rear admiral and then to vice-admiral, which only goes to show that no one back home really blamed him for his unfortunate run of mutinous luck. To be fair to him, the Nore mutiny was not about him personally; indeed, captains were expelled from their ships from time to time, and the Rum Punch Rebellion was really a fight between the old guard, who had got used to their perks, and a government on the other side of the world that wanted to rein them in.

Nevertheless, Bligh is still causing havoc at sea today. The *Exxon Valdez* oil spill of 1989 occurred after the ship hit Bligh Reef. It was named by Captain Cook during his third and final voyage, after his sailing master, one William Bligh.

16

Bang!

There is no terror in a bang, only in the anticipation of it.

Alfred Hitchcock, quoted in *Halliwell's Filmgoer's Companion* (1984)

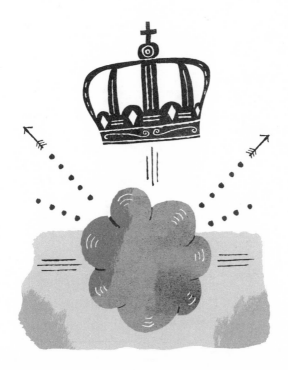

How long did the gunfight at the OK Corral last?

Despite being immortalised in novels and movies, the gunfight at the OK Corral on the afternoon of Wednesday, 26 October 1881, lasted only about thirty seconds. During that time, between twenty and thirty shots were fired from a range of about ten feet. At the end of it, however, Billy Clanton and Frank and Tom McLaury were left dead or dying. Three members of the Clanton gang survived unscathed by very wisely running away when the shooting started: Billy's brother Ike, who was probably unarmed; Billy Claiborne (again probably unarmed); and Wes Fuller. On the other side, Wyatt Earp emerged unscathed, Doc Holliday received a graze to the hip, whilst Virgil Earp and Morgan Earp received wounds in the calf and back respectively.

Billy Clanton and the McLaurys were buried at the Boot Hill Cemetery in Tombstone. There are at least eighteen Boot Hill cemeteries in the US, the name being given to burial grounds for those who 'died with their boots on' or, in other words, died a violent death. These cemeteries were also used for paupers' graves.

How could Annie Oakley have prevented the First World War?

Phoebe Ann Mosey was born in 1860 into a poor family in Ohio, and from the age of nine learnt to shoot game to provide an income for her mother and siblings. So good in fact did Phoebe become at shooting that she began taking part in local competitions with sharpshooters, and it was through one of these that she met her future husband and began her famous career. Starting out as her husband's assistant, she soon outshone him and he became her manager instead. By the time the two of them joined Buffalo Bill's Wild West Show in 1885, she had taken the professional name Annie Oakley and her name was known across the USA. In 1887 the show toured Europe and attracted royal patronage, including a performance given for Queen Victoria. It also was on this tour that Annie briefly, and unknowingly, got her chance to change history.

Crown Prince Wilhelm, very shortly to become Kaiser Wilhelm II, had heard of her famous trick in which she shot the ash off the end of a cigarette held in her husband's teeth. He insisted that she perform the trick on him but, perhaps unwilling to take too great a risk, she persuaded him to hold the cigarette in his hand rather than between his lips. She then became perhaps the only person ever to point a loaded firearm at Wilhelm. It is a tragedy for world history that she proved that, even under these stressful conditions, she was an excellent shot. She hit the ash on the cigarette, leaving the Shakespeare-loving Kaiser (see pages 240–1) unscathed – something she is later claimed to have quite regretted.

Who ruined the Parthenon?

The Parthenon had stood on the Acropolis of Athens since the fifth century BC and survived being converted into a Christian church in the sixth century AD as well as a mosque following the Turkish capture of Athens in 1458. Whilst both Christians and Muslims had made some alterations to the building, it remained remarkably intact until 1687. In that year the Venetians, under Francesco Morosini, attacked Athens and the defending Ottomans fortified the Acropolis, turning the Parthenon into a gunpowder magazine. The result was predictable. On 26 September a Venetian mortar battery, set up on the Hill of Philopapus, opened fire on the Acropolis. One mortar achieved a direct hit on the powder magazine in the Parthenon and the building exploded. All the internal structures were destroyed, the tops were ripped from many of the pillars on the south side and the roof collapsed. In the process, many of the famous sculptures on the building were hurled to the ground and broken. Shortly after this act of vandalism, Morosini did capture the city and returned to Venice loaded with plaudits (as well as bits of the Parthenon). In 1688 he was elected doge.

What was 'cudgel play'?

Whilst we like to think of the Tudors playing tennis and perhaps doing a spot of hunting, the ordinary games of the era, played at fairs and on holidays, were a little more basic. Take cudgel play, a game so simple that it might in fact appear stupid. Two combatants would attack each other with wooden clubs. The first combatant to bleed was the loser. That's it – it doesn't take long to learn the rules. For those looking for something more civilised, there was Dun in the Mire in which a log was placed in a bog or muddy puddle and two players would each try to retrieve it whilst also attempting to prevent the other from doing so by hitting and punching them and, if the opportunity arose, dropping the log on their feet.

Which assassination attempt was inspired by a bad poem?

Queen Victoria was not perhaps quite as popular with the people of her huge empire as history would have us believe. In fact, she was subject to seven assassination attempts, although most of these might be classed more as extreme attempts to gain royal attention.

The first took place in 1842 when Edward Oxford attacked the just-married Victoria as she was riding on Constitution Hill in London. Oxford fired two shots at the queen, both of which missed, and he was quickly wrestled to the ground. He was tried for treason but was found to be insane and committed to the Bethlehem Hospital (Bedlam) until 1864 when all that institution's criminal patients were moved to Broadmoor. Two years later he was offered a discharge and agreed to emigrate to Australia.

In 1844, John Francis had another go, firing a pistol at the queen as she rode in a carriage through St James's Park. He was manfully thrown to the ground by Police Constable William Trounce and hauled before the bench on a charge of treason. In this case Prince Albert was sure that the man wasn't insane, declaring that he was 'a thorough scamp', which seems like an extraordinarily polite way of describing someone who has just tried to murder your wife. The jury agreed that he was a thoroughly bad man and found him guilty. He was sentenced to death but, after much deliberation, this was commuted to transportation for life.

Shortly after this, a young lad by the name of John William Bean fired a gun at the queen, although it was loaded only with tobacco and paper, making it more of a novelty cigarette than a weapon. By now Prince Albert felt that shooting the queen was becoming a popular pastime amongst attention-seekers who knew that, as the penalty for treason was death, most juries would pity them for trying something so futile and declare them insane rather than see them hang. So the 1842 Treason Act was passed, making it a misdemeanour to throw things at the queen, hit her or point a gun at her, punishable by up to seven years' transportation or three years' imprisonment (with or without hard labour) and the option of a good flogging.

Fortunately for young Master Bean, he was tried just after the Act came in and so, instead of hanging or spending a life in Bedlam, he received eighteen months in prison. Neither he, nor any other individual convicted under the Act, was ever flogged. The new Act didn't deter everyone, however. In 1849, William Hamilton was transported for seven years for firing a powder-filled pistol at the queen on Constitution Hill. He claimed that he wanted to alarm her – which he did.

Then in 1850 it was William Pate's turn. William was unlike the other potential assassins, who were generally young men, often just boys, hoping to make a bit of a splash. Pate, a former army lieutenant, fancied himself as something of a dandy and he took the opportunity, whilst walking in Piccadilly, to hit the passing queen over the head with his cane – one of the few occasions when Victoria was actually hurt by one of her assailants. Prince Albert concluded that the man was 'manifestly deranged' but the jury disagreed and Pate was shipped off to the colonies.

Two more attempts followed. In 1872 Arthur O'Connor tried the old 'fire an empty pistol at the queen to alarm her' routine again. He was promptly leapt on by the ever-faithful John Brown who received a gold medal from Victoria for his trouble. O'Connor received a year in prison.

Ten years later the outcome was a little different. Roderick Maclean fired a loaded pistol at the monarch as she rode through Windsor because, so he claimed in court, he had received a rather curt reply to the poem he had sent her. Such was the public outrage that Maclean was tried for treason. Not surprisingly, the jury found him not guilty on the grounds of insanity and he was committed to Broadmoor. The queen was furious, demanding to know how a man could be found 'not guilty but insane' when she had seen him fire the bullet herself; as far as she was concerned he was clearly guilty, regardless of whether or not he was mad. Despite the pleading of the legal profession, who tried to explain that a crime requires criminal intent, Victoria would not be moved and so it was that the following year the law was changed to allow a verdict of 'guilty but insane'. The assassination attempt inspired the doggerel poet William McGonagall to write 'Attempted Assassination of the Queen', which many consider to be the worst poem in the English language and almost certainly worse than the one from Maclean that left Victoria so unimpressed.

Which English king exploded?

According to the chronicler Ordericus Vitalis, William the Conqueror had a very unseemly end. He had fallen sick at Rouen after receiving abdominal injuries from his saddle pommel when he fell off his horse at the siege of Mantes, and was taken to a small lodge just outside the city. There, his condition rapidly worsened and he became racked with stomach pains. Realising

that his time had come, he summoned his sons and nobles and
made preparation for what he knew would be a messy succession.

According to Vitalis, William didn't hold out much hope for
his soul either, telling them:

> I tremble, my friends, when I reflect on the grievous sins which
> burden my conscience, and now, about to be summoned before
> the awful tribunal of God, I know not what I ought to do. I was
> bred to arms from my childhood, and am stained from the rivers
> of blood I have shed. It is out of my power to count all the
> injuries which I have caused during the sixty-four [he was actu-
> ally probably fifty-nine] years of my troubled life.

He did, however – at least according to the rather pro-William
chroniclers who recorded the event – make lengthy confessions,
divide up his lands and extensive treasure, and decide what should
be done with some of his more troublesome prisoners, before
finally expiring on 9 September 1087.

It was now that events started to get a little unseemly. The
nobles who had been with the king immediately fled back to their
own estates to secure them against any possible conflict over the
succession, leaving the king's body in the charge of their retainers.
Depending on how you look at it, these individuals now either
quite sensibly took the opportunity to improve their pension
prospects in what had suddenly become a considerably more uncertain world, or behaved rather badly. According to Vitalis, 'the inferior servants, observing that their masters had disappeared, laid
hands on the arms, the plate, the robes, the linen, and all the royal
furniture, and leaving the corpse almost naked on the floor of the
house, they hastened away.'

Eventually a local knight brought the dead king's rapidly putre-
fying and swollen body to St Stephen's church in Caen for burial.
However, there were to be further delays. During the funeral procession a fire broke out in the town and most of the mourners left to
put it out. When the service finally began it was immediately inter-
rupted by a local man called Ascelin who loudly announced that

he owned the land on which William was to be buried but had never been paid for it. Eventually he was given sixty shillings and the service continued. The remaining monks who were not putting out fires or paying off irate landowners then tried to squeeze William's now very bloated corpse into a stone sarcophagus but, as Vitalis says, *'they were obliged to use some violence in forcing [the body] in, . . . so that, as the king was very corpulent, the bowels burst, and an intolerable stench affected the bystanders . . . The priests therefore hurried the conclusion of the funeral service and retired as soon as possible, in great alarm, to their respective abodes.'*

William's body was finally interred at Caen and remained there until 1562 when his tomb was completely destroyed by Calvinists. Only his left thigh bone was saved from destruction, which was later reinterred in a new tomb. This too fell prey to rioters during the French revolution in 1793 and now only a stone slab marks where William the Conqueror once lay.

What nineteenth-century game involved smashing snail shells?

The name 'conker' comes from the nineteenth-century dialectal word *conker* meaning snail shell, as the game was originally played using garden snail shells. A regional variant used hazelnuts. The first recorded game of conkers using horse chestnuts was on the Isle of Wight in 1848. Conkers are also known regionally as 'obbly-onkers' or 'cheggies'. The World Conker Championships began by accident in Ashton in 1965 when a group of regulars at the local pub were prevented from going fishing by bad weather. They decided to play conkers instead, giving the entrance fees to charity and instituting a small prize for the winner.

Who were the Stanton Harcourt Lovers?

On 1 September 1718, Alexander Pope, the poet and critic, sat in his study composing a letter. That day, however, his subject was not the great sweep of the arts nor the politics of society but an incident that he had witnessed in a small Oxfordshire village. He tells the story best in his own words:

I have a mind to fill the rest of this paper with an accident that happened just under my eyes, and has made a great impression on me. I have past [sic] part of this summer at an old romantic seat of my Lord Harcourt's, which he lent me. It overlooks a common field, where, under the shade of a haycock, sat two lovers, as constant as ever were found in Romance, beneath a spreading beech. The name of the one (let it sound as it will) was John Hewet, of the other Sarah Drew. John was a well-set man, about five-and-twenty; Sarah a brown [dark-complexioned, though maybe rustically suntanned] woman of eighteen.

John had for several months borne the labour of the day in the same field with Sarah: when she milked, it was his morning and evening charge to bring the cows to her pail. Their love was the talk, but not the scandal, of the neighbourhood; for all they aimed at was the blameless possession of each other in marriage.

It was but this very morning that he obtained her parents' consent, and it was but till the next week that they were to await to be happy. Perhaps this very day, in the intervals of their work, they were talking of their wedding-clothes; and John was now matching several kinds of poppies and field flowers to her complexion, to make her a present of knots for the day.

While they were thus employed (it was on the last day of July), a terrible storm of thunder and lightning arose, that drove the labourers to what shelter the trees or hedges afforded. Sarah, frightened and out of breath, sunk down on a haycock, and John (who never separated from her) sate by her side, having raked two or three heaps together to secure her. Immediately there was heard so loud a crack as if Heaven had burst asunder.

The labourers, all solicitous for each other's safety, called to one another; those who were nearest our lovers, hearing no answer, stepped to the place where they lay: they first saw a little smoke,

220

and after, this faithful pair; – John, with one arm about his Sarah's neck, and the other held over her face, as if to screen her from the lightning. They were struck dead, and already grown stiff and cold in this tender posture. There was no mark or discolouring on their bodies, only that Sarah's eyebrow was a little singed, and a small spot appeared between her breasts. They were buried the next day in one grave, in the parish of Stanton-Harcourt, in Oxfordshire, where my Lord Harcourt, at my request, has erected a monument over them.

NEAR THIS PLACE LIE THE BODIES OF
JOHN HEWET AND SARAH DREW,
AN INDUSTRIOUS YOUNG MAN AND VIRTUOUS MAIDEN
OF THE PARISH
CONTRACTED IN MARRIAGE
WHO BEING WITH MANY OTHERS AT HARVEST
WORK, WERE BOTH IN ONE INSTANT KILLED
BY LIGHTNING ON THE LAST DAY OF JULY
1718

How did the Earl of Cardigan satisfy Captain Johnson?

It may seem rather odd that Lord Brudenell, also known as the 7th Earl of Cardigan (he of the Charge of the Light Brigade, see pages 263–5), should offer to fight a duel with a man whose wife he had already stolen but then Brudenell was an unusual man. In June 1824, Johnstone had started divorce proceedings, citing Brudenell as co-respondent. Brudenell offered no defence and didn't appear in court. There was very little he could say in his defence, really, as he was living in Versailles with Mrs Johnstone at the time. So Johnstone won his case and was awarded £1,000 in damages, but Brudenell, with the sort of misplaced ideas of chivalry that would dog him all his life, offered the aggrieved husband the additional 'satisfaction' of a duel. Johnstone, well aware that a dead man can't spend £1,000 and that he had also relieved himself of a very expensive wife, simply replied: *'Tell Lord Brudenell he has already given me satisfaction: The satisfaction of having removed the most damn bad-tempered and extravagant bitch in the kingdom.'*

Lord Brudenell and Elizabeth Johnstone were eventually married in May 1824. The union proved a disaster, however, as Elizabeth was indeed extravagant, bad-tempered and allegedly promiscuous, a bit like her new husband in fact. The marriage ended in 1846 when Brudenell left his wife for another woman.

What was the Popgun Plot?

The Popgun Plot wasn't really a plot at all. Allegedly it was a dastardly plan to assassinate King George III by firing a poisoned dart at him from the pit of a theatre during a performance although there's no real evidence that anything like this was ever planned by anyone. What the plot did do was to throw into the public spotlight the members of the London Corresponding Society, a radical political group who promoted civil rights and whom the government suspected of subversion.

In fact the Society was really quite respectable and the spies that the government infiltrated into its midst – which wasn't terribly difficult; you just had to pay a penny a week to join – were forced to create plots in order to discredit it. In May 1794, the 'discovery' of the Popgun Plot brought accusations of high treason against thirteen members of the Society. Other members were summoned to appear under oath before the Privy Council, including James Parkinson, the doctor who first described Parkinson's disease. Of them all, only three were ever brought to trial and all three were, not surprisingly, acquitted as there was no evidence. The plot that wasn't had served its purpose, however, and the fear of prosecution kept new members away. Finally in 1799 the Society was banned altogether.

17

Unlucky

Some folk want their luck buttered.

Thomas Hardy, *The Mayor of Casterbridge* (1886), chapter 13

What was the Ball of the Burning Men?

This unfortunate incident was definitely not the sort of party you'd want to get invited to.

In the first week of 1393 the French court decided to celebrate the forthcoming third marriage of one of the queen's ladies-in-waiting with a party. As part of the festivities, the king, Charles VI, known rather worryingly to history as Charles the Mad (see pages 100–1), decided that he and a few friends would dress up as wild men, chain themselves together and dance around. Keen to look the part, the king ordered costumes made of linen soaked in pitch on to which were stuck strands of frayed hemp, making them look appropriately hairy and wild. It was also pointed out that they bore a striking resemblance to unlit candles and so all naked flames were banned from the event.

It seems, however, that no one had mentioned this to the king's brother, Louis, Duc d'Orléans, who appeared during the revels at the Hôtel St Pol with a lighted torch. Sadly the inevitable happened. One of the dancing wild men strayed too close to the torch and promptly burst into flames. As he careered around trying to put himself out, he soon set light to other dancers and pandemonium ensued. At this point the heroic Duchesse de Berri, who was only fourteen at the time, came to the fore. She recognised King Charles and hid him under her skirts, thus protecting him from the flames. The others were not so lucky. The combination of pitch and hemp burnt furiously and whilst one dancer managed to save himself by jumping into a barrel of water, the Comte de Joigny burnt to death on the spot. Yvain de Foix and Aimery Poitiers died of their burns two days later and Huguet de Guisay, who was blamed for coming up with the whole silly idea, followed them to the grave the following day. The event went down in history as the Bal des Ardents – the 'Ball of the Burning Men'.

The Interesting Bits

How did a dinner-party aside lead to a resignation?

Dinner parties can be social minefields as one of Britain's most able politicians found when an off-the-cuff comment at one brought about his fall from grace.

Richard Haldane, Viscount Haldane, had already had a distinguished career by the time war broke out. Having been born and raised in Scotland, he had studied at Edinburgh and Göttingen universities before reading Law in London. As a liberal imperialist he was a member of the Coefficients Dining Club, which brought together social reformers, including the poet Henry Newbolt (who had written his famous 'Vitae Lampada' after the attempt to rescue Gordon from the Mahdi), the philosopher Bertrand Russell and H. G. Wells. Lord Haldane had been a prominent MP, helped to found the London School of Economics, been Secretary of State for War and Chancellor of Bristol University, as well as overseeing the founding the British Expeditionary Force, the Imperial General Staff, the Officer Training Corps and the Territorial Army.

In April 1913, at a dinner party held by Mrs Humphry Ward to introduce him to some German professors, Lord Haldane had casually mentioned that he thought of the classroom in Göttingen where the philosopher Rudolph Lötze had taught him, as his 'spiritual home'. At the outbreak of war, Professor Oncken of Heidelberg skewed this rather, claiming that Lord Haldane had said that Germany was his spiritual home – which would be an odd thing for a Scot to say who had spent so much of his life preparing his country for war with Germany. In the jingoistic atmosphere of the early days of the war, some parts of the press seized on this, plus the fact that Lord Haldane spoke fluent German, to claim that he was a German sympathiser. Haldane was promptly dropped from Asquith's 1915 coalition government.

You can't keep a good man down, however, and despite this he went on to found the British Institute of Adult Education, secure Birkbeck College's admission to the University of London, and become Chancellor of St Andrews University, whilst still finding time to publish a book on the philosophical implications of Einstein's theory of relativity. In 1924 he also returned to his old job as Lord Chancellor, this time for the first Labour government. As the only member of that cabinet with any previous cabinet experience, he used his advantage to tell them that smoking was allowed in cabinet meetings (which it hadn't been), allowing him to smoke during them.

Who was Tumbledown Dick?

'Tumbledown' isn't the sort of title anyone would really want for themselves unless they were a clown but that's precisely what a number of Richard Cromwell's contemporaries thought he was.

As the son of the Lord Protector Oliver Cromwell, or Oliver ap Robert as he should properly be known (see page 20), Dick was always in a tricky position. Despite his father's protestations that England was a Commonwealth, everyone knew that it was largely run by Cromwell himself who was a king in all but name. Indeed, the constitution required that Oliver nominate a successor and, under somewhat dubious circumstances, that successor proved to be Dick.

He immediately inherited a number of problems. The country was heavily in debt and parliament was refusing to grant new taxes, telling the Protector to reduce costs. The army, however, which thought that it was running the show, needed more money and told Dick to raise more taxes to pay them. With parliament pulling one way and the army the other, it would have been a difficult situation even for a master politician but, as his father had noted before, Dick wasn't that. Eventually the army, fearing that its budget was about to be cut, ordered him to dissolve parliament. When he refused, the army mustered in St James to help him change his mind.

Refusing to leave Whitehall for fear of arrest as a debtor (and possibly under military house arrest anyway), Dick dissolved the old parliament and re-established the Rump Parliament. This was a clever move as it granted him a pension and paid off his debts in return for his resignation as Lord Protector. In July 1659,

Tumbledown Dick left Whitehall to return to his country house at Hursley in Hampshire before fleeing to France. Around 1681, with the monarchy well and truly re-established, he finally returned to England and lived out his days in Finchley, dying there in 1712.

Who has the record for the shortest reign?

Dom Luis of Portugal's is perhaps one of the unhappier entries in the book of Royal records. Luis's father, King Carlos I, had come to the throne of Portugal in 1889 but his reign was marked by social unrest. His extramarital affairs and financial extravagance made him unpopular, particularly as the country twice went bankrupt under his reign, as did his appointment of an authoritarian government. On 1 February 1908 as the royal family were returning to the palace in Lisbon, shots were fired at their carriage as it passed through Terreiro do Paço Square. Carlos was hit and died instantly, leaving his heir Luis Felipé as king. Unfortunately he had been mortally wounded too and, after reigning, uncrowned, for just twenty minutes, he also died.

Even Luis Felipé's single claim to fame is disputed. Following the 'July Revolution' of 1830 in France, Charles X was forced to abdicate by a delegation of the people sent to the Tuileries. At the moment that he signed the abdication document, his heir, Louis Antoine, became King Louis XIX. Louis XIX, however, was not at all sure that he wanted to be king and an extraordinary scene ensued, in which the former King Charles sat crying in the corner whilst Louis XIX's wife desperately tried to persuade her husband to accept the throne. After twenty minutes Louis tired of this drama and abdicated as well.

How did King Baldwin of Jerusalem pay off his crusader knights?

During the late eleventh century, Sicily had become a Norman kingdom, taken from the Muslim rulers by the sons of the crusader,

Tancred. Whilst one son continued to make inroads into southern Italy – where the pope had granted him all the land he could conquer – the other remained to rule Sicily. On his death in 1101, the kingdom fell to his son Roger II. As he was still a child, the country was governed on his behalf by his father's third wife, Adelaide.

Sicily was a rich province at the time, having been well governed by its previous Muslim rulers, many of whom were kept on after the Norman conquest to run the country. The royal family of Sicily presided over the most ethnically diverse and religiously tolerant kingdom in mediaeval Europe, which welcomed not only Orthodox and Roman Catholics but Muslim and Jewish scholars and artists as well. By the standards of the late eleventh century there really wasn't anywhere more civilised to be. But as Roger II grew up, it became clear to his mother that her rule of the island was soon to come to an end and so she began looking for another husband.

Of the available candidates perhaps the least likely and certainly the least desirable was Baldwin, King of Jerusalem. Jerusalem had been taken from the Muslims during the Crusade but it was surrounded by Muslim kingdoms, making its defence very expensive. Furthermore, the city was still full of crusader knights who, without pay or booty, were just as likely to turn against Baldwin as they were against Islam. At this, Baldwin's most awkward moment, Adelaide came on to the scene.

Obviously unaware of Baldwin's reputation or financial situation, she agreed to marry him and set off from Sicily in 1113 with a resplendent fleet of ships. Onlookers were amazed at the gold- and silver-plated prow of her galley, the carpets of gold thread, and the rest of her dazzling dowry, which had cost Sicily a substantial proportion of its wealth. When Adelaide arrived in Jerusalem she was quickly married to Baldwin, who immediately began to distribute her dowry to pay off his debtors. What she could not realise was that her use to Baldwin would last only as long as her dowry. In 1117, Baldwin fell ill and announced that he believed

his sickness was caused by the fact that his marriage was biga-
mous. All the time that Adelaide had been in Jerusalem, so had
Baldwin's Armenian wife Arda, whom he had placed in a nunnery
when the opportunity arose to get his hands on Adelaide's money
– although he claimed that he had put her away because she had
been raped by pirates. Apparently now filled with repentance, he
was granted an annulment and Adelaide was packed off back to
her son's court in Sicily, impoverished, unmarried and financially
undesirable.

Who gave his name to nationalistic zealotry?

Nicholas Chauvin is remembered today for the one word that he
brought to the English language – chauvinism. Separating the real
Chauvin from the mythical is no easy matter but he appears in
fact to have been a rather brave soldier in the First Army of the
French Republic and then latterly in Napoleon's Grande Armée.
Having enlisted at eighteen, he fought fervently for the new France,
being wounded seventeen times and becoming badly disfigured in
the process. Indeed, so valiant was Chauvin that Napoleon himself
awarded him a pension – along with a nice sword. After the fall
of Napoleon, however, a wave of disenchantment swept over
France. Men like Chauvin, who had shown such idealism and
unswerving loyalty, were ridiculed and Chauvin himself was cruelly
caricatured in plays as a blindly nationalistic fool. His largely
invented exploits and opinions, as disseminated in these plays, led
to the coining of the word chauvinism to describe unthinking
nationalistic zeal.

What happened to Good King Wenceslas?

Good King Wenceslas, for all his trudging through the snow with
ready meals for hungry peasants, ended up being murdered by his
own brother.

When Wenceslas, a Christian prince in the Bohemian royal

household, reached the age of thirteen, his father died and he came under the influence of his Christian grandmother, St Ludmila. She did her best to keep the young duke away from his mother, Drahomíra, who happened to be a pagan, as were many of the nobles in the country. The family tensions finally came to a head when Drahomíra had her mother-in-law strangled in 921 and became Regent for her son.

Her attempts to convert Wenceslas back to the 'old faith' seem to have failed, however, and when he was old enough to take charge of Bohemia for himself he promptly exiled his mother and went about converting his country to Christianity. This was easier said than done. In the first place Bohemia had been happily pagan for a long time and a lot of people didn't really see the benefits of converting. More worryingly for the nobles, Wenceslas was allying himself with the Holy Roman Empire as part of his evangelising plan and many thought that this would lead to Bohemia's absorption into the empire, which was highly likely.

So the pagan Bohemians cast around for an alternative leader and luckily found one close to home in the form of Wenceslas's own brother, Boleslav, who happened to be a pagan too. Now all they had to do was get rid of Wenceslas. By all accounts Boleslav was a violent and stormy individual. It is said that when his request to build a stone castle at the confluence of two rivers was turned down on the grounds that castles should be built only of wood, he decapitated the elder who voiced this opposition with one stroke of his sword – making one of the bloodier planning committee meetings in history.

Boleslav, aware that it would be difficult to remove Wenceslas whilst he remained in Prague, decided to lure him to his own residence at Stara Boleslav. At the feast of Cosmas and Damian, Boleslav invited Wenceslas to a celebration on the pretext of dedicating the church in his castle to the two saints. Wenceslas, aware of the plan, nevertheless went to the banquet.

At this point the biographies of Wenceslas head into the realms of hagiography, adding a lot of improbable and colourful details.

As the banquet progressed, the Boleslav faction became more agitated and three times rose to attack Wenceslas, only to sit down again. The biographer Christian says that this was the work of God who wished to preserve the king until the following day, which was not at that time dedicated to a saint, providing a useful vacancy.

Foiled in their initial plan, the conspirators resolved to assassinate Wenceslas the following morning on his way to church. As he approached the church, the priest locked the door against him and Wenceslas was surrounded by Boleslav and his men. The king is then said to have embraced his brother, saying, 'May Christ invite thee to His eternal feast as thou hast so generously entertained me and my friends.' Boleslav replied by drawing his sword and saying, '*Yesterday I served thee as I could, today behold how brother serves brother.*' With this he struck a blow at the king's head, but, according to Christian, the sword glanced off. Boleslav was terrified but struck again, only to see Wenceslas catch the sword in his bare hand, saying, '*Thou dost ill to strike me!*' This either says something about the quality of Boleslav's sword or the imagination of Wenceslas's biographer. Wenceslas then took the sword and threw it at his brother's feet, saying, '*Man, condemned by thine own judgment seest thou not that I could crush thee like an insect? But the right hand of the servant of God may not be stained with the blood of a brother.*' He then picked up the sword and returned it to his brother before hastening towards the church. Boleslav, however, pursued him and, aided by his friends, cut Wenceslas down at the door of the church.

So is this all true? Well, Boleslav has gone down in history as 'Boleslav the Cruel' but there's not much evidence that he reintroduced paganism to Bohemia. Indeed, his son was known as 'Boleslav the Pious' and his daughter became a nun. He does seem likely to have been the murderer of Wenceslas, however, and his son, who was born on the night Wenceslas died, had the nickname 'Stratchkvas', meaning 'dreadful feast', which seems to implicate Dad. In truth the murder probably had much more to do with Wenceslas's pro-Holy Roman attitude, which was making Bohemia just another province of the empire and which Boleslav wanted to resist. Certainly the first thing Boleslav did after his brother's death was go to war with the empire. Wenceslas, the duke who threatened to destroy Bohemian identity, rather ironically became the patron saint of his people.

Why might it be dangerous to drink weak beer?

Thomas Thetcher, according to his tombstone outside Winchester Cathedral, made the fatal mistake of drinking beer that wasn't strong enough on a hot day. All that we know about Thomas comes from his tombstone, which has been lovingly preserved and, where necessary, replaced by generations of Hampshire Grenadiers – the regiment to which Thomas belonged. The stone begins with the basic facts of the case:

> IN MEMORY OF THOMAS THETCHER
> A GRENADIER IN THE NORTH REGIMENT
> OF HANTS MILITIA, WHO DIED OF A
> VIOLENT FEVER CONTRACTED BY DRINKING
> SMALL BEER WHEN HOT ON THE 12TH MAY 1764
> AGED 26 YEARS . . .

Small beer was a common drink throughout the mediaeval period and well into the nineteenth century, as the boiling of the water used to make it and the presence of a low level of alcohol in it killed bacteria and generally made it much safer than water. Just how small beer killed Thomas is uncertain although a series of letters in 1999 to the distinguished *New England Journal of Medicine* suggested 'deglutition syncope', a condition where drinking cold liquids can lead to fainting.

Thomas's fellow soldiers were less interested in the exact cause and more in the lessons to be drawn from it. The tombstone goes on: *'In grateful remembrance of whose universal good will towards his Comrades, this Stone is placed here at their expense, as a small testimony of their regard and concern.*' Then it breaks into verse:

> Here sleeps in Peace a Hampshire Grenadier
> Who caught his death by drinking cold small beer
> Soldiers be wise from his untimely fall
> And when ye're hot drink strong or not at all.

Having turned the story of Thomas from a warning against drink to an exhortation to drink something stronger, the Hampshire Grenadiers have been keen to preserve their monument, adding other suitable lines as and when necessary. The gravestone continues with an affectionate rededication:

> THIS MEMORIAL BEING DECAY'D WAS RESTOR'D BY THE
> OFFICERS OF THE GARRISON A.D. 1781.

> AN HONEST SOLDIER NEVER IS FORGOT
> WHETHER HE DIE BY MUSKET OR BY POT.

Since then the North Hampshire Militia and the Royal Hampshire Regiment have both taken their turns in replacing the stone when it has decayed. Today an annual service is still held at the graveside.

What made William the Miserable so unhappy?

William was the son of Robert, Duke of Normandy, and grandson of the explosive William the Conqueror (see pages 217–19) and should therefore have been a pretty powerful figure in twelfth-century European politics. Although he should have inherited the wealthy duchy of Normandy, this was sequestered by his uncle, Henry I, who captured and imprisoned Robert in 1106. Robert was kept in such great luxury that he rather took to it and made no attempt to escape, leaving his son to wander around Europe. William made several attempts to regain his duchy but they all failed and for twenty years he was homeless. Eventually he became engaged to the daughter of the Count of Anjou, which meant that he could look forward to a sizeable dowry and inheritance from the match, but the marriage was blocked at the last minute by dear old Uncle Henry.

Then, in 1128, the Count of Flanders died without an heir and William managed to persuade the French king to back his somewhat tenuous claim to the title. The French king gave William an army and he marched to Flanders. In the meantime, the nobles of Flanders had already chosen a new count, Thierry of Alsace. The two sides clashed at Thielt where, in a brilliant manoeuvre, William outflanked and defeated Thierry, which was about the only good piece of fortune in his entire life. William now ruled Flanders and soon heard that the nobles of Normandy had asked for him as their duke (rather than Matilda, Henry's daughter). William immediately made plans to take up the dukedom, but on his way came upon a small skirmishing party of Uncle Henry's troops. William received a cut in the fight, which turned septic, and he died in agony five days later.

18

How Did That Happen?

It happened one day, about noon . . .

Daniel Defoe, *Robinson Crusoe* (1719)

How was an island won by drug dealing?

The Opium Wars fought between the British and Chinese are certainly not Britain's proudest moment. These days we might assume that they were an attempt by Britain to stop the spread of opium use in the empire but in fact the exact reverse was true.

During the first half of the nineteenth century, trade between Britain and China was difficult but lucrative. As the Qing dynasty allowed trade only through state-appointed monopolies in Canton, it wasn't worth the British selling huge quantities of cheap goods there as they did in India. Instead, they needed high-value trade so they sold silver to China and the Chinese sold tea to the British. But to keep up the supply of silver, Britain had to buy the metal in Europe, which was expensive, so the British cast around for another commodity to sell. That was where opium came in. Opium was highly addictive and, although expensive, its growing was subsidised by the British in India, who exported the whole crop to China, despite a nominal ban on the drug that had been in place since 1729.

Between 1821 and 1837, exports increased fivefold and the Qing dynasty became alarmed, not only at the flow of silver now going the 'wrong way' to pay for the opium, but also by the fact that they had 2 million addicts. Not surprisingly the Chinese petitioned the British to stop this appalling trade and initially it looked as if that would be that.

Then things got complicated. Some British sailors killed a Chinese man near Kowloon and the Chinese authorities demanded that they be handed over for trial. They also demanded that all traders henceforth sign a bond, on pain of death, promising not to smuggle opium and to be subject to Chinese law. The British refused and blockaded trade with China. War kicked off when the Chinese navy attempted to protect a British ship that wanted to trade with China and was happy to sign the 'no opium bond'. This incensed the British government, the fleet engaged and many Chinese ships were lost. Eventually the Chinese were forced to sign the Treaty of Nanking, which opened more ports to British ships and forced the Qing dynasty to pay reparations for the cost of the war as well as the opium losses. Hong Kong was also ceded to the British into the bargain. Even then the British weren't really satisfied and in 1856, following a nasty incident with an insult offered to a flag, they had another go in the Second Opium War (see pages 202–3).

Why do Americans count like pirates?

After the Revolutionary War, the young USA found itself chronically short of currency and was forced to reintroduce the Spanish pillar dollar as legal tender. The pillar dollar was a silver coin whose bullion value was eight reals. As the coin was worth its weight in silver, if anyone wanted a smaller denomination, such as one real, they simply cut the coin into eight pieces – hence the favourite term of pirates and their parrots, 'pieces of eight'. In the USA these pieces were known as bits and hence 'two bits', or two eighths of a dollar, was the equivalent of a quarter-dollar, so a quarter became known, as it still is, as two bits. The pillar dollar remained legal tender in the USA until 1857 and the New York Stock Exchange continued to value stocks in eighths of a dollar (effectively pieces of eight) until 1997.

Why did a war lead to the renaming of a Shakespeare play?

It was 1917 and the British were not overly popular with the bullet-dodging Kaiser (see pages 213–14), due to the ongoing First World War. When he heard that the British royal family intended to change its name from the rather German-sounding 'Saxe-Coburg-Gotha' to 'Windsor' in a bid to distance themselves from their German ancestry, the Kaiser was apoplectic. But what could he do? He could hardly start a war – he'd already done that – so he decided to take his revenge via that icon of Britishness, William Shakespeare. Leafing through the playwright's collected works, he came across the perfect candidate, the 1602 comedy *The Merry Wives of Windsor*. The Kaiser announced forthwith that he was immediately commissioning a new play: *The Merry Wives of Saxe-Coburg-Gotha*.

How did Erik Bloodaxe get his name?

Many early Scandinavian leaders took (or were given) epithets that said something about who they were, from the fairly obvious 'Gorm the Old' to the more puzzling 'Ivarr the Boneless'. Erik falls comfortably into the first category.

On the death of their father Harald Finehair, the first king of Norway, his sons quickly set about trying to consolidate their own positions by murdering each other. The first victim was Bjørn the Seaman, who was surrounded whilst having a drink at Tønsberg by Erik and his men. According to Harald Harfager's saga, Bjørn and his friends put up a good fight but in the end Erik killed him, which didn't make Erik too popular in that part of the country. Olaf, another (half) brother, then tried to make himself king of eastern Norway, supported by another (half) brother, Sigrød, which rather annoyed Erik. The three men met in battle just outside Tønsberg where Erik notched up another two dead brothers and gained the Latin title 'brother-slayer' or the rather more visual Viking title 'bloodaxe'. Unfortunately for Erik, his run of fratricidal luck was about to run out. In 933 the youngest brother, Haakon, returned from England and ousted Erik, who was forced to flee to Northumbria where he became king with his capital at Jorvik (York). He died in battle, as someone called Bloodaxe probably should, at Stainmoor in 954. Haakon meanwhile became king of all Norway and received the much nicer title, 'Haakon the Good'.

Why did Joan of Arc fight the English?

At the time of Joan of Arc's campaign, France was legally a possession of the descendants of Henry V of England, as laid out in the Treaty of Troyes, which had been signed by the French king, Charles VI (see pages 100–1), following the defeat of his army at Agincourt. In the treaty Charles had declared his son illegitimate (which was quite likely) and made the children of his son-in-law, Henry V, his heirs – so what did Joan have to complain about? The simple reason was that when Charles had signed the document, he was completely mad.

The first attack of the schizophrenia from which Charles would suffer for the rest of his life did not occur until 1392, during a campaign against the man who had attempted to assassinate one of his councillors. On 5 August, a very sultry summer's day, the king and his entourage were riding towards the Breton borders. Charles, who had drunk a great deal of wine, was wearing a thick velvet jacket and a velvet hat, which in itself was bizarre enough. His brother and uncles were with him but at a distance as the road was very dusty.

When the group reached the edge of the forest of Le Mans, a roughly dressed man stepped out from behind a tree and seized the bridle of the king's horse, shouting, 'Ride no further, noble king! Turn back! You are destroyed!' The king's attendants forced the man to release the bridle but strangely enough he was not arrested, perhaps because they simply assumed him to be deranged.

Later that day, as the cavalcade was emerging from the forest into the open plain, one of the king's pages, drowsy with the heat, dropped the king's lance, which fell on to his neighbour's steel helmet with a clatter. Charles was startled by the sound and drew his sword, shouting, 'Forward against the traitors! They wish to deliver me to the enemy!' He then struck out at all those around him, killing four or five of his own knights, including the Chevalier de Polignac. The Duke of Burgundy shouted, 'My God, the king is out of his mind! Hold him, someone!' Charles was eventually disarmed and taken down from his horse. He lay prostrate on the ground, speechless, his eyes rolling wildly from side to side. Eventually he was placed on an ox-cart and taken back to Le Mans.

This incident marked the beginning of a series of episodes of madness in which the king would variously forget who he and his family and friends were, and he spent his nights running through his palaces howling like a wolf. Towards the end of his life he also became delusional, believing that he was made of glass and might shatter if touched. As a result many in France, including Joan of Arc, believed that his signature on the Treaty of Troyes wasn't worth the paper it was written on and a campaign began to restore the French monarchy to a French ruler.

Why did Lady Godiva get her kit off?

Lady Godiva, or Godgifu to give her her Anglo-Saxon name, was a real historical character, although stories about her dress sense have been wildly exaggerated in later centuries. She was the wife of Earl Leofric of Mercia, a successful and by all accounts rather pious noble who managed to steer a political path through the reigns of Cnut, Harold Harefoot, Harthacnut and Edward the Confessor – something that would impress you if you'd met any of them. According to the legend, however, he was a harsh land-lord who had inflicted heavy taxes upon the people of Coventry, much to the disgust of his wife. In the earliest version of the tale, recorded by Roger of Wendover around the late twelfth or early thirteenth centuries, Leofric, exasperated by Godiva's nagging, eventually agreed to lift the taxes if she would ride naked through the market in Coventry in front of all the citizens. He clearly thought that she would never do something so humiliating but she, with a flourish, let down her floor-length hair, which he obviously hadn't noticed she'd grown but which handily covered her modesty. She then mounted her horse and, accompanied by two knights, rode through Coventry in front of all and sundry, none of whom got a glimpse of anything more saucy than a bit of leg. Leofric therefore kept his word and waived the taxes. So it would be fair to say that Godiva rode through Coventry naked for tax reasons.

In still later versions of the story, Godiva protected her modesty by issuing a decree that everyone in Coventry should stay indoors whilst she rode through town so that no one would see her. By the seventeenth century this story had received a new wrinkle when one inhabitant, Thomas by name, is said to have decided to bore a hole in the shutters of his house so that he could glimpse the lovely Godiva as she rode past. Unfortunately for Thomas, as she rode into view he was struck blind, and at that moment the legend of 'Peeping Tom' was born.

None of this actually bears much relation to the real Godiva, though. Coventry was not subject to particularly harsh or arbitrary taxes more than anywhere else and the town was probably a personal possession of Godiva's rather than Leofric's (important Saxon women held land in their own right). Indeed, Godiva is one of only a handful of Anglo-Saxon landowners who managed to hold on to their property after the Norman conquest. Nor would it have been that impressive to ride through the city naked as Coventry was really more of a hamlet at the time. Indeed, in the Domesday survey of 1086, only sixty-nine families are recorded as living there, and amongst their houses there was nowhere suitable for Leofric and Godiva to have being staying whilst they had the famous argument anyway. In truth, Godiva and her husband were pious benefactors of the Church and no harsher landlords than any other. All early sources agree that Godiva was a generous and good woman and none mentions the naked ride, which you might think they would have done if it had happened. If there is a grain of truth in the Godiva story, it is perhaps that she, as the owner of Coventry, rode through the village as a penitent (i.e. in plain dress) as part of a benefaction to the monastery there.

How was the Unknown Soldier chosen?

The story of how an unknown soldier could become a country's greatest hero began in 1920 in the fields of France and Belgium.

The First World War had been unlike any before it. Four years of mechanised slaughter had left 7.5 million soldiers dead. Some had been identified and buried, many were mutilated beyond recognition, whilst others simply sank for ever into the suffocating mud of the trenches.

Each year the farmers who tilled the former battle lines reaped a gruesome harvest – a sombre reminder of the thousands more who would never be found.

As a mark of respect for these thousands of lost souls, a strange and secret ceremony was decided upon. The unmarked remains of four British soldiers were exhumed – one from each of the four great battlefields. Draped in Union flags, the four anonymous bodies were set before a blindfolded army officer. Whichever body that officer pointed to would be the Unknown Soldier.

Placed in an oak coffin, these humble remains were sent back to a hero's welcome in Britain and a state funeral in Westminster Abbey with full military honours. It was a ceremony for more than the man who lay within; rather, it was one for all those whose names or resting places might never be known.

In the seven days that this unknown soldier lay in state, over 1 million people came to pay their respects.

Who introduced the 'economy coffin'?

The Habsburg emperor Joseph II of Austria was not the luckiest of monarchs, nor, come to think of it, was his sister, Marie Antoinette. Unlike Marie, however, Joseph was a bit of a reformer and is often classed as one of the 'enlightened despots'. This simply means that although he didn't have only his own interests at heart, he still imposed his ideas on other people regardless. Whilst those ideas were often progressive and logical, he took little account of the customs and traditions of his subjects and hence most of his good ideas came to nothing. Even his own self-penned epitaph read, '*Here Lies Joseph Who Was Unfortunate in All His Undertakings.*'

And Joseph had a lot of undertakings. In fact, by the end of his ten-year reign he'd issued over 6,000 decrees, which included such enlightened acts as abolishing serfdom (which he saw as unproductive and inhumane), introducing free hospital treatment for paupers, and granting toleration to Protestants. Mixed in with these laudable moves, however, were some less popular ones, including the introduction of German as the universal language of the empire, despite the fact that a large proportion of his people didn't speak it. Other laws of his were considered simply meddling. In the interests of hygiene, Joseph ordered that peasants could not drink spring water without first adding vinegar, nor could they bathe in the Danube under any circumstances. Gingerbread was banned on the grounds that it was bad for the digestion. Girls brought up in state institutions were forbidden to wear corsets in case it damaged their potential to bear children, whilst failed suicides were put in lunatic asylums for having recklessly disregarded their duty to the state to stay alive. Never a superstitious man, he downgraded witchcraft trials to the same status as fraud, and abolished state censorship for everything except pornography, aggressive atheism and superstitious writings. All of this was generally popular, but he also banned relics, pilgrimages and the wearing of lucky charms, prohibitions that in largely Catholic dominions were greatly resisted.

One of the few cases where Joseph was actually forced into the retraction of a policy, however, was in his introduction of economy coffins. In 1784, he came to the conclusion that coffins were a ludicrous luxury that further impoverished the poor. His thinking was perfectly sound at one level – coffins were not only expensive to make but also, frankly, a waste of money and good wood as they were buried as soon as they were used. So Joseph replaced them with a reusable 'economy model' with a trapdoor at one end. The coffin bore the occupant to the grave where the trapdoor opened and the body, wrapped in a sack, was deposited in the ground. The coffin itself could then be used again. Joseph's people didn't share his utilitarian principles and there were riots on the streets of Vienna where the burial of the dead in sacks was considered an outrageous insult to the departed. Joseph was eventually forced into repealing the law and is himself buried in a normal coffin in the imperial crypt in Vienna, although he chose one made of copper as it was cheaper than the more usual bronze.

How did Calamity Jane get her name?

Martha Jane Burke (née Canary) was better known in her day as Calamity Jane. Sorting out the biographical details of her life is tricky as she was rather prone to exaggeration in her own memoirs. We know that she was born in 1855 in Missouri and that both her parents had died by the time she was twelve. In 1870 she signed on as a US army scout (although it is unclear whether she actually enlisted in the army) and over the next six years she was involved in a number of campaigns in the Indian Wars. During this time she claimed that she was under Custer's command but this seems unlikely.

It was during this period that she got her nickname 'Calamity', although there are two versions of how this came about. She claims in her *Life and Adventures of Calamity Jane* that, during the splendidly named Nursey Pursey Indian Outbreak, her unit was ambushed and her commander, Captain Egan, shot. She turned to see him reeling in the saddle and, galloping back, caught him, swung him on to her horse and rode the two of them to the safety of the nearest fort. When Captain Egan recovered, he supposedly christened her Calamity, presumably for saving him from one. The alternative story, prevalent even during her lifetime, was that she got the name due to her repeated warnings that a calamity would befall anyone who crossed her.

In 1876, Calamity ended up in the gold-strike town of Deadwood, South Dakota, where she met Wild Bill Hickok whom she later claimed she had married and had borne a daughter. In truth Wild Bill was shot dead in a saloon not long after they met and was at the time newly and happily married, so this is fairly improbable. Being associated with Wild Bill never hurt the reputation of a frontierswoman, however, particularly one who was already becoming the focus of early magazine stories about 'how the West was won'. In 1891, Calamity did marry but not happily and five years later she began touring with the new 'Wild West' shows. Her erratic behaviour and alcoholism did not endear her to show managers and eventually she returned to Deadwood, where she died in poverty in 1903. Her last wish was granted and she was buried next to Wild Bill Hickok.

Who lost her husband because of a forged stamp?

Mary Robinson was the fifteen-year-old daughter of the innkeeper of the Fish Hotel at Buttermere when she was catapulted to fame after appearing in the book *A Fortnight's Ramble in the Lakes in Westmorland, Lancashire and Cumberland* (1792), in which Joseph Palmer described her as the epitome of beauty:

> On our going into it the girl flew away as swift as a mountain sheep, and it was not till our return from Scale Force that we could say that we first saw her. She brought in part of our dinner and seemed to be about fifteen. Her hair was thick and long, of a dark brown, and though unadorned with ringlets did not seem to want them; her face was a fine oval, with full eyes, and lips as red as vermillion, her cheeks had more of the lily than the rose.

She became something of an icon for Thomas De Quincey and Samuel Taylor Coleridge as a representation of innocent beauty. She also came to the attention of John Hatfield. He was in the Lakes going about his usual business, which was swindling. Posing as Colonel Alexander Hope MP, brother of the Earl of Hopetoun, he was in the process of persuading a rich heiress to marry him when he met Mary. Although she was considerably less wealthy, he seems to have become besotted with her so he abandoned his fraudulent scheme and persuaded Mary to marry him. The two were wed at Lorton church on 2 October 1802 and, thanks to the

Beauty of Buttermere's fame, the event made it into the London papers, courtesy of Coleridge who, as their 'Keswick correspondent', described the event for the London *Sun*.

At this point things began to unravel for Colonel Alexander Hope MP. The *Sun* discovered that he was, in fact, an undischarged bankrupt who was already married to a woman in Tiverton and who had run up numerous fraudulent debts in the Lake District, whilst the real Colonel Hope was actually in Vienna.

At this point John Hatfield did what any swindler would and promptly ran away, first to Ravenglass, where he hid on a sloop, and then to Wales via Chester. Here, however, the Bow Street Runners caught up with him, and he was arrested and taken to London. Magistrates there concluded that he had sealed and franked letters in the name of an MP and hence avoided paying postage. This was forgery, a capital offence, and he was sent to Carlisle to be tried. After an eight-hour trial he was found guilty and sentenced to death by hanging.

Mary Robinson fared better. William Wordsworth was greatly touched by the case and wrote in his *The Prelude* (Book 7):

> And how, unfaithful to a virtuous wife
> Deserted and deceived, the spoiler came,
> And woo'd the artless daughter of the hills
> And wedded her, in cruel mockery
> Of love and marriage bonds . . .

She later married a local farmer, initially taking over the running of the Fish Hotel before moving to Caldbeck, where she died around 1837.

Who used a lot of hot air to escape a siege?

The siege of Paris marked the end-game for France in the Franco-Prussian War when Prussian forces surrounded the capital between September 1870 and January 1871, following their capture of Napoleon III. With no rail or road routes open, communication with the outside world appeared impossible and the Parisians' fate seemed sealed, until a group of aeronauts approached the Post Office with a plan. They suggested that the way out of Paris was by balloon. The French already had a long history of balloon flight; indeed, the first manned balloon flight took to the skies of Paris in 1783. Although it was slow and no one could guarantee where one might end up, it was a way of passing over the Prussian troops who hadn't yet thought up any form of anti-aircraft weapon. In fact, the French Minister of the Interior, Léon Gambetta, had already made perhaps the slowest getaway in history when he fled Paris in October in the balloon *Armand-Barbès*, landing at Tours.

The Post Office liked the idea and, on 23 September, Jules Durouf floated out over enemy lines in his balloon *La Neptune*, carrying the city's mail. As he drifted over the bewildered Prussians, he took the opportunity to drop his visiting cards on them and just over three hours later he landed safely behind their lines. Return mail proved a little trickier, however, as the balloon's direction depended entirely on the wind, and unless the wind was blowing in the direction of Paris (and kept doing so), the mail could end up anywhere. The solution found was to send out carrier pigeons in the balloons, which would then fly back into the city with the replies.

Soon there was a balloon shortage in the city as none of those that had left had made it back. A flurry of balloon construction took place to feed the desire of Parisians to send news (and themselves, if they could afford it) out of their besieged capital. Combined with a lack of experienced pilots, this made for some dangerous journeys. Two flights disappeared completely and many others landed actually in the Prussian lines. One overshot and ended up 800 miles away in Norway.

By the end of the siege, sixty-six balloons had escaped from Paris, carrying 2 million letters, 102 people, over 500 homing pigeons and 5 dogs that were supposed to take dispatches back to Paris, like the pigeons, but which never arrived.

19

Who?

'Whom are you?' he asked, for he had attended business college.

George Ade, 'The Steel Box', in the *Chicago Record*, 16 March 1898

Who relieved Khartoum?

Khartoum was relieved thanks to the good offices of a travel agent. After General Gordon got himself into a tight corner in Khartoum during the Mahdist uprising of 1883–5, the British government, under intense pressure from the press, were finally forced to consider military options for getting him out. The problem was that Gordon and his men were in the middle of the Sudan, besieged on all sides by around 50,000 men. The man put in charge of the relief, Sir Garnet Wolseley, had to work out how to get his forces from Alexandria on Egypt's Mediterranean coast, where they had disembarked, all the way up the Nile to Khartoum, over a thousand miles to the south. Wolseley had small boats to navigate the many cataracts but these needed to be towed for the greater part of their journey as his Canadian pioneers could hardly be expected to paddle them the whole way.

Many would have waited for specialist steamers to be brought but Wolseley was in a hurry so he did what any impatient tourist in Egypt would do. He went to the offices of Thomas Cook and arranged to charter holiday boats for his army as far south as was possible. Thomas Cook & Sons – then in the hands of John Mason Cook, the founder's son who was known as 'the second greatest man in Egypt' – eagerly accepted and the expeditionary force was conveyed in flotillas of ninety boats each as far as Sarras. Of course, Thomas Cook still had a tourist business to run so, capitalising on the grand sight of the British army in full battle array gliding gracefully upriver, he sold tickets for tourists to accompany the expedition as far as the first cataract at Aswan. Unfortunately Wolseley's relief force arrived too late to save Gordon but Thomas Cook still did very well out of the deal, charging the British government a staggering £500,000 for the trip, enough to ensure that Thomas Cook would go on to become the first name in world travel.

Why were there 212 fatalities at the first boy scout camp?

There wasn't much dybbing and dobbing at Robert Baden-Powell's first scout camp as the camp in question was in Mafeking and took place during a particularly nasty siege in the Second Boer War. Baden-Powell had been sent to Cape Colony to raise two new regiments to fight the Boers who at this point seemed to be winning their war against the British Empire. He was already a well-known figure thanks to the publication, in book form and in newspaper articles, of his role in the Ashanti and Zulu campaigns. He had also managed a stint in secret intelligence, collecting news from around the Mediterranean whilst disguised as a butterfly collector. But by the time he arrived in Cape Colony in 1899, now a lieutenant-colonel, he had still not made the impression he hoped for. Mafeking would change that.

Baden-Powell met considerable resistance in the Cape and, with the Boers closing in, eventually concluded that the best form of attack was defence. Taking and fortifying the strategically important town of Mafeking, he held it against Boer besiegers with a force of about 2,000, including a unit of boys who served as messengers and orderlies. Outgunned and outnumbered, Baden-Powell was forced to use every trick and stratagem he knew, including ostentatiously laying a field of (fake) mines and getting his troops to act as though they were picking their way through (imaginary) barbed wire to keep the besiegers at bay.

After a siege lasting 217 days, and costing 212 lives amongst Baden-Powell's men, they were relieved by the arrival of a British force that included his own brother, Major Baden Fletcher Smyth Powell (who changed his name by royal licence in 1902 to the even more elaborate Baden Fletcher Smyth Baden-Powell).

As the Boer War had been going badly for the British, the news of Baden-Powell's plucky resistance at Mafeking, and its heroic relief, caused the British press to go wild. Baden-Powell was fêted as a hero and the verb to 'maffick' (to wildly celebrate) briefly entered the English language, at least in the minds of journalists. His famous exploits in keeping the Boers at bay also made his book, *Aids to Scouting for NCOs and Men*, an unexpected best-seller and, following a meeting with the founder of the Boys' Brigade, he agreed to rewrite this book for children. Although there is no evidence that the 'boy scouts' used at Mafeking were directly organised by Baden-Powell, he does seem to have been impressed by their resilience and he mentions them in the first chapter of *Scouting for Boys*. This, too, was a great success and as a result scout groups began spontaneously forming all over the country. Under the guidance of Baden-Powell and his wife, this grew into the international Scouting and Guiding movement which now has over thirty-eight million members.

Baden-Powell is buried near his last home in Kenya. His grave carries the trail sign of a circle with a dot in the middle, meaning, 'I have gone home.'

Which world leader drew the poster for Teddy's Perspiration Powder?

Quite a few world leaders have considered themselves to be great artists too, notably Nero, who toured the festivals of Greece, winning plaudits and laurels with only the help of his innate genius and a heavily armed bodyguard to intimidate the judges. Not all aspiring artists have had it quite so easy, however, particularly one young man hammering on the door of the Vienna Fine Art School in 1907. He took the entrance examination that year but, greatly to his own surprise, was rejected on the grounds that his test drawing was 'unsatisfactory'. He therefore tried again the following year but did not even make the grade to sit the examination. Thus it was that the brilliant career of one young man was smothered before it had even begun.

He spent another five years in Vienna, living hand-to-mouth (as many a great artist has done), although he did get through an inordinate number of cream cakes, and in that time produced by his own reckoning over a thousand watercolours. As few of these sold, he was reduced to painting advertising hoardings for local shopkeepers, including one for Teddy's Perspiration Powder, a jolly image of Santa selling coloured candles, and the magnificent spire of St Stephen's Cathedral rising out of a pile of soap cakes. Eventually he decided to cut his losses and leave the city of his artistic dreams. The First World War was looming and Adolf Hitler was going to enlist. A new career awaited.

Which Hollywood star was kidnapped after his death?

Charlie Chaplin, screen idol of the silent era, finally hung up his hat and cane on Christmas Day 1977 and was laid to rest in his Alpine home at Corsier-sur-Vevey in Switzerland. And there the greatest of silent stories should have ended. It was three months later, however, that his widow Oona received the first of several unusual phone calls.

The man on the end of the line had something that he thought Oona might want. But it wasn't a memento of her husband, a photograph, a letter or a keepsake. The man on the phone was offering to sell her Charlie himself.

Switzerland is a quiet country not used to kidnapping or grave robbing, yet its most famous resident had suffered both. Charlie Chaplin's body had been stolen. Late one night, two unknown persons had broken into the cemetery at Corsier-sur-Vevey, dug up Charlie's body and taken him away. The voice on the phone said that he was near by, but that it would cost $600,000 for Oona to see him again. The caller said he'd ring back – and that was his mistake.

Oona informed the police, a trap was set for the kidnappers and Oona's phone line was tapped. After several more phone calls, the ransom had come down to $250,000 and the police had traced the callers to a phone in Lausanne.

One final phone call and the trap sprang shut. On the line was a Polish car mechanic, aged twenty-four, and his accomplice. After intensive interrogation, the grave-robbers revealed the whereabouts of Charlie's body – in a cornfield in nearby Villeneive. The kidnappers went to prison and Charlie Chaplin was reburied in a steel vault under six feet of concrete to prevent any repeat performances.

Who was 'The Man They Couldn't Hang'?

On the night of 15 November 1884, the cook awoke at The Glen in Babbacombe, Devon, to find her room filling with smoke. Rushing downstairs, she found the battered remains of her employer, Emma Ann Whitehead Keyse, whose clothes had been doused in oil and set alight.

The police took the usual step of assuming that in such cases it was the butler who had done it but, in the absence of a butler, questioned the cook and her half-brother, John Lee, who was acting as Miss Keyse's footman. Lee claimed that he had tried valiantly to put out the fire and was distraught to hear of his mistress's death, crying to the local constable, 'I have lost my best friend.' This was probably not far from the truth as Miss Keyse had taken pity on Lee, a former naval rating with a history of petty theft, and had employed him when few others would.

To the police, however, this smacked of crocodile tears. Lee had been found with blood on his clothing and, in the pantry where he was known to have been shortly before the fire, they found an empty oil canister. Lee claimed that the blood was his own (from breaking a window to let the smoke out) but couldn't explain the oil canister. He was arrested and charged with murder.

At the trial it came out that Miss Keyse had recently cut Lee's wages because he was suspected of theft and in the jury's mind this settled the matter. Lee had gone to his employer in a fit of pique and had beaten her to death, then setting light to her body to cover his tracks. The judge sentenced him to death by hanging and that should have been the end of John 'Babbacombe' Lee.

But it wasn't. As Lee was taken from the dock he shouted, 'I am innocent. The Lord will never permit me to be executed.' And he wasn't far off. The night before his execution, Lee was told that a reprieve was out of the question. He replied that his half-sister could even now clear him if she would 'say the word', but the word never came.

Just before 8 a.m. on Monday, 23 February 1885, executioner John Berry led Lee on to the gallows at Exeter prison. He stood the condemned man over the trapdoor, tied his legs together above the ankles, placed a white hood over his head, looped the noose around his neck and stood back. After a few moments he seized the lever that opened the trapdoor and pulled it. At this moment the bolts that held the door shut should have been drawn, the door sprung open and Lee dropped through, breaking his neck as the rope around it snapped taut.

But instead nothing happened. Lee remained standing on the trapdoor, still very much alive. This was all rather embarrassing for the executioner, who liked to do a professional job. Rather gruesomely, he and a warder then stamped on the doors to try to get them to open, but this rather Gothic tarantella failed to work either. Keen not to inconvenience his client again, he removed the noose and hood from Lee and moved him off the trapdoor. He then tied a flour bag weighing the same as Lee to the rope and tested the mechanism. The bolts shot, the door opened and the flour bag plummeted to its doom. With growing confidence he then replaced Lee, plus hood and noose, over the trapdoor and tried again.

Berry pulled the lever once more – and nothing happened. Lee was again taken off the gallows whilst the executioner summoned a prison engineer to examine the mechanism. They called in the carpenter who planed the edges of the trapdoor and greased the bolts. Another flour bag was strung up, the lever was pulled and everything worked perfectly.

By now the scene could probably have been described as 'tense'. Lee was once again marched on to the trapdoor, hooded and the noose placed around his neck. Berry pulled the lever, the bolts were heard to shoot and . . . nothing. The chaplain was already on his fourth rendition of the burial service, which is more times than anyone hopes to hear it, and both he and the prison surgeon urged the governor to put an end to this cruel and unusual treatment.

So at this point it was decided to send a messenger to London to inform the Home Secretary and request advice. In the meantime, one report claims that John Lee tucked into the executioner's breakfast, which poor old John Berry didn't really fancy. The official report (from the chaplain), which was probably more reliable, says that Lee was taken back to his cell, dazed and confused, crying, 'Why am I not to die?'

It was nine hours later that the messenger returned with the news that the Home Secretary had commuted Lee's sentence to life imprisonment. Lee was released in 1907 after serving twenty-two years.

The rest of his life is shrouded in mystery. He married in 1909 and seems for a time to have made a living telling his notorious story. Researchers then disagree as to whether he abandoned his wife and two children and went to Milwaukee, or stayed in England, dying in a West Country workhouse. But was he saved by divine intervention? The report on the mechanism, sent to the Under-Secretary of State from the Sheriff of Devon two days after the incident, says that the ironwork of the release mechanism had been found to be faulty, but John 'Babbacombe' Lee maintained to the end that he, an innocent man, had been saved by the hand of God.

Who was deposed in the November Revolution?

The November Revolution of 1918 is rather forgotten about these days, taking place in the dying days of the First World War, but it is the revolution that brought about peace. It happened in Germany.

The revolution began in late October amongst the German fleet lying at anchor off Wilhelmshaven. Although Germany was exhausted and most of its people knew that the war was lost, the ever-optimistic Admiral Hipper was still planning one last great battle against the British navy. Needless to say, this pointless waste of life was not all that popular amongst the men of the fleet and when the order to put to sea was issued several ships mutinied. This initial revolt proved short-lived and when some torpedo boats were brought up, the crews surrendered. Nevertheless, the High Command was shaken enough to rescind the order to battle and return the fleet to Kiel.

Convinced that they were back in control, the commanders now ordered the ringleaders amongst the mutineers to be arrested and brought to trial, but they had misread the situation. Back in Kiel large number of sailors, many of them members of the left-wing Social Democracy Party (SPD), now began rallying to the mutineers' cause, and by the afternoon of 3 November several thousand protesters, including large numbers of union members, were parading through the city, demanding the release of the sailors and, more importantly, an end to the war. When, fatally, this demonstration was fired upon by the army, it quickly turned into open revolt. By the following morning many navy and army units were refusing to obey orders and the imprisoned sailors were finally freed. It was too late, however, to prevent the spread of the revolt, which had already reached Wilhelmshaven, and, in ever-increasing numbers of towns, public and military institutions began falling under the control of councils of soldiers and union-ists.

Over the next few days the royal heads of all the German states, starting with the king of Bavaria, abdicated, leaving only the Kaiser. In Berlin, Friedrich Ebert, the leader of the SPD, hoping to prevent a communist revolution, asked the Kaiser to abdicate. The Kaiser refused, believing that he could end the revolt by force, but with soldiers' and workers' councils springing up in Berlin itself and a general strike having been called, Ebert couldn't wait. This time he sent the Kaiser an ultimatum. By now the army at the front was refusing to fight and even the guards regiment was refusing to obey orders, but the Kaiser still hoped that he might at least retain his title as king of Prussia. Exasperated, the liberal chancellor, Prince Maximilian of Baden, simply took matters into his own hands, sending a telegram announcing the Kaiser's abdication. He then resigned himself. The Kaiser responded by running away to the Netherlands, only signing the official abdication document in exile several weeks later. He remained there until his death in 1941. Many in the German government continued to believe that the monarchy itself could be saved, just with a new head, but by now the crowds were not satisfied even with the news of the Kaiser's abdication. In order to try to draw attention away from attempts to set up a socialist state, the SPD were forced to declare the monarchy abolished. A German republic was announced, with Ebert as its leader. Thus it was that the rule of the kaisers ended and the ill-fated Weimar Republic was born.

Who was Dirty Dick?

The original Dirty Dick was an ironmonger called Nathaniel Bentley, known as 'The Beau of Leadenhall Street'. Life was not to be kind to Dick and when his bride-to-be died on the night before their wedding, he sealed up the room in which he had prepared their wedding banquet and became a recluse. Refusing to wash or change his clothes, he soon became a famous, if tragic, character in the City. After fifty years in business, Bentley finally retired in 1804 and moved away, when it was discovered that he had made his shop on Leadenhall Street into a shrine to lost love. The interior was as though half a century had not passed. Everything had been left where it was on that terrible evening. Even his cats lay where they had died, and inside the locked room the desiccated remains of the never-eaten wedding banquet still stood on the dust-covered table.

The English love an eccentric and by this time Dirty Dick was already a celebrity, inspiring the landlord of the Old Port Wine

Shop in Bishopsgate to buy the contents of his ironmongers, lock, stock and barrel, carefully transporting it in its filthy state to his pub, which he renamed Dirty Dick's. This peculiar attraction remained on show in the City until the 1980s when the collection fell foul of health and safety regulations and had to be cleaned up. Dirty Dick's memory lives on, however, preserved in the pub's name and immortalised in Dickens' *Great Expectations*, in which he was the inspiration for Miss Havisham.

When did a one-armed sailor meet an iron duke?

On 12 September 1805 two men sat waiting for an interview with the Secretary for War and the Colonies, Lord Castlereagh (see pages 133–4), in an ante-room of the Colonial Office in Downing Street. Both being military men, the two fell to talking. One was a naval man and the other a soldier, although it was the navy that had the best, if not all, of the conversation. Indeed, the army man later noted of the other: '*He entered at once into conversation with me, if I can call it conversation, for it was almost all on his side and all about himself and, in reality, a style so vain and so silly as to surprise and almost disgust me.*'

What baffled the army man was that it had dawned on him during the 'conversation' that the one-armed admiral who was expounding on his own greatness was Lord Nelson whom he had been led to believe was a much more civilised chap. After a while Nelson himself seems to have become aware that the major-general he was talking to was a little uncomfortable. Excusing himself, he left the room for a moment and went to enquire about the identity of the listener to his monologue. The reply came back that it was the Honourable Sir Arthur Wellesley – the future field marshal and Duke of Wellington. With that Nelson changed tack completely. Realising that he was face to face with the other great hero of his age, he returned to the waiting room and, as Wellesley later put it, '*his charlatan style had quite vanished . . . and certainly for the last half or three quarters of an hour, I don't know that*

I ever had a conversation that interested me more . . . I saw enough to be satisfied that he was really a very superior man; but certainly a more sudden or complete metamorphosis I never saw.'

It was the only time that the two men ever met. Just over five weeks later, Nelson was killed at the Battle of Trafalgar.

Who was remembered more for his woollies than his wars?

In his early adulthood, James Thomas Brudenell, 7th Earl of Cardigan, was a striking figure: tall, blond haired, blue eyed. He had a reputation as a daring horseman, excelled at swordsmanship, was a fine shot and something of a ladies' man (see pages 221–2). He was not academically talented, however, and, having failed to take a degree at Christchurch College, Oxford, began his career as he intended to go on by purchasing positions, first as an MP and then in the army. As Cecil Woodham-Smith says in *The Reason Why* (1953): *'The melancholy truth was that his glorious golden head had nothing in it.'*

In May 1824, at the age of twenty-seven, Brudenell joined the army as a cornet in the 8th Hussars through the influence of the Duke of York. He then bought a lieutenancy in January 1825, and a captaincy in June 1826, becoming a major in August 1830. During this time he became known for his pedantic insistence on what he considered to be correct protocol and appearance, together with a willingness to duel over just about anything. In December 1830, Cardigan bought a lieutenant-colonelcy and in 1832 he transferred to the 15th King's Hussars. Here junior officers in the regiment who differed with Cardigan soon discovered how far he would go to get his own way. Captain Augustus Wathen was court-martialled (but found not guilty) in 1833, mainly because he alerted superiors to Cardigan's overpurchasing of new uniforms. Cardigan was relieved of command.

Only through the influence of relations – his brother-in-law was the queen's chamberlain – and another purchase of rank was

Cardigan able to continue in the army, securing the command of the 11th Light Dragoons in 1837–8. His tenure with the 11th was just as stormy and unpleasant as it had been with the 15th Hussars. Cardigan couldn't stand officers who had served in India, and the 11th – having been stationed there for seventeen years – was full of them. Cardigan waged a war of attrition with them, denigrating them, reprimanding them and excluding them from social functions.

This eventually led to the 'Black Bottle' affair. In May 1840, Cardigan ordered the arrest of Captain Reynolds for placing wine on the mess-table in a black bottle instead of a decanter. Soon afterwards he met another Captain Reynolds from the regiment and, having rather taken against the name, had him arrested for impertinence. An account of this event appeared in the *Morning Chronicle*, written by Captain Harvey Tuckett; Cardigan promptly challenged Tuckett to a duel. At the second shot, Captain Tuckett was wounded. Public feeling ran strongly against Cardigan, who demanded the right to be tried by his peers. The trial took place on 16 February and by the end of the day it was all over. Cardigan was acquitted on a technicality and retained the command of his regiment until he was promoted to major-general on 20 June 1854.

None of this made him terribly popular with his regiment but what Cardigan did do for them, which also made his name, was to buy them all new uniforms. Indeed, of his private income of £40,000 a year he put aside £10,000 to fit out his men, making them the best-dressed unit in the army, although these spectacular uniforms made him a figure of fun in the press.

But it was at the outbreak of the Crimean War (see pages 30–1) that Cardigan made his lasting contribution to British history. Unwilling to see his regiment fighting in just any old uniform, he commissioned and bought for each of his men a new style of jacket, which soon became known as the 'cardigan'.

At the siege of Balaclava he led his cardiganed men in the Charge of the Light Brigade, being the first man in (and the first man out) of the 'Valley of Death'. Of those who took part, less than half returned. His habit of living aboard his yacht during the campaign (whilst Lord Lucan lived alongside his men) aroused much ill feeling, leading to reports that he recklessly led the famous charge, sloping off afterwards to his yacht to unwind with a bath and a bottle of champagne. Neither allegation is really true.

When he returned to England he insisted (with some success) on being fêted as a hero. Having explained his heroism personally to the queen, he retired to his seat of Deene Park and spent the rest of his life collecting various decorations for bravery and telling everyone about how thoroughly splendid he was. Despite these efforts, his moment of glory at Balaclava has gone down in history as one of the greatest military blunders of the age and his name lives on for his contribution to woollens, not warfare.

Which twentieth-century British king was murdered?

George V was not a man to mince his words, certainly not when he was feeling poorly. A famous story relates that, as he lay on his deathbed, some courtiers tried to cheer the dying king by suggesting that he would soon be well enough to visit Bognor Regis. Aware that he would never rise from his bed again, he caustically replied, 'Bugger Bognor!' and promptly expired.

Sadly this is probably untrue. The king's librarian, Sir Owen Morshead, told a different variant of the story. He claims that when the good burghers of Craigwell came to see the king to ask whether they might change its name to Bognor Regis, the king told his private secretary (who presented the petition), 'Bugger Bognor!' The ever-diplomatic Private Secretary translated this back to the citizens of Craigwell as, 'His Majesty would be graciously pleased to grant your request.'

Perhaps more interesting than George V's last words is the fact that he was murdered (well, technically speaking). On 15 January 1936, the king had retired to his bedroom at Sandringham, feeling ill. By 20 January he was comatose and clearly dying but still clinging to life, which presented his doctor, Lord Dawson, with a problem. He didn't want the king's family left in limbo for days. In Dawson's opinion, the world at large would be better served by hearing of the king's death in the morning papers rather than in what he sniffily referred to as 'the evening journals'. So he decided to kill him. Conveniently, the King was entirely insensible and felt nothing. Having written the famous bulletin, 'The life of the king is moving peacefully to its close,' on his menu card at dinner, he went upstairs to hurry it along a bit. His Sandringham diaries, first brought to light by Francis Watson in 1986, reveal how he did it: *'I therefore decided to determine the end and injected (myself) morphia gr.3/4 and shortly afterwards cocaine gr.1 into the distended jugular vein: 'myself' because it was obvious that Sister B [the king's nurse] was disturbed by the procedure.'*

This did the trick and the king died peacefully, surrounded by his family, at about five minutes to midnight, in good time to catch the headlines in the morning broadsheets. Later that year Dawson voted against a euthanasia bill passing through the House of Lords.

20

A Bit of Politics

Politics is perhaps the only profession for which no preparation is thought necessary.

Robert Louis Stevenson

What 'grisly' weapon did Germany unleash on Russia in 1917?

When Winston Churchill wrote, '*It was with a sense of awe that they turned upon Russia the most grisly of all weapons,*' he was referring to the very strange events of April 1917.

With the First World War raging across Europe, the February Revolution in Russia that had removed the tsar had left Lenin in the wrong place, stuck in neutral Switzerland. Desperate to get back home and take the lead in the establishment of a communist state, Lenin begged his Swiss friends to negotiate passage for him across Germany. This was problematic, first, because there was a war going on, in which Germany and Russia were enemies, something that normally precludes taking a train trip between the two countries. Second, there was the difficulty of Lenin himself. As the shock waves of the February Revolution rocked Europe, few politicians in the West doubted that Lenin's Marxism was one of the most potent weapons available. In his turn, Lenin had a low opinion of most of the war's protagonists; indeed, he thought that the war had nothing to do with ordinary people (other than killing them by the thousands). This put the German government in an interesting position. At one level they would have loved Lenin to return home and use his influence to make Russia withdraw from the war. However, the risk was that his Marxist ideas might infect Germany en route, in which case the German people might end up, like the Russians, thinking that the war was an aristocratic, ruling-class disaster. Neither the Kaiser nor the government particularly wanted to share the fate of the recently deposed, and soon to be shot, Russian royal family.

Lenin was too good a weapon not to use, however, and so the Germans settled on a plan. They would allow him to travel across their country but his communist ideas would have to be kept in quarantine to prevent them influencing the German people. Lenin and his entourage were put on a sealed train, like some form of highly infectious bacillus, and transported in locked carriages until they reached Russia. Germany had unleashed communism on Russia and it was that which Churchill, never a great fan of Marxism, was recording.

How did GOM become MOG?

Prime Minister William Gladstone had been rather affectionately known as the GOM – Grand Old Man – by his followers, although Disraeli, who had a way with words (see pages 124 and 128–9), once said that the initials should stand for 'God's Only Mistake'. It was, however, the death of General Gordon at Khartoum, owing to the late arrival of a Thomas Cook tour (see page 253), that brought about the reversal in both the initials and Gladstone's fortunes. Gordon was a wilful and manipulative character who preferred to send dispatches to the London newspapers rather than to his government masters. A messianic and mystical Christian, he had first gone to Sudan as a governor for the Ottoman Empire, intent on abolishing slavery, rather than as a British general.

After Egypt went bankrupt and the Muslim Mahdist uprising began in Sudan, Gordon brilliantly managed to manipulate the British press and population into clamouring for his return to the country. Gladstone, who disliked Gordon's reckless attitude and self-promotion, initially resisted but finally acceded to calls in 1884 to send the general to Khartoum, but only to evacuate the city. Gordon, of course, had absolutely no intention of presiding over a retreat and, having evacuated the women and children, began fortifying the city for a stand-off with the Muslim army of the Mahdi. A flurry of telegrams were sent from London to Khartoum, ordering a withdrawal, but Gordon ignored them and, after the telegraphic cable was cut, no further messages were received from him. Under intense pressure, Gladstone was again forced to acquiesce to public opinion and arrange a relief expedition to rescue the wayward general.

That force, which formed the basis for A. E. W. Mason's story

The Four Feathers, reached Khartoum just too late. The Mahdist forces had already attacked and seized the city, and Gordon had been decapitated on the steps of his headquarters. The only information about what had actually happened inside the city came from the reports of a few survivors plus Gordon's own diary, which of course portrayed him as a hero. News of his death reached London on 5 February 1885. Gordon had his final revenge on Gladstone. As the newspapers screamed 'Too Late' under fanciful pictures of Gordon heroically fighting to the last, Queen Victoria sent an uncoded telegram to the Prime Minister, openly criticising his government's failure to support the empire and the heroes who had created it. Gladstone, who had been known to a generation as the GOM, was rebranded the MOG – Murderer of Gordon. Four months later he resigned.

Whom did the British emancipate in 1829?

Not slaves – that was in 1833 – but Catholics. Catholics in England had been in hot water ever since the pope issued the 1575 Bull Regnans in Excelsis, which stated that God would be quite happy for any good Catholic to kill Queen Elizabeth I. Needless to say, this had increased tensions between Catholics and the state, which came to a head in the Gunpowder Plot of 1605 (see page 51), in which a group of Catholic conspirators attempted to blow up the king and parliament. After this, Catholicism was heavily suppressed and its priests were imprisoned and executed. Furthermore, to make sure that Catholics didn't sneak back into favour, a rather nervy parliament passed laws preventing Catholics from marrying into the royal family, holding public office, buying land, inheriting property and, just for good measure, voting.

Whilst some of these measures were revoked in the late eighteenth century, George III bitterly opposed them as he thought they put him in breach of his coronation oath. It was only in 1829, when Ireland threatened to withdraw from the Union, that the Duke of Wellington and Sir Robert Peel finally pushed through an Emancipation Bill. But just in case newly emancipated Catholics became too confident, the Act that required the compulsory celebration of Bonfire Night (commemorating the crushing of Catholic opposition) on 5 November remained on the statute books until 1859.

Who was Britain's first female MP?

The first woman to win a parliamentary seat was Constance, Countess Markiewicz, who won a seat for Sinn Fein in the December 1918 election.

Constance Gore-Booth, as she was born, was an unlikely radical. The daughter of an Arctic explorer with estates in Ireland and the wife of a Polish count, she was in some ways the epitome of the establishment. Having studied art at the Slade School in London, Constance and her husband settled in Dublin where she met leading Irish independence leaders as well as mixing with the English ruling classes. Indeed, she attended her first Sinn Fein meeting in a ball gown and tiara, having come straight from a state function at Dublin Castle. Constance soon became involved in both women's suffrage and the Irish independence movement, standing for Sinn Fein in Manchester in 1908 against Winston Churchill, an election that she lost. By the following year her views had hardened and she had formed a paramilitary boys' brigade to teach teenagers how to use firearms in a future armed uprising. By 1913, Constance's husband had retreated to the Ukraine, possibly due to his wife's radical activity, and he would never return to Ireland. Three years later she was taking an active part in the Easter Rising for which she received a death sentence that was commuted to life imprisonment on account of her sex. On hearing this news, she reportedly said to an officer at Kilmainham gaol, '*I do wish you lot had the decency to shoot me.*'

She was released the following year as part of a general amnesty but again imprisoned, this time for an alleged involvement in pro-German activities (speaking against conscription) in 1918. On her release she stood for St Patrick's, a Dublin constituency, a seat that she won, making her the first woman elected to the British House of Commons. In line with Sinn Fein's policy, however, she refused to take up her seat. She died in 1927 with her estranged husband back at her side, after a long career in Irish politics, having become the first woman to hold a cabinet office in Irish history (and she would be the last until 1979).

What was the Addled Parliament?

The Addled Parliament was the second parliament of the reign of James I, which sat in 1614. Its main purpose, as far as James was concerned, was to vote him money although this was actually the last thing that this group of MPs had any intention of doing. For eight weeks the parliament sat, during which time it refused to bring forward any tax-raising measures and instead grumbled loudly about the impositions that the Crown had already placed on it. Most famously, the MP for Hereford, John Hoskyns, took the opportunity to give a highly inflammatory speech against the king's Scottish supporters, making a veiled reference to the thirteenth-century Sicilian Vespers – an anti-Angevin massacre – and suggesting that the Scots might find themselves in a similarly sticky situation if they hung around for too long. Four days later James decided he'd had enough and dissolved parliament, sending Hoskyns to the Tower for good measure.

In all its time sitting, the parliament had brought forward not a single piece of legislation – hence it became known as the Addled Parliament. James was reported to have commented, 'I am surprised my ancestors should ever have permitted such an institution to come into existence.'

What did the 1832 Reform Act reform?

The 1832 Act abolished the 'rotten boroughs' that had become something of a democratic scandal. Rotten boroughs were constituencies that could return MPs to parliament but which had few or no voters, making it possible for landowners or their nominees to be 'elected' to parliament without opposition (see page 124). Most famous amongst these was Old Sarum, a site that returned two MPs but had been largely abandoned since the fourteenth century when its bishopric had moved to the new site of Salisbury. The 1831 return listed only three houses and eleven voters in the borough but in fact there were no genuine inhabitants at all. The voters themselves consisted of certain 'householders' who all lived elsewhere, as their nominal Old Sarum 'homes', which gave them their voting rights, had decayed many centuries previously into nothing more than patches of grass, which they owned or rented. Old Sarum, like many rotten boroughs, was owned by a wealthy family who played the system to ensure that they could always have a representative in parliament and hence a role in the running of the country. In Old Sarum's case, that family was the Pitts, with Pitt the Elder 'representing' the constituency from 1735 until 1747. He actually only became MP for the borough because his family had bought two boroughs and his older brother, Thomas, had been elected to both. Thomas had decided to sit for his Okehampton constituency, meaning that Old Sarum could be given to his little brother. Other rotten boroughs included Dunwich in Suffolk, which was largely underwater, and Gatton in Surrey, which had only seven registered voters and one actual inhabitant.

By the 1830s this obviously corrupt system was in dire need of reform, not least because whilst fifty-six rotten boroughs each returned two MPs for almost no inhabitants, the new industrial cities of Manchester and Birmingham had no MPs whatsoever. The 1832 Reform Act finally abolished all the rotten boroughs and cut the number of MPs elected by another thirty-two small constituencies. One unexpected side-effect of the Act, however, was to create the Women's Suffrage movement, as another clause specifically prohibited women from voting – something that had never previously been explicit in law.

Which country was ruled by a baker?

This unusual state of affairs came about due to King Christian II's love of the common people. In an age when aristocrats and royalty kept very much to themselves, Christian, who would briefly become king of Norway, Sweden and Denmark in the Union of Kalmar (1520–21), really did love his people. In particular he loved Dyveke Sigbritsdattir, the daughter of a Norwegian baker of Dutch extraction. She had been noticed by the Norwegian chancellor around 1509 and recommended to the king who met her at a ball and promptly fell in love. Nor was this pretty Norwegian girl all he got from the deal. Her mother, Sigbrit Willoms, had also caught the chancellor's attention, not so much for her looks as for her astute business sense, and she soon became an adviser to the king.

Having a baker's wife whispering in the ear of the monarch was not at the time exactly considered the done thing by the aristocrats of Scandinavia or Europe as a whole and moves were taken to 'rectify' the situation. In the summer of 1517, Dyveke suddenly died and was very probably murdered. One tale suggests that she was poisoned whilst at Elsinore (the castle in which Shakespeare set his play *Hamlet*) by a vengeful governor of Copenhagen whose advances had been rejected and who had sent her a bowl of poisoned cherries to settle the score. More likely she was poisoned by Scandinavian nobles or perhaps even by the Holy Roman Emperor (whose sister was married to Christian).

This tragedy didn't have the desired effect, however. Her mother's star continued to rise. Sigbrit ended up in charge of the whole of the king's finances and hence largely held sway over three Scandinavian countries. Christian seems to have much preferred the honest advice of this middle-class businesswoman to the suggestions of his own nobles, and she in turn soon filled the king's inner circle with her own friends. She too had her suspicions about the death of her daughter, for which the magnate, Torben Oxe, was quickly arrested on the king's orders and executed. Just to show how popular she now was amongst the old nobility, they referred to her as *'the foul-mouthed Dutch sorceress who hath bewitched the king'*. She was in fact simply a straight-talking baker and the insult didn't seem to bother her in the slightest. What did bother her was the large-scale uprising against the king, partly caused by the Bloodbath of Stockholm, which had not gone down well in Sweden. When Christian fled the throne she went too, escaping with him back to Holland. Nothing further is heard of her.

What was the Barebone's Parliament?

The Barebone's Parliament was the last attempt of the Commonwealth to find an acceptable form of government for the nation before the installation of Oliver Cromwell as Lord Protector. Despite calling itself the Parliament of Saints, it was neither a representative nor an effective body. None of its members was elected; they were directly nominated either by Cromwell himself or by the Army Council of Officers. Most of these nominees were wealthy tradesmen and religious fundamentalists who had little if any experience of government and quickly showed themselves to be incapable of agreeing on anything.

Just how highly the parliament was regarded by the folk on the street can be seen from a broadsheet description, calling them 'Pettifoggers, Innkeepers, Millwrights, Stockingmongers and such a rabble as never had hopes to be of a Grand Jury'. Amongst this illustrious group was a man with the splendid name of Praise-God Barebone, a leather merchant and puritanical preacher from London whose sermons had a habit of provoking a combination of ridicule and violence from his audience. Despite the fact that there is no evidence that he ever took part in a single debate, the enemies of this parliament thought him representative of its failings and dubbed it 'Barebone's Parliament'. Eventually, in December 1653, the moderate faction in the House tired of the endless wrangling and took a petition to Cromwell, declaring that the parliament was no longer helpful to the Commonwealth. Those radicals who were still refusing to step aside were confronted by soldiers who politely suggested that they might care to leave. Needless to say, they took the hint.

What present did Denmark give Sweden?

Some people say it with flowers but, in 1814, Denmark said it with an entire country as, under the terms of the Treaty of Kiel, its government gave Norway to Sweden. The king of Sweden at the time was Jean-Baptiste Bernadotte, formerly one of Napoleon's marshals, who had rather unexpectedly been offered the throne and, even more unexpectedly, accepted. Having had an argument with Napoleon about a military retreat (for which he was stripped of his command), Bernadotte had taken up the offer to become king of Sweden and promptly changed sides, joining Britain and Prussia in alliance against France.

Denmark–Norway meanwhile had managed to get embroiled in the Napoleonic Wars on the French side, thanks to its partici-pation in the Gunboat War against Britain. Events did not turn out well for Denmark–Norway and, by January 1814, Denmark had not only lost its fleet but stood on the brink of being invaded. To protect his country, King Frederick VI of Denmark (the son of the cuckolded, rack-loving Christian VII – see pages 194–6) had to think quickly. What did he have that he could use to appease the victors? Then it hit him – Norway. So he gave Norway to Bernadotte's Sweden (although managing to keep Greenland, Iceland and the Faeroe Islands for Denmark) and on 18 January he wrote a letter to the people of Norway, releasing them from their fealty to him. This was then ratified in the Treaty of Kiel.

No one had really asked the Norwegians what they thought about this and in truth they had been hoping for a little more independence. The Danish viceroy in Norway, Christian Frederick, was all in favour of going it alone and, having declared himself Regent, went about setting up a Norwegian constitution. To say that Bernadotte and Sweden were a little piqued would be an understatement. The Norwegians had also rather forgotten that by breaking a key provision of the Treaty of Kiel, they effectively put themselves at war with all the European allies who were fighting Napoleon. In fact, not all the Norwegians were entirely enamoured of the idea of having Christian Frederick as their king either – he was, after all, a hereditary prince of Denmark and many believed that he might simply be planning to reunite Norway with that country.

After much diplomatic wrangling and a short war, Christian Frederick abdicated and Bernadotte declared himself king of Sweden *and* Norway. This was ratified by the Norwegian parliament, and Sweden and Norway were united. Things didn't turn out too badly for Christian Frederick either. In 1839 he became King Christian VIII of Denmark, and his great-grand-nephew became king of Norway when that country finally achieved independence in 1905.

What was the family relationship between Wellington and Napoleon?

The ruling classes in nineteenth-century Europe made up a surprisingly small group, which could lead to all sorts of diplomatic awkwardness when politics and marriage collided.

Take the Duke of Wellington, one of Britain's greatest generals and the nemesis of Napoleon Bonaparte. What is less well known is that he was related to his arch-enemy, by marriage at least. Wellington had an older brother, Richard, who had spent much of his life living with a French actress, Hyacinthe-Gabrielle Roland, with whom he had a daughter, Anne (who also happens to be an ancestor of Elizabeth Bowes-Lyon, the late Queen Mother, but that's another story). After the death of Hyacinthe-Gabrielle, Richard married Marianne Patterson (whose mother was a grand-daughter of Charles Carroll of Carrollton, the last surviving signatory of the American Declaration of Independence, but that is another story too). This marriage was initially not very popular with the Duke of Wellington as he too was 'ill with love' for Marianne.

Anyway, Marianne had previously been married to Robert Patterson, whose sister was Elizabeth Patterson, and *her* first marriage had been to Jerome Bonaparte, brother of Napoleon. Just as Wellington was a bit upset about his sibling's marital choice, so Napoleon was also none too pleased with Jerome's, and he ordered his brother to return to France (whilst at the same time banning Elizabeth from landing on continental European soil). Jerome gave in to his brother's bullying and the marriage to Elizabeth was annulled. He later married Catharina of Württemberg and became king of Westphalia.

Who was crowned in the Hall of Mirrors in Versailles?

Not a French monarch but a German one. The Prussian king, Wilhelm I, was proclaimed German emperor there on 18 January 1871, an event that marked the end of the North German Confederation and the beginning of the German Empire, also sometimes known as the Second Reich. The reason that a French palace was chosen for such a German event was that, at the time, it was the headquarters of the German army during the Franco-Prussian War.

Wilhelm, by all accounts, didn't enjoy the event much; indeed, you might say that he was a shade ungrateful, writing to his wife that evening: *'I have just come back from the Emperor charade. I cannot tell you how utterly depressed I have been feeling in these last days, partly because of the high responsibility, partly because of the pain of the Prussian title being superseded.'* In fact, the whole event proved rather unlucky really. On the same day, 18 January, some forty-eight years later, the Paris peace conference opened in the same room, at which the Second Reich was dismantled and the seeds of the Third were sown.

Who nearly became king of America?

The Newburgh letter could have changed American history at a stroke. It was addressed to George Washington at his camp at Newburgh on 22 May 1782, as the general and his army waited for the revolutionary war to be concluded. (The fighting had ended at Yorktown in 1781 but the Treaty of Paris wasn't signed until 1783.) Considering the hardship and bloodshed that the nascent United States had just gone through to relieve itself of a monarch, the contents of this letter must have come as something of a surprise to Washington: its author, Colonel Lewis Nicola, asked the great man whether he would care to become America's first king. In his letter he explained that republics were weak, and whilst the general would naturally shy away from such a grand title as king, Nicola thought that Washington could carry it off to some advantage – provided he was a constitutional monarch and not a tyrant.

The real reason for the letter lies elsewhere. With the war nearing its official end, many in the army were increasingly worried that they would now never be paid (which many of them weren't) as the fledgling states couldn't and wouldn't fund the cost of this. The offer of kingship to Washington hence marks the first step in the 'Newburgh conspiracy', an attempted military coup that would have ensured that the army that had fought so hard never lost its income or its influence. However, substituting one King George for another didn't appeal to Washington and he declined. Seven years later he became the first President of the United States of America.

ACKNOWLEDGEMENTS

This book is a collection of historical curiosities that I have gathered over the last twelve years as I went about writing books, making documentaries and advising on films. As such, it includes the thoughts and suggestions of hundreds of people whom I've been fortunate enough to work with along the way. Without the help of the many academics and researchers I've quizzed and, on rare occasions, bought drinks for, it would be a thinner and far less appealing tome than, I hope, it is. In particular in recent years it has been, and remains, a pleasure to work with John Lloyd and the whole *QI* team, who go to such great lengths to prove that there is nothing in history, science or the universe as a whole that is of itself boring, just things that have yet to be explained properly.

For suggesting particular stories for this book, I should add my special thanks to my father, Dr Matt Lee, Gordon Pollard, Stuart Hill, Paul Gott and Barrie Howe. This would also still be a half-baked idea rather than a fully baked book were it not for Roland Philipps, Rowan Yapp and Lucy Dixon at John Murray, Julian Alexander at LAW and Richard Foreman at Chalke, who have worked their magic once again. Furthermore, it would be a grey and dusty volume were it not for the wonderful illustrations produced by Martin Haake.

Finally, as always, I want to thank Steph and Connie, who continue to put up with a husband and father who still hasn't managed to get a proper job after all these years but who manage to make that look like the most normal thing in the world.

INDEX

The Interesting Bits

The Interesting Bits